The Body of Il Duce

The Body of
IL DUCE

MUSSOLINI'S CORPSE

AND THE

FORTUNES OF ITALY

SERGIO LUZZATTO

Translated by Frederika Randall

METROPOLITAN BOOKS

Henry Holt and Company · New York

Metropolitan Books
Henry Holt and Company, LLC
Publishers since 1866
175 Fifth Avenue
New York, New York 10010

Metropolitan Books ® and ® are registered
trademarks of Henry Holt and Company, LLC.

Originally published in Italy in 1998 under the title *Il corpo del duce*
by Giulio Einaudi editore s.p.a., Torino.

Library of Congress Cataloging-in-Publication Data

Luzzatto, Sergio, 1963–
    [Corpo del duce. English]
    The body of Il Duce : Mussolini's corpse and the fortunes of Italy /
by Sergio Luzzatto; translated by Frederika Randall.—1st American ed.
        p. cm.
    Includes bibliographical references and index.
    ISBN-13: 978-0-8050-6646-3
    ISBN-10: 0-8050-6646-2
    1. Mussolini, Benito, 1883–1945–Death and burial.   2. Heads of
state—Italy—Death.   3. Italy—Politics and government—1945–1976.
4. Politics and culture—Italy—History—20th century.   I. Title.
DG575.M8L8913 2005 945.091'092—dc22   2004061102

Henry Holt books are available for special promotions and
premiums. For details contact: Director, Special Markets.

First U.S. Edition 2005

Designed by Victoria Hartman

Printed in the United States of America
1   3   5   7   9   10   8   6   4   2

There are some experiences, even very abstract or spiritual ones, that are lived only *through the body*. If the body belongs to another, so does the experience.

What the bodies of our fathers experienced, our own cannot. We can try to imagine, we can reconstruct and interpret; we can write a history, that is. But the reason history interests us so passionately (and more than any other science) is because the most important element in it irrevocably eludes us.

—Pier Paolo Pasolini, *Petrolio*

Contents

The Body of Il Duce

Prologue

No previous event in Italian history comes close to the horror at Piazzale Loreto. Even tribes of cannibals do not visit such atrocities on the dead. We cannot say that the murderers stand for progress; they represent a descent into primitive bestiality. . . . Nor can we say that the war was the cause of their ferocity, since the lynch mob of Piazzale Loreto never saw the trenches. These are the shirkers, the deserters, the boys too young to have gone to war.

STRANGE AS IT may seem, these lines are not a news report from Milan at the end of April 1945, when the Resistance and the Allies had just liberated the city from the Germans. This is not a crowd driven wild by the suffering and privations of World War II; the victims are not Benito Mussolini and other Fascist Party bosses; the lynch mob is not a group of partisans. No, the events in question took place earlier, in June 1920, during the great wave of strikes and political unrest known as the *biennio rosso*, the "red years" of 1919–20. The dead person was an anonymous

Carabinieri officer, Giuseppe Ugolini, who just happened to be crossing Milan's Piazzale Loreto. The perpetrators were Socialist and anarchist militants who had grown violent after a long general strike, infuriated by the government's repressive response. Benito Mussolini did play a role, but not as the victim. The editor of the Fascist daily *Il Popolo d'Italia*, Mussolini was the writer, the source of the commentary.

The conjunction is remarkable, a rare find for a historian: an editorial written by Mussolini himself (accomplished journalist that he was) on the tortured fate that awaited him twenty-five years later at the very same piazza. The connection is pure coincidence, of course; Mussolini wrote these lines just as he was preparing to put the *fasci,* the Fascist combat groups he controlled, at Prime Minister Giovanni Giolitti's disposition to squelch the threat of a pro-Bolshevik revolt. His piece in *Il Popolo d'Italia* thus properly belongs to the study of the origins of the Fascist regime, not to the history of Il Duce's dead body.[1] And yet his "tribes of cannibals" editorial is as good as any place to begin such a history, if only because Mussolini's words underscore—with all the intensity of pure chance—the intrinsically tragic dimension of his life. A man unaware he is passing judgment, twenty-five years in advance, on the precise and terrible circumstances of his own demise: is this not the stuff of tragedy?

In Mussolini's writings there are other premonitions of what he once called his "grotesque and sublime" destiny as a public figure who would be both widely loved and despised.[2] "I would have to be extremely disingenuous to ask to be left in peace after my death," he wrote, for "there can be no peace at the gravesides of those who lead the great transformations we call revolutions."[3] Yet, lest coincidence lead us astray, a reminder: that Benito Mussolini died a violent death at the hands of Communist partisans outside the gates of a villa near Lake Como was not the mark of predestination. Nor was the violence visited on his corpse, the way his body was strung up in view before the people of Milan. This does not mean, however, that we should ignore Mussolini's past when trying to understand his postmortem life. Out of that past comes the historical logic of his death, the restless fate of his corpse in the early postwar years, and the impact his body—his dead body—would exert on Italian life and the Italian imagination.

It was Mussolini himself who first structured his life story under the double aegis of life and death—or even more extravagantly, of death and resurrection. From his earliest experiences as a soldier in the trenches of the Great War, Mussolini cast himself in a large public role, in the sense that this particular soldier was a prominent personage, a leader in the movement calling for Italy to enter the war on the side of the Allies. But he was public also in the sense that he represented the common man, because he was risking his life just like the humblest foot soldier. When he was gravely wounded, Mussolini skillfully used his convalescence as a propaganda tool, suggesting a kind of imaginary descent into the realm of the dead. His subsequent recovery—seen as an act of duty to those who had fallen in battle—earned him the eternal gratitude of bereaved mothers and widows. Mussolini had arisen from the inferno of the battlefields by passing the highest test—he had shed blood. In his struggle to give Italians a better future, Il Duce had risked dying even before he was born.

The prehistory of Il Duce's corpse must begin with World War I for another reason as well: after the victory, the bodies of the wounded and the dead dominated all political discussion surrounding the Great War. As editor of *Il Popolo d'Italia* Mussolini was quick to occupy this ground; as early as December 1917 he identified the war wounded as the vanguard of the mass of war veterans who would make up a postwar "trench-ocracy." When the guns finally fell silent, the celebration of the rite of the Unknown Soldier suggested how large a role the body had come to play in postwar European politics. In Italy this emphasis was the result of Fascism's decision to build its legitimacy and its political platform on the tragedy of the Great War, drawing from blood already spilled the mandate to spill new blood. Mussolini emerged from the trenches bearing the stigmata of the fallen, brought back to life by the will of the nation. But with him also came a vocabulary and an armory of violence that would provide the pillars of a new civil religion: physical aggression against opponents, the destruction of their meeting places, and murder as a legitimate political weapon. Mussolini's opponents similarly employed religious symbolism, using terms like *Calvary, resurrection, holocaust,* and *transcendence.* Life, violence, and the sacred became tightly interwoven in Italy after World War I.

Thus Mussolini's body assumed political significance even before the rise of Il Duce and his seizure of power, in October 1922. For many Fascist sympathizers, especially survivors of the battlefield, Mussolini's flesh and blood symbolized the just cause they had fought for and promised victory to a generation that was ready to join ranks in a military Fascist party. Not all of Mussolini's supporters felt this way: Giuseppe Bottai, a veteran of the Arditi, the elite combat unit formed during the Great War, wanted to separate Fascism from its embodiment in the party leader. But the writer Curzio Malaparte was surely closer to mainstream Fascist opinion when he advocated militancy by calling on his leaders: "Oh, Mussolini, you old hard ass, when are you going to kick up some dust?"[4] Mussolini's opponents also attached great importance to his physical self. They were keen to see his body become a corpse; to them, it was a symbol they wanted buried. Thus, after the general elections of October 1919 (a disaster for the Fascists), Socialist militants staged a mock funeral for Mussolini in the streets of Milan. Similarly, a journalist for the Socialist daily *Avanti!* wrote a macabre satire of a crime story, reporting that "a corpse found in the waters of the Naviglio was identified as that of Benito Mussolini."[5]

Less than five years later, in August 1924, the language of bodies became brutal when a real corpse, that of Socialist deputy Giacomo Matteotti, one of Mussolini's fiercest opponents, turned up in the woods outside Rome two months after his disappearance. The violence done to Matteotti's body was primitive. Long before they beat him to death, the Fascist thugs made it their business to physically abuse the Socialist leader. He was battered repeatedly, the violence eventually culminating in sexual assault. For the Fascists, bringing Matteotti down meant destroying his body. When he was found, a rumor circulated in the Roman press that his genitals had been mutilated. Although it was false, that rumor suggests the depths of the political fight, how brutal it had become. Not a fistfight, not even a wrestling match, politics now demanded crushing, dismembering, even devouring the opponent. "We'll make sausages of Matteotti's flesh," some Fascist militants are said to have chanted after the deputy's murder—a boast that would echo down the years; a quarter of a century later the rumor that the assassins had sliced off Matteotti's genitals and displayed them as a victory trophy was still alive.[6] Sausages, trophies—Matteotti's flesh was treated with the same profane disregard that many of Mussolini's followers had developed in the trenches of the war, where they were forced to eat, drink, and sleep in the slurry of dead bodies. The trenches had forced a cohabitation between survivor and victim that had pushed the veterans' knowledge of death beyond the obscene and the grotesque.

In the anti-Fascist imagination, Mussolini's demise began to take shape the day Matteotti's body was found. At night, under cover of darkness on the streets of Rome, red paint was applied to pictures of Mussolini, drops of blood trickling down the Fascist leader's throat. Twenty years before he was removed from office in a coup, Mussolini was already murdered in effigy. The fantasies were not always so violent, but dreams of Mussolini's death would persist among those Italians who remained in opposition to the Fascist regime—Italians like the country priest from Puglia who spent his evenings working on an ambitious poem laced with references to Erasmus, in which Saint Peter halts Mussolini at the gates of Paradise and condemns him to perdition with "the insults of Earth, Heaven and Hell."[7] The priest set the distinguished anti-Fascist historian Gaetano Salvemini to reflecting on the epochal significance of Matteotti's murder. Whether Mussolini was directly responsible for Matteotti's death or not, Salvemini thought, the murder was clearly going to haunt him for the rest of his days. "There are two dead here, Matteotti and Mussolini," wrote Ugo Ojetti, one of the most perceptive journalists of the time, "and Italy is divided between those who mourn the one and those who mourn the other."[8]

Much has been said about the circumstances that made Mussolini's political survival possible, and even helped consolidate his power, after Matteotti's assassination. But despite the recent attention of historians, we know less about the ways in which the anti-Fascists expressed their grief at the death of the Socialist deputy. In the first weeks after Matteotti's disappearance, writers and politicians paid homage in strongly religious terms. Matteotti was an apostle. His portrait was passed around like an icon. Filippo Turati, the Socialist Party secretary, turned emphatically to the rhetoric of religion when he spoke in Parliament: "In vain they will have mutilated him (if so they have), in vain subjected him to barbarous insults. In vain his kind, grave face will have been disfigured. Now he is whole again. The miracle of Galilee has come to pass a second time." The tomb is empty now; the dead man rises, Turati went on. He rises with the face of historical vengeance; he looks past the mere murderers toward the man who ordered his execution. No longer victim, Matteotti is now executioner. "Dying, Giacomo Matteotti has had the better of them."[9] The longer it took to find his corpse, the more charismatic a guide he would become to his followers, Turati predicted.

The anti-Fascists' expressions of grief were uncannily like the rituals accorded Mussolini's body by the neo-Fascists after World War II. No less striking are the parallels between the measures taken by the Fascist regime to inhibit the cult of Matteotti and those used by the republic to block the cult of Mussolini. In each case the aim was to prevent the faithful from building a shrine at the scene of the crime—near the Tiber in Rome, where Matteotti was kidnapped, or by Lake Como, where Mussolini was shot. And with both men, the campaign to obtain a burial site set off a cycle of pilgrimages, police crackdowns, and clashes between Fascists and anti-Fascists. Whether the destination was Matteotti's birthplace of Fratta Polesine in the 1920s or Mussolini's birthplace of Predappio in the 1950s, the dynamic was similar. In each case there was also a plan to steal the corpse and move it, a plan motivated more by political calculations than by compassion for the remains.

All of this will be discussed in detail. But it is important to be aware of the postmortem parallels between Matteotti and Mussolini. In twentieth-century history, Mussolini's was not the only body to be worshipped as a sacred relic. Nor was the Fascist regime alone in trying to impose an oblivion of memory on its adversaries.

THE DEAD NOT only drag us down, they also live on. So Turati warned Mussolini, and his warning was taken up in various ways by anti-Fascists in the 1920s and 1930s. The more cultivated among them borrowed a phrase Marx was fond of—*le mort saisit le vif*—to express their hope that the murderer would face the victim's retributive justice. For others, the equation was simple: Mussolini was guilty of killing Matteotti. In any event, the 1924 murder and a famous speech of Mussolini's, delivered in Parliament on January 3, 1925, in which he assumed political responsibility, remained engraved in the collective memory of many as proof of Fascist criminality. Among younger people, especially of the working class, Matteotti's murder generated a rage and grief that led many to an anti-Fascist vocation. The murder also became the stuff of legend: one Roman artist, decades later, would trace his lifelong Communist militancy to the "terrible shock" he experienced while taking a walk in the woods just as Matteotti's body was discovered "with his head hacked off."[10]

More radically, the Matteotti crime fueled the anti-Fascist appetite to assassinate Mussolini. From the earliest hours following the Socialist deputy's disappearance, the belief that Mussolini was involved prompted plans to take the dictator's life. A group called the Friends of the People, heavily infiltrated by the police, began to plot. There was a certain amount of naïveté among the conspirators, who variously turned to an astrologer to guide them and then to a mysterious countess who had her own plan to poison Il Duce. In an equally romantic scenario, it was decided that if the attempt on Mussolini's life were to fail, Peppino, Ricciotti, and Sante Garibaldi, grandsons of Giuseppe Garibaldi, one of the founders of modern Italy, would step in and lead a national uprising. Creaky as these old-fashioned intrigues were, they reflected widespread sentiment in the anti-Fascist pockets of Italy, a longing for lost liberties linked to the wish to see Mussolini's end, and a determination to bring it about.

Matteotti's murder remained the driving force behind this passion and commitment. Gaetano Salvemini, a prominent historian, journalist, and former Socialist deputy, became an eager conspirator in Friends of the People. Exiled in 1925 for anti-Fascist activity, this university professor spent his time hunched over the available documents like a medieval monk, determined to prove Mussolini's complicity in the killing. Salvemini, who devoted the greater part of his life to fighting Mussolini's physical and symbolic survival, would be involved in the long odyssey of Il Duce's body as few anti-Fascists were. For Sandro Pertini, Socialist leader and later president of the republic, his relentless struggle against Mussolini began in 1925 when he placed a wreath on a city monument in Savona to honor Matteotti.

Even children were marked by the memory of the Matteotti crime. The young son of a miner in Racalmuto, Sicily, the future writer Leonardo Sciascia, remembered that his aunt, a seamstress, had a picture of the murdered Socialist hidden in a basket among her spools of thread and scraps of cloth. When young Leonardo, then three or four, insisted on taking it out, she warned him darkly never to say a word about the portrait to anyone. Matteotti, she told him, had been ordered murdered by *him*.[11] Thereafter, Mussolini's existence was a burning problem for Sciascia. At just ten, he suffered bouts of insomnia after one of the many attempts on Il Duce's life failed. And throughout his life, Sciascia would ponder the fatal nexus of a harsh destiny and the prediction of one: "A man who dies tragically is, at any moment of his life, a man who will die tragically."[12]

POLITICAL INSTITUTIONS AND their symbols do not always evolve in tandem. Formally, the Italian republic was established on January 1, 1948, when Italy's newly minted constitution went into effect. In a broader sense it was born on June 2, 1946, with the referendum in which the majority of Italians voted against the monarchy. But in terms of deep popular sentiment the republic was born on April 29, 1945, when the people of Milan and the partisan brigades came together to celebrate the death of Il Duce. That day the anti-Fascists assigned Mussolini's corpse the tragic job of making a statement about the polis. Strung upside down in front of a gas station in Piazzale Loreto, Mussolini's body declared the victory of the Resistance and announced that the pact between Il Duce and the Italian people was over. Gone were the cult of the superman, the reign of violence, the imperial ambitions, the king's complicity with a provincial upstart. Il Duce's body merits a historical study if only because it was on his corpse that the new Italy pledged itself to a pacific, democratic, republican future.

The founding fathers of the Italian republic were fully aware of the great symbolic value vested in the death of the tyrant. At the same time, the savage scene at Piazzale Loreto immediately became a kind of taboo for the Committee of National Liberation, the organization uniting the Resistance forces. To the extent that Mussolini's battered body bore the horrors of a civil war, it told a tale that was not altogether presentable as a founding myth for the young republic. How to remember Il Duce without making reference to the fact that he had been strung up in a public square? Moreover, what to say about the cheering crowd that stood around his corpse? Was there any difference between the jeering crowd in Piazzale Loreto and the people who had cheered Mussolini for twenty years in Rome's Piazza Venezia? Between Italy of the Crucifixion and Italy of the Hosannah?

DRAMATICALLY PRESENT IN the days of the Liberation, Mussolini's corpse was singularly absent in the early years of post-war Italy. In the summer of 1946 the authorities decided to hide the body, once they had reclaimed it from the neo-Fascists who had spirited it out of Milan. Only in 1957 were the mortal remains of Mussolini returned to his family and buried in the family crypt. Between the absolute transparency of the body hanging in the piazza in 1945 and the decadelong blackout following 1946, the contrast was striking. For more than ten years after the dictator was executed, the republic did not feel sufficiently confident to permit a final resting place where Fascist adherents could celebrate their nostalgic rites. Italy's fledgling republican institutions feared a corpse's symbolic power.

With no body at hand, Italians threw themselves into trying to divine the whereabouts of Il Duce's remains, an exercise that left ample trace in the literature of the late 1940s and early 1950s. Imaginative flights of fancy were mixed with the torment of memory, although real self-examination was lacking. Two philosophies—two mutually exclusive approaches, mirror images of each other—grew up around the body of Mussolini. One was secular, unforgiving; the other inclined to Christian pardon for the dictator and his followers. In many ways, Benito Mussolini's life after death reflects the peculiar political life of the Italian republic—torn between intransigence and indulgence, radicalism and opportunism, the obligation of memory and the art of forgetfulness.

1

TOUGH TO ERADICATE

For twenty years after Mussolini's March on Rome of October 1922—when thousands of Fascists converged on the capital and propelled their leader to power—the majority of Italians passionately loved Il Duce. Indeed, the mainstay of popular consensus for the Fascist regime was the personal charisma of Mussolini. The fact that King Victor Emanuel III was a mediocre figure both physically and politically allowed Il Duce to occupy the public stage as the vigorous personification of power. It was not the distinguished Savoy king but the son of a blacksmith from Romagna who dominated the reality and imagination of Italy between the wars.

For a tourist visiting the capital, a glimpse of Il Duce on his balcony in Rome's Piazza Venezia was as important, if not more, than a visit to St. Peter's to see the pope. The dictator's tireless motion did the rest, multiplying his appearances in Italy's streets and squares. Crowds gathered along the railway lines where Mussolini's train was expected, hoping to catch sight of the illustrious traveler through the window. "Il Duce is tireless, and the people never tire of seeing him," one propagandist wrote.[1] Most Italians wanted to measure themselves against Il Duce's physical presence and were proud of it. "You are Italy!" shouted one Roman admirer after an attempt on Il Duce's life, a cry immediately taken up by the cheering crowd. Fascist Italy identified Mussolini's bodily self with power, and the people identified physically with their leader. As one caricaturist put it, Il Duce's body was a gigantic "commonplace" of Italian life.[2]

Common as it was, Mussolini's body was also extraordinary, making any public showing exceptional, an epiphany. So much so that one of the literary conventions of the Fascist period was to describe Il Duce's appearance. The huge cranium, the high curved forehead, the powerful jaws, the protruding nose, the bushy eyebrows, the large dark eyes: both in the size of the features and in the impact of the profile, Mussolini's head warranted the title of supreme ruler. But Il Duce's presence was all the more impressive because he was not only ideal man but flesh and blood. So his Fascist followers were invited to look beyond the mask of power for the human face of the dictator: his deep gaze, his soft voice, his youthful smile. Even the blind could see Il Duce's gentle nature. Carlo Delcroix, blinded in the war and head of the National Association of Injured Veterans, described his leader: "I have never seen Il Duce but I do not believe the harsh descriptions I've heard. Perhaps he shows himself at his most natural to those who cannot see, but I have never perceived that terrible look on his face that artists and writers attribute to him."[3]

Attractive and human as it was, Il Duce's body was to be observed only from afar. As scholars of absolute monarchy have made clear, the distance between a ruler and his subjects is a basic element of power. Nevertheless, the story of Mussolini's body (and Hitler's, for that matter) cannot be compared to that of

Both in the size of the features and in the impact of the profile, Mussolini's head warranted the title of supreme ruler. Il Duce, circa 1939. (*Istituto Luce*)

sovereigns by divine right. One of the tenets of royal power in medieval and modern Europe was the dynastic principle, by which the monarchy outlived the mortal king (summed up in the familiar French phrase "The king is dead; long live the king"). In the twentieth century, however, the power of charismatic leaders was based on the uniqueness of the man at the top: after the dictator, the deluge. In the Western tradition the sovereign's physical self was secondary to his political role. In Fascist and Nazi ideology, the leader's authority derived directly from his body.

Even more than in the Third Reich, the body of the dictator in Fascist Italy became an instrument of rule, thanks partly to Mussolini's voice and his oratorical skills but also to other, nonverbal means of communication. Swiveling his eyes, contracting his jaw so his lower lip jutted out, spreading his legs, and putting his hands on his hips, Il Duce communicated through body language. Furthermore, like the ancient Romans he claimed for his ancestors, Mussolini was not embarrassed to be seen bare-chested. Nor—unlike Hitler, who was tough on his portraitists—did he seek to control the many and varied representations of him. So the dictates of propaganda and the vanity of the leader combined to turn Mussolini's body into the ideal of Fascist virility, the epitome of modern masculinity. The journalist Indro Montanelli, among others, wrote lyrically of the sensualness of the leader's body. Even fully dressed Il Duce appeared naked, impervious to drapery and clothing. "We rip off the clothing," he wrote, "going after the inimitable essentialness of this Man, who vibrates and pulsates with a formidable humanity."[4]

But the infinite metamorphoses of Il Duce—from ruler to journalist, from knight on horseback to peasant farmer, from motorcyclist to airplane pilot, from faithful husband and father to Don Juan—were not merely the work of the regime's propaganda machine. They were also the product of Italians' collective fantasies. Like lovers in Stendhal, the men and women of Fascist Italy first imagined their ideal love object, then made Mussolini correspond to it. The Fascist press freely indulged in this form of projection. According to Franco Ciarlantini, author of *Mussolini in the Imagination*, numerous citizens of Savona, far from the battlefields, claimed to remember the wounded Mussolini being brought to the hospital during the Great War—seriously injured but in such high spirits that he was able to make the other patients, the doctors, and even the chaplain laugh. An Italian American in California swore he had seen the founder of Fascism in 1919 in Milan, playing with a hand grenade to test the courage of each new convert to the cause, to see if he was made of the stuff of a Fascist. A woman from Versilia, the mother of a seriously ill child, was certain that Il Duce would cure her boy because Mussolini "is now in charge of the Balilla," the Fascist youth organization. A boy from Merano, walking to Rome barefoot, told police he had taken off his shoes because he feared he would get them dirty and need a shoeshine just when he was to meet Mussolini.

The impact of Il Duce's body on children's imagination was vital since the children of the 1920s and 1930s were the future soldiers of the 1940s (and adults of the 1950s: enchanted by the living Mussolini's physical presence, they became passionate witnesses to the adventures of his corpse). The dictator as they imagined him was obviously the product of a process of indoctrination by teachers and parents. Mothers and fathers willingly guided their offspring, as did teachers, who assigned edifying writing topics such as "How I Imagine Il Duce." The indoctrination went beyond school essays. In school libraries, children found books that placed the Fascist revolution within the great events of national history, situating Mussolini in a centuries-long line of great leaders. When the school year was over, they would be sent off to summer camp with a picture of Il Duce in their knapsacks.

How spontaneous their devotion ultimately was is hard to tell. Certainly, there was excitement and a desire to be present when Il Duce came to visit an Italian city. The boys in the Balilla youth groups and the girls in the Piccole Italiane shined the metallic M decorating their uniforms. There was a mystical quality in the relationship between these young citizens and their leader. Like adults, children saw Il Duce's public presence as a religious offering, a sort of sacred host. "If only I could receive you along with Jesus," a young Florentine girl, Margherita V., wrote to Mussolini on the day of her first communion, May 8, 1936. "If only you could enter on my tongue, sit on my chest, rest on my poor heart."[5]

The worship of the leader's body explains in part the strong theatrical vein in totalitarian regimes in general and Fascism in particular. Not only did Il Duce embody power, he acted it out. That is not to say that Mussolini's popularity was due solely to his skill as an actor, as anti-Fascists liked to think. Countless witnesses testified to the fascination Il Duce was able to exert on those who met him. One of the most expressive accounts was written in 1931 by the author Vitaliano Brancati, a young man at the time: "[Mussolini] is a monolith, all of a piece. If that piece is situated in a room, the room revolves around it; if it is situated in a crowd, the crowd bubbles up around it; if it is situated in the midst of a people, they make a pyramid around it."[6] Fourteen years after Brancati wrote those words, the crowd at a large Italian square circled around Mussolini the monolith and beat him ferociously. The pyramid of people enjoyed the vision of his dead body hanging upside down in front of a gas station. Between the two extremes of collective feeling—love for Il Duce's body and hatred for his corpse—lies the history of postwar Italy, where Fascism, anti-Fascism, and post-Fascism intersect.

IN A COURTROOM in Chieti on March 16, 1926, four years after Mussolini's ascent to power, Amerigo Dumini and accomplices went on trial for the murder of Matteotti. Mussolini intended to turn the court proceedings into something much more than the prosecution of Matteotti's killers; he wanted to put the anti-Fascist opposition on trial. Thus, no less of a figure than the Fascist Party's national secretary, Roberto Farinacci, was appointed Dumini's defense lawyer. Il Duce also hoped that the trial would show how little Italians cared about the murder, or so a note he wrote—"We must not let Italy go back to its Matteotti obsession"—suggests. As it happened, one of the spectators as the trial opened was an unstable Irishwoman, Violet Gibson, determined to avenge the murder of Matteotti by killing the dictator. A few days later she tried to carry out the assassination on a street in Rome. Her bullet grazed Mussolini, and she was saved from the fury of the crowd only by the police. The same day someone put fresh flowers in front of Matteotti's image, and no policeman tried to stop him. (Throughout the two decades of Mussolini's rule, the funerals and commemorations of "subversives" remained a constant challenge to Il Duce.)

Attempts on Mussolini's life such as Gibson's merely strengthened his position, as they forced Italians to imagine a future without him. It was a future that frightened the majority, who feared becoming embroiled in a civil war. As a high-ranking Fascist official, Luigi Federzoni, observed, the regime was only as vital as its leader, "and that is the tragic greatness as well as the only real weakness of our situation."[7] For Italians, the sociologist Roberto

Michels commented, Mussolini's death was the equivalent of Italy's death. Proof that such thoughts occurred to many ordinary citizens is to be found in Il Duce's archives. After Gibson's attempt on Mussolini's life, a fourteen-year-old girl from a good family wrote to Il Duce to express her relief that he had survived and her hatred of the would-be assassin. "Why couldn't you strangle that murderous woman who injured you, divine spirit? Why couldn't you remove her forever from Italian soil, now that it has been touched by your pure blood, by your great, good, honest blood from Romagna?" The passionate adolescent's letter continued, "Oh, Duce, my life is dedicated to you," concluding with the signature of Clara Petacci, Mussolini's future mistress.[8]

In September 1926 an anarchist marble cutter from Carrara, Gino Lucetti, made another attempt on Mussolini's life. Following the attempts of Friends of the People and Violet Gibson, this was the third failed effort, and it contributed to a popular impression that Il Duce enjoyed the protection of divine Providence. Fearing that Mussolini would soon wear a mystical halo if he survived yet another attack, anti-Fascist leaders in exile condemned the notion of assassination. They were backed in this by the most distinguished of Italy's anti-Fascist intellectuals, beginning with Salvemini, who was still smarting from his experience with Friends of the People. A few days after Lucetti tried his hand, Salvemini wrote in the *Manchester Guardian* that nothing could be more favorable to the military-capitalist alliance controlling Italy than a successful attempt on Mussolini's life. If Matteotti's murderer were out of the way, argued Salvemini, his successor would have no blood on his hands—a situation detrimental to the anti-Fascists. "The death of Mussolini would be an incomparable gift to the Fascist regime," the historian continued.[9]

Somehow it escaped the normally astute Salvemini that Il Duce's was no ordinary body. Exiled from Italy, the historian was out of touch with the charisma of the Fascist leader. True, in 1926, the cult of Il Duce was only beginning to reach its height. That was the year Margherita Sarfatti published her hagiographic treatment, *Dux;* the same period saw the first of many printings of an influential biography by the journalist Giorgio Pini. A vigorous debate about realism in figure painting and sculpture had also begun, the most important figure under discussion being that of Mussolini. A highly sophisticated Fascist intellectual, Giuseppe Bottai, soon found himself alone in criticizing an official art made up of "horrible busts of decorated plaster" and of "colored prints of Il Duce in absurd postures."[10] Before long, advertisers were competing with artists to transform the dictator into a design object. Between 1925 and 1926 two satirical magazines, *L'Asino* and *Il Becco giallo,* ceased publication. The moment had arrived in which Mussolini's image would no longer be an object of satire.

A few weeks after the Lucetti attack, there was another. An attempt to shoot Mussolini in Bologna on October 31, 1926, signaled the end of democratic Italy. All political parties except for the National Fascist Party were outlawed; the opposition press was suppressed; the death penalty was reinstated for political offenses; a secret police, the OVRA, was created, as was a special tribunal for crimes against the state. Despite decades of historical research, the facts of the Bologna assassination attempt remain hazy. According to the Fascist police, the would-be assassin was a sixteen-year-old anarchist militant named Anteo Zamboni, who barely missed Mussolini and was lynched on the spot by Fascist supporters. The anti-Fascist version of events is that the young man was the innocent victim of a plot hatched by the Fascist Party itself.

Zamboni's father and aunt were convicted as co-conspirators, and during their sentencing at the tribunal for crimes against the state, the judges cited rumors of an assassination plot circulating in Bologna before Mussolini's visit. But whether or not the shots were announced in advance, the lynching certainly was. A photograph taken near Porta Saragozza on October 30, 1926, the day before the attempt, shows a cart being pushed by a band of Blackshirts. The names of Mussolini's previous failed assassins appears on the side of the cart, with a poster showing a straw man hanging from a rope—a clear warning to anyone who might try again. The next day, after Anteo Zamboni had been stabbed to death, his killers did indeed try to string him up on a lamppost. They were dissuaded only by the powerful local Fascist boss Italo Balbo, who proudly advised that "Fascists don't hang the dead." According to Sisto Zamboni, Anteo's uncle, "Matteotti's murderers were among the lynch squad," and indeed, Albino Volpi, a Milanese Fascist militant implicated in the Matteotti crime, was part of the group that killed Zamboni.[11]

As news of the assassination attempt spread across Italy, it unleashed a wave of violence. It was raw violence, the sort that the *squadristi*, the paramilitary groups that enacted the Fascist party's crudest impulses, had learned from the Arditi during the war—a military-parade show of might and a cruel celebration of the physical destruction of the enemy. There were attacks on the homes of several parliamentary deputies who had protested after Matteotti's death. In Sardinia, Emilio Lussu, a leader of the anti-Fascist Partito d'Azione, the Action Party, opened fire on a group who had arrived to kill him; one young *squadrista* died. Alcide De Gasperi, head of the Catholic Partito Popolare, the Popular Party (and for many years prime minister in postwar Italy), was threatened by Fascist militants as he traveled on a train. On another train, Antonio Gramsci, secretary general of the Italian Communist Party, met some of the Fascist *squadristi* who had been in Bologna that day. According to Gramsci, an angry crowd of Fascists boarded the train and some, who came to sit in his carriage, pridefully showed off their knives running red with blood: "After they murdered Anteo Zamboni, the Fascists lined up in front of that innocent young man's body and stabbed him so as to take home their bloodstained trophies."[12] Gramsci was arrested and imprisoned only days later, an experience that eventually killed him.

THREE DAYS BEFORE the events in Bologna, Mussolini, celebrating the fourth anniversary of the March on Rome, told the crowd gathered under his balcony that his watchword was "a verb, to endure"—to endure day after day, month after month, year after year, letting his opponents' attacks fall away like "vile slime" as they hit the wall of Fascist resolve and tenacity.[13] Rhetoric aside, Mussolini's watchword points to a greater mission than politics, one that Il Duce genuinely perceived as ageless, a will to power defying time and reaching for eternity. Eternity here is not to be confused with immortality; to say something is dead does not mean it cannot last. Like other twentieth-century totalitarian regimes, Fascism tried to cloak the body of its charismatic leader with the durability of a monument, to turn Il Duce into a lasting entity not much different from the embalmed corpses of Soviet memory.

And like other twentieth-century revolutionaries, Mussolini dreamed of being eternal, sometimes to foolish effect, as when Fascist propagandists sought to conceal the fact that he was aging and kept quiet about the birth of his grandchildren. The exhortation to endure also tested the regime's legal experts, who struggled with the question of succession. How were they to decide whether the title of Duce was transferable to others without questioning Mussolini's immortality? The debate—such as it was, given the participants' connection to the regime—testifies to the poverty of juridical thought in the period. One Fascist legal expert felt no shame in asserting that Mussolini was Italy's "eternal

Il Duce the eternal, Piazza Venezia, October 28, 1934.   (*Istituto Luce*)

Duce."[14] Journalist Berto Ricci had a subtler interpretation. "We believe in the *Dictator perpetuus,*" he wrote, "but not in the perpetual dictatorship."[15]

That Mussolini's dictatorship would be eternal was just what the anti-Fascists had begun to fear. So they periodically waxed enthusiastic about rumors of Il Duce's poor health, rumors that circulated all the more vigorously the harder the regime tried to silence them. The opposition especially cultivated the "myth of the ulcer" that writer Leonardo Sciascia later recounted. As far away as the provinces as Racalmuto, Sicily, Sciascia's hometown, people had heard about Mussolini's "galloping" ulcer "and they were as enthralled by that gallop as by the cliffhanging end of a Western." One local anti-Fascist made sure to go down to the village station in 1937 when Mussolini's train came through. "He went to see how far the ulcer had galloped," but against his hopes found Il Duce in excellent physical form. "Ulcer, my foot," the man confessed to his friends, "that man is going to live for a hundred years."[16]

For all the promise of the galloping ulcer, the anti-Fascists never gave up on the hope of a liberating bullet. In 1927 the special tribunal for crimes against the state heard more than 160 cases that involved the accused's speaking favorably about an attempt on Mussolini's life. While the court issued its harshest sentences in the places where the workers' movement had flourished before Fascism, the tribunal's proceedings suggest that the crime of wishing Mussolini dead was not confined to his radical working-class opponents. Anti-Fascist tongues were loosened, it seems, whenever there was news of someone's actually trying to kill Il Duce. Thus a rush of cases followed the assassination attempts of 1926; after a few years of relative silence, a new spate of attempts in 1931–32 prompted more cases. Of course, it would be unwise to overstate the political significance of this verbal crime against the Fascist state. An offender could just as easily be a careless drunk or someone mentally ill as a coolly rational anti-Fascist. Still, there is no gainsaying the truth that emerges from the tribunal's archives: every corner of Italy and every social class harbored enthusiasts in favor of Il Duce's assassination.

Among those indicted for applauding the Friends of the People's 1926 attempt were two peasants from Trapani, Sicily; another two from near Verona; a mechanic from Vercelli, in Piedmont; a field hand from Trieste; a traveling salesman from Palermo; and an electrician from Tivoli. Admirers of Anteo Zamboni included a farm owner from Istria; a waiter from Perugia; a day laborer from Siena; a bricklayer from Vacri, near Chieti, in Abruzzo; a housewife from Merano; a mechanic from Bologna;

two factory workers from Brescia; an engineer from Russi, in Emilia-Romagna; a priest from Pontemaggiore Belsisto, near Palermo; a farmer from near Padua; an agricultural laborer from the Marches working in Friuli; a glazier from Mondovi, in Piedmont; an accountant from Modena; and a student from Avellino. Cheers for Violet Gibson came from a vintner from the Roman Hills; a farmer from Alessandria, in Piedmont; a road inspector from Chiesanova, near Padua; a decorator in Turin; and a sailor from Pesaro. Gino Lucetti's effort to kill Mussolini won support from a fellow marble cutter from Avenza, in Tuscany; a white-collar worker from Lodi, in Lombardy; an accountant from Milan; a field hand from Brunico, in Alto Adige; and a bricklayer from Arezzo. A parish priest from near Salerno was denounced along with a friend when he told two Fascist militiamen, "We're not mad at you, poor fellows, but at Mussolini, who makes you act like bandits. . . . Whoever gets rid of him is going to get a golden trophy."[17]

The crime of wishing Mussolini dead was not the only insult to Il Duce processed by the tribunal. Sometimes the charge was "offenses against the head of state." A single remark could bring multiple charges. Pasquale Spagnuolo, a farmer from near Aquila, made the following comment in 1928: "Fascism won't last more than ten years and you'll see that Mussolini and the four bums still loyal to him will come to a fine end." For these few words Spagnuolo was charged on three counts: speaking in favor of assassination, causing offense to the head of state, and spreading subversive propaganda.[18] But beyond the fine points of judicial process, the tribunal records reveal the level of hatred toward Mussolini: "Kill the toad-faced, monkey-faced bum," "Wring his neck like a chicken's," "Split his heart in two."[19] In Mantua, someone named Ulderico Carnevali predicted in 1931 that "soon we will see Mussolini strung up in a public square."[20] That same year—the high-water mark of popular anti-Fascism—seventeen-year-old bricklayer Leopoldo Piantino was charged with writing "Death to Mussolini" in a book in the Turin prison library.

Without the messages left to us by these faceless opponents of the regime, the prehistory of Mussolini's dead body would be incomplete. Talk, however, was just the tip of the iceberg; would-be assassins surely had plans. The mere idea that someone was scheming to kill Il Duce obsessed the regime's police, who filled archives with reports on suspected murder plots. True, OVRA and its henchmen had an interest in finding plots everywhere so as to justify their existence. Nevertheless, the police files are instructive for the light they shed on the sometimes grotesque paranoia of Mussolini's safekeepers. Such paranoia was by no means unique to Fascist chief of police Arturo Bocchini and his aides; it was shared by heads of security the world over, as it is now. But in Mussolini's Italy, paranoia reached such extremes that it is an indicator of historical significance. As the OVRA police knew better than anyone else, even at a time of sweeping consensus for the regime, Mussolini's body was one that many imagined as dead.

In 1928 Fascist informers in Paris reported a plot to kill Il Duce with "a large dose of bacteria" and recommended chemical analysis of Mussolini's drinking water, the carpets in his office, and other potential sources of infection. In 1930 those same sources reported plans for "an assassination device to be hidden in an animal, perhaps a stuffed dog or a lady's fox fur." In 1931 the police foiled the sale of some acres of agricultural land in Romagna, on a tip that it was to be used to plant a bomb along Il Duce's most-traveled route. A few years later an informer revealed a murder plan that involved "a pencil capable of launching a sharp needle tipped with a powerful poison." Another spy for OVRA, aware of Mussolini's weakness for women, reported that he was to be murdered in the bedroom by "a beautiful, sexy female." If the police informers are to be believed, the prize for ingenuity would go to the would-be killers who intended to exploit Mussolini's vanity and his passion for his likeness: a 1933 plan reported from Paris involved a "bust bomb" destined to explode weeks after its installation in Palazzo Venezia.[21]

While the police force's imagination was sometimes overheated, anti-Fascist conspirators were not lacking. Their schemes became ever more complex after the failures of 1926 and they were increasingly at risk of infiltration by the police. In April 1929, when Sandro Pertini was arrested in Pisa following a period of exile in France, the Socialist leader had come to OVRA's attention for a plot to plant a powerful time bomb in the sewer system of Palazzo Venezia. The plan had been suspended because one of his colleagues, Ernesto Rossi, a veteran anti-Fascist, had learned that the drains in question were under police surveillance. Neither in this case nor in others did the failure of one plot mean the conspirators renounced their plans to murder Mussolini, especially once the anti-Fascists began to see how tightly the regime's hold was tied to the person of Mussolini. As Rossi later put it, all good anti-Fascists thought that assassination was the only solution, although it would mean their certain deaths.

In his 1930 book *The Chain*, published in Paris, Emilio Lussu, cofounder of the anti-Fascist movement Giustizia e Libertà (Justice and Liberty), sharply rejected the wait-and-see attitude of some opponents and urged efforts to kill Il Duce. Because the opposition had not adopted violence as a political weapon, argued Lussu, its leaders had been exiled and sometimes murdered. But now the time had come to change direction. Lussu was ready to put his ideas into action. First he tried to hire a killer with a long-range precision rifle, then he got involved in an amateurish assassination plot with Michele Schirru, a Sardinian anarchist who ultimately faced the firing squad.[22] Lussu's enthusiasm was contagious among anti-Fascists abroad. In September 1931, OVRA's agents in Paris were clearly worried. "All hopes among the community of anti-Fascists . . . now lie in the disappearance of the chief," said one dispatch.[23] A few months later the Roman police arrested Angelo Sbardellotto, an anarchist militant who had planned to shoot Il Duce on June 2, 1932, the day the ashes of Anita Garibaldi, Giuseppe Garibaldi's wife, were to be transferred to the capital. It was a heavily symbolic choice of occasion, for the murder of Mussolini would coincide with the moment he had chosen to appropriate the democratic legacy of Italy's unification. As it was, Sbardellotto failed and, like Schirru, was condemned to die. In both cases, the tribunal for crimes against the state turned to the clause of the Fascist penal code that applied the same sentence for an assassination plot as for a successful murder.

The years that followed were particularly hard for anti-Fascist exiles. In 1932, on the tenth anniversary of the March on Rome, the regime offered an amnesty to Italians exiled abroad, and to many an Italian, the choice not to return to Italy now seemed a choice of victimhood. Meanwhile the myth of Mussolini's invulnerability grew as the bullets multiplied but Il Duce remained untouched. Even Lussu abandoned the assassination strategy in his writings on the theory of insurrection. At home, there were still some anti-Fascists who continued to defy the tribunal for crimes against the state, but the 1930s, the high point of the regime's consensus, saw fewer of them. There was, however, an increase in sentences for damaging an image of Il Duce—a print, photograph, or postcard. Felice Arrigoni, an Alfa Romeo mechanic from Milan, was brought before the tribunal after he tried to stop a colleague from hanging a portrait of Mussolini in the shop. "Do you have to hang that thing here? It turns my stomach," Arrigoni was reported to have said. "Mussolini really has a shitface."[24] There were many more such cases, elementary acts of protest against an icon that Fascist propaganda was disseminating ever more widely.

In the anti-Fascist imagination, fantasies about Il Duce's death varied according to the individual's sociocultural background. To the educated, history offered an obvious figure of comparison, Cola di Rienzo, a medieval Roman rabble-rouser who emerged from humble origins to lead the people before plunging back into ignominy. Throughout the 1930s various opponents cited the similarity, which made even more sense after the war, when Mussolini's corpse met its implacable fate at Piazzale Loreto. As rulers, Mussolini, the son of a blacksmith, and Cola di Rienzo, the son of an innkeeper, were linked by their plebian origins to a precarious destiny. Other educated Italians dreamed of taking advantage of their position to eliminate Mussolini personally. The writer Alberto Moravia advised his friend Roberto Ducci, son of a high-ranking navy official, to shoot Il Duce at close range just as Mussolini was awarding him a prize at a ceremony. And the archaeologist Ranuccio Bianchi Bandinelli dreamed of assassinating Il Duce as he showed Hitler and Mussolini around Florence during a 1938 state visit.

ON THE EVE of World War II, the prehistory of Il Duce's dead body became intertwined with Italian foreign policy. Although Italy had signed a mutual intervention agreement with Germany, Italians wondered about Il Duce's real intentions: would he keep Italy out of the European conflict or wait for a propitious moment to join the fray at the side of his powerful German ally?

Mussolini's prestige seesawed wildly during this time of uncertainty, with public opinion ranging from rage at a leader who seemed unable to protect his country from an inevitable war to fear of losing the one man who could guarantee the country's future. As early as September 1939, an OVRA informer from Florence reported Mussolini as "morally dead, in the sense that there seems to be no trust in his political acumen."[25] In the months that followed there were rumors that Il Duce was dead or dying. One elaborate story had Mussolini "embalmed with his right arm raised in the Roman salute" so that he could be wheeled out onto the balcony of Palazzo Venezia, concealing his inability to walk.[26] The fantasy showed how widely Il Duce was seen as a human monument.

If the police archives are any gauge, Mussolini's prestige survived Italy's entry into the war and well into 1941; even the country's setbacks in France, Greece, and elsewhere failed to damage Il Duce's image as the country's savior: he was seen as fallible only insofar as he was surrounded by mediocre Fascist officials. This perspective was strongest in the center-south of the country, where the war had the least impact; in the industrial north, insults were hurled at Mussolini ("Il Duce is a crackpot"), followed by outright threats. In February 1941, a worker at the Fiat Grandi Motori factory named Alfredo Colombi was heard expressing the following fantasy: "At the end of the war I'm going to put him in a cage and show him off for five lire a head, and I'm sure I'll become a millionaire."[27] Colombi's boast cost him a five-year sentence in *confino,* the Fascist regime's internal exile in a remote part of Italy. But within a few months men like Alfredo Colombi were multiplying throughout the cities of Italy as it came under heavy bombing. Ten years of Mussolini's rhetoric about Fascist efficiency crumbled under the evidence that the antiaircraft system was woefully unprepared. The supreme commander's uniform seemed to fit him less with every passing day. It is not by chance that Fascist propaganda showed fewer and fewer portraits of Mussolini in his soldierly role.

The final blow came with Italy's heavy losses at the Soviet front. Even the Church began to distance itself from the regime; the clergy, in particular, lent its moral backing to the people rather than to Il Duce. At a time of shortages and suffering, religious sympathy was no longer seen as due the leader once known as the "man of divine Providence." The plight of Mussolini was of no interest to mothers concerned with their children and grieving for their dead. In a letter to her husband in Germany that was intercepted by the censors, a Ligurian woman wrote: "The king and queen came to inspect the damage in Genoa and the crowd booed them, calling for the other one with the bald head. They say Il Duce has cancer; let us hope that it is true."[28] In the fall of 1942 there were new rumors that Mussolini was in poor health. This time they contained a modicum of truth, as Il Duce was suffering from gastric problems. Overall, police records from the period show a major reversal in public opinion. Mussolini was seen no longer as bold, honest, and wise but as cowardly, thievish, insane. Perhaps he had syphilis and was still running after Clara Petacci and various actresses and who knew who else?

Mussolini a coward, dishonest, unfaithful—these accusations are worth keeping in mind, since they would stick and reverberate powerfully after Il Duce's fall from grace. In the months that led up to his ouster from the government on July 25, 1943, the Italians' relationship to Il Duce seemed reduced to one long meditation on death. On the streets of Milan, an OVRA informer said, the "death to Mussolini" graffiti were often not even painted over. The name of Milan's department store UPIM was now invoked as a macabre invitation, the letters standing for *"Uniamoci per impiccare Mussolini"*—"Let's get together and hang Mussolini." In Rome, the police reported, people lining up outside shops to buy food as early as 4:00 A.M. cursed him and called for his death. Similar wishes were widespread in the country as well. A farm woman from near Cuneo, in Piedmont, wrote to her brother, a soldier, hoping to evade the censor: "To tell the truth, when I'm shifting manure I get so angry about the war that if I had someone here I would stick my pitchfork in his stomach. My dear, I cannot tell you who that someone is, but you understand, don't you?"[29] Farmers in the area were reported as saying, "If only we could kill Mussolini, we would burn him alive."[30]

In the winter of 1942, Gaetano Salvemini was not the only anti-Fascist intellectual exiled in the United States to ponder Mussolini's death.[31] The question tormented Vincenzo Vacirca, an important opponent of the regime. Largely forgotten today, Vacirca was a Socialist deputy at the time of the March on Rome, one of Mussolini's toughest adversaries even before the Matteotti murder, and one of the first to leave the country. Having escaped to America, Vacirca used his energies as a journalist for the New York Italian-language newspaper *Il Nuovo Mondo*, trying to reconcile the various strands of anti-Fascism in the States—the anarchists, the Communists, and the liberal Socialists. He also wrote a book with a prescient title, *Mussolini: The Story of a Corpse*, which he finished in 1934 but was not able to bring out until 1942.

In an epilogue Vacirca sought to explain why he was publishing the book despite its being out of date. He was eager, he said, to tell Americans the truth about Mussolini in the run-up to an Allied landing in Italy—to tell them more than the mixture of fact and fantasy in so many of the books published by English and American journalists during the years of Il Duce's rule. Although he had written the book about "a man who is alive," Vacirca intended the work as "the autopsy of a moral corpse." In his most moving chapter, he intertwines the story of Mussolini's live body with the tragic episode of Matteotti's corpse, a dead body that took a long time to be found, "since the corpse of an assassinated man is a terrifying accuser." It tells us all about the crime: the number of wounds, the weapon used, the degree of premeditation, the torture imposed and on which parts of the body.[32]

Nearly twenty years after Matteotti's murder, Vacirca remembered every detail of the collective anguish the Italian people had lived through during the weeks following his disappearance. Every morning forty million Italians woke up and asked themselves whether the body had been found. "Everyone could see it," he wrote, "and everyone had an obsessive image floating in his dream space."[33] When the body was discovered, he recalled, Mussolini carefully avoided any public mention of Matteotti, so powerful was the dead man's aura.

From the title of his book on through, Vacirca treated Mussolini as if he were a dead man. This reflected a fundamental difference between his view of the dictatorship and that of his better-known compatriot Gaetano Salvemini, who was also in the United States. As Salvemini saw it, Mussolini would continue to dominate the political scene as long as he was alive. A dictator like Mussolini, Salvemini argued, could not just be deposed and retire to private life like an ordinary president of a democratic republic. Nor could he take refuge abroad because no country would be willing to harbor him. In Salvemini's reasoning, the writing was on the wall: "Mussolini . . . will remain where he is, or he must be assassinated."[34] But who, Salvemini continued, would get rid of Il Duce? Only a military coup d'état would remove him, one that would physically eliminate him and dissolve the Fascist Party and other Fascist institutions. Such a coup could obviously occur only if the army commanders were to take the initiative. In his most thoughtful essay of the period, "What to Do with Italy?," Salvemini wondered if they would.

Then, on July 25, 1943, Mussolini was abruptly removed from office on the king's orders. Il Duce's meekness before the Carabinieri sent by Victor Emanuel III made him seem almost a caricature of himself. The following day, in various cities, he was cursed, mocked, and murdered in effigy. In Rome, busts of him (often made of cheap metal rather than bronze) were tied to the backs of streetcars and dragged along, clattering like empty cans. In the all-too-graphic testimony of novelist Aldo Palazzeschi, young Romans showered portraits of Mussolini with "all that their bold, sturdy bodies could muster" and Il Duce's noble features disappeared under "everything the human body contained in the way of refuse and excrement."[35] The fury of the crowd was not limited to such abuse. There were cries for a guillotine to be set up in Piazza Venezia, for a military trial to be followed by the cruelest possible execution.

In Milan, the atmosphere was much the same. A column of Alfa Romeo workers headed downtown, dragging a bust of Mussolini. Out came a woman who put two fingers in Il Duce's bronze eyes, spit on the statue, and screamed, "Murderer! This is for my son whom you sent to die in the war."[36] The scene is all the more striking because it would be repeated by Milanese women two years later in front of Il Duce's actual body. A letter from a Milanese resident tells of another enthusiastic incident: "Everyone was cheering and clapping because they had taken a statue of Mussolini and hanged it."[37] The iconoclastic fury of the Milanese extended to scurrilous songs like this one: "If on the night Il Duce was conceived / Donna Rosa, illuminated by divine light / Had offered the Predappio blacksmith / Instead of her front her backside / Then someone would have been buggered that night / But not the whole of Italy."[38] Meanwhile the walls of Milan were covered with graffiti, "some of it actually very clever," one police officer admitted.[39]

Il Duce the fallen as Verrocchio's Colleoni, Venice, December 1944. (*Istituto Luce*)

From the archives come examples of the anti-Fascist fury and homicidal intentions the police had been denouncing for years. "The donkey from Predappio has stopped braying," read one slogan. "Mussolini has slain the sons of Italy. Long live Matteotti. Matteotti, you are not dead, because the dead are those who are forgotten, while you live on in the minds of all and you will be revenged. Cut off his head," it continued. Another comment played on the letters of Mussolini's surname: *"Morirai Ucciso Solo Senza Onore Liberando Italia Nostra Independente"* (You will die alone and without honor, liberating our dear independent Italy). Other graffiti referred to the shameful way Il Duce had exited the political stage, without any resistance on his part or that of other Fascist officials: "The hangman has disappeared. Note: We're looking for a pig that's run away from Rome. A large reward for the finder. . . . All his followers are in the toilet with a bad case of the runs." Mussolini, one graffiti writer complained, had failed miserably to save his honor: "The scoundrel has disappeared without even the courage to do himself in." But perhaps the most striking of the slogans are those that refer to Il Duce as if he had died. "He's finally dead," read one scrawled comment, while another said, "He wanted to be Caesar but he died Vespasiano," referring to the Roman emperor whose name in Italian is shorthand for public toilet.[40]

For half a century, Italian historians, mostly nonacademics, have pondered how Italy went to sleep a Fascist country on July 25, 1943, and awoke an anti-Fascist country the next day. This supposed change of heart is one of postwar Italy's great clichés, reinforced by tales of the saturnalia that took place across the land on July 26. An observer of the events in Rome told of a "well-known actress wearing only her pajamas and a large dose of libido" who was dragged and tossed around by the young men of Via del Tritone.[41] That not all Italians waited for Mussolini's fall before cursing him and calling for his death is a useful corrective to the historical myth. Moreover, the number of participants in the celebrations of July 26 was relatively small. Even in Milan, the anti-Fascist marches were joined by only a few hundred people. Nowhere in Italy could the demonstrations that day be described as mass events. And the large number of participants who were killed (eighty-six dead and more than three hundred injured between July 26 and August 1) suggests how the new government headed by former army chief of staff Field Marshal Pietro Badoglio approached the demonstrations: the marchers were criminals, not average Italians.

There is every reason to believe that the fall of Il Duce was

"He wanted to be Caesar but he died Vespasiano," referring to the Roman emperor whose name in Italian is shorthand for "public toilet." (*Foto Publifoto/ Olympia*)

welcomed not only by longtime anti-Fascists but by some of the same Italians who had once cheered him under the balcony of Palazzo Venezia. Nevertheless, the marches of July 26 should be seen less as an abrupt change of heart by Italians than as the culmination of twenty years of antiregime sentiments. Those who had talked about assassinating Mussolini over the previous two decades were a minority, just as the people celebrating his downfall and killing his effigy were a minority. While there is no certain evidence the two minorities were one and the same, there are grounds for thinking they were largely composed of the same

kinds of people: visceral anti-Fascists who came out on behalf of
no political parties but mobilized along generational or professional lines. This was an Italy moved less by political platforms
than by symbolic gestures—by place-names, for example: already
by July 27 there was a Piazza Giacomo Matteotti in Rome and a
Via Matteotti in Milan.

THE ANONYMOUS GRAFFITI writers of Milan were not far
wrong when they spoke of Mussolini as a dead man. In many
ways the dictator, although he survived the coup that deposed
him, was a figure who had outlived his purpose. His adventures
of the summer of 1943—fifty days in confinement on the remote
island of Ponza and the Gran Sasso peak in Abruzzo; Hitler's order to free him, followed by a swashbuckling jailbreak from the
Gran Sasso carried out by Otto Skorzeny, a German pilot—only
added to that impression. On July 28 the Socialist leader Pietro
Nenni, himself confined to Ponza, stood by as Il Duce was
brought to the island. "He is a defeated man," Nenni wrote in his
diary, "a hero who has fallen from his paper throne and is rolling
in the dust."⁴² How could Il Duce see it differently, given the
news of demonstrations and burning effigies that followed his
ouster? In a letter to his sister Edvige at the end of August, Mussolini called himself "a bag of bones and muscles in a state of organic decay." He was "three-quarters dead," he wrote.⁴³ Having
been for twenty years the physical symbol of the regime, Il Duce
perceived his political decline as bodily decrepitude. On the night
of September 11, he tried to slash his wrists.

After his escape from prison at the Gran Sasso, in the fall of
1943, Mussolini was installed as the head of the German-backed
Italian Social Republic in northern Italy, headquartered at Salò,
while southern Italy, under Field Marshal Badoglio, had surren-

dered to the Allies. Yet many Italians—whether in Rome, in Mussolini's birthplace of Predappio, in the south, liberated by the Allies, or even in the German-occupied north—believed that the real Duce was dead. According to Vincenzo Costa, a senior official of the Republic of Salò, Mussolini was widely thought to have passed away or been imprisoned by Hitler in Germany; the Duce installed at Lake Garda was said to be a body double. The same conviction was shared, according to a young Blackshirt, by the clients of a provincial brothel. The philosopher Benedetto Croce noted that these suppositions were widespread in Naples. "The very rumor that he is dead, which goes around from time to time, suggests that he really is dead in the hearts of many."[44] In the spring of 1944, Mussolini also reportedly believed that the rumors of his death indicated a popular wish.

Thus the fate of Il Duce during the six hundred days of the Social Republic was to live on to show he was not dead. To some of the less motivated Italian soldiers of the Hitler-backed regime, Mussolini's destiny was pathetic. One young artilleryman recounted to a friend a visit to his barracks by Il Duce: "He amused us when he was reviewing the troops. He waggled his backside around like a girl in heat, and some of the officers, seeing him doing that, could barely stop themselves from laughing."[45] However, Il Duce's situation was tragic for the true believers of the Italian Social Republic: the men who had signed up to prove to their idol that the real Italy was not the spineless nation that had surrendered to the Allies, that Fascism had raised at least a few courageous youths ready to honor the war pact with Hitler, people who knew what a hero's death was, who had no fear of finding themselves wearing "a wooden overcoat" lined with "zinc fur," as one Blackshirt memorably put it.[46]

The most passionate followers of the Social Republic never ceased worshipping the body of Il Duce. The women enrolled as

"Who was that man who talked like him, moved like him, whom we had seen so many times in the newsreels, but who wasn't him?" Mussolini inspecting his troops, the Republic of Salò, March 1945. (*Istituto Luce*)

auxiliaries, in particular, adored their new Christ risen for the salvation of the country, still venerating his image and thrilling to his voice. But Mussolini, now aging at sixty, was increasingly difficult to present as an icon, to the point that the Salò regime allowed few of his photos to circulate. Apart from military occasions, Il Duce appeared less and less in public, spending his time holed up in his headquarters at Villa Feltrinelli in the village of Gargnano. Those who encountered him came away initially with the impression of a man unchanged. There were the same strong facial expressions, the same jerky gestures, the same habit of pursing his lips and sticking them out after saying a few words. Still, the sense that this was the Mussolini of old quickly gave way to uneasy uncertainty. "Who was that man who talked like him, moved like him, whom we had seen so many times in the newsreels, but who wasn't him?" asked one young Blackshirt from Rome, Carlo Mazzantini, who saw in Il Duce a self-impersonation.[47] For writer and journalist Leo Longanesi, a cruel fantasy he'd once harbored seemed to have come true: Mussolini is back in Predappio, living on charity, and his friends invite him to the bar. "Benito, we'll buy you a drink," they say, "but first you have to do your famous Blackshirt speech." So Il Duce, hands on hips, strides to the center of the applauding circle to ape himself.[48]

"Never before has a bankrupt man been called upon to take charge of his own bankruptcy," jurist Salvatore Satta wrote;[49] yet this was Mussolini's fate, the hardest Providence could assign: to rise from his own ashes. Postwar neo-Fascist writers would depict Salò as a place of punishment curiously devoid of any crime. Mussolini had sacrificed himself, given himself over to the Germans to spare Italy further suffering. This interpretation of Mussolini's final years was later taken up by revisionist historians: Il Duce as the helpless and impotent head of a puppet state; as the ever more bored lover of his mistress, Claretta Petacci; as a grandfather indulging his growing number of grandchildren; as a grieving father haunted by the death of his son-in-law, ex–foreign minister Galeazzo Ciano, who was executed by the Social Republic for supporting Mussolini's ouster in 1943. While each of these personas contained some degree of truth, taken together they added up to a false picture. It wasn't true that the head of the Social Republic was not—and did not want to be—anybody's dictator.

Between 1943 and 1945, Mussolini proposed at least one political initiative, a "socialization" plan to turn workers into the owners of companies through their labor federations. He also began a media campaign to burnish his image, starting with a series of articles signed "The Globetrotter" that appeared in the *Corriere della Sera* in the spring of 1944. Collected in a book entitled *The Story of a Year*, first published by the newspaper and then by the Mondadori publishing house, Mussolini's volume was one of the rare best sellers in a year when reading books was not a priority for Italians. In it Il Duce told his version of the fall of Fascism and the rise of the Social Republic—his ouster on July 25, 1943, his arrest and imprisonment, the shame he felt when Badoglio signed the armistice with the Allies, his arguments for why the German-backed Republic of Salò was the responsible choice for Italy. But he also told the story of his, of Il Duce's, body. Mussolini began with his injuries in the Great War, when he lay in the hospital at Ronchi, his "body riddled with shrapnel." He continued through Il Duce's "many duels," the "incredibly tedious" attempts on his life, and a series of car and airplane accidents that put his body to the test of history. That he escaped with his life, Mussolini suggested, was partly due to his "iron skull."

Tempting as it is to read this account ironically, that would be a mistake. Twenty years of Fascism had shown that the body of Il Duce was a serious matter. Nevertheless there is something old hat about the book, as, for example, when Mussolini boasts about his "Panzer-style" head. Dozens of regime hacks and poet laureates had made the same claim, likening his head to "a square bullet, a box of good explosives, a cubic will to rule."[50] When Il Duce took the praise up himself he was merely invoking an old futurist dream of remaking the human body in metal. But there is also the incongruity of his making these claims for himself, claims previously advanced only by his admirers. It is unusual for a leader to have to write an appreciation of his own physical attributes and seems desperate, after he has been cruelly murdered symbolically. If the fairy tale had a moral, it was that this was a leader who was "tough to eradicate."[51] The message was far from irrelevant, for Mussolini's intention was to prolong his life.

The Globetrotter's articles were written with a purpose that would have been clear to people immersed in the political climate of the moment. Mussolini's version of events was meant to send a signal of rapprochement to the forces in the Resistance front that Il Duce considered most moderate and most likely to negotiate with him: the Socialists and the Christian Democrats. Thus, when the philosopher Giovanni Gentile, a former Fascist minister and supporter of the Social Republic, was murdered in April 1944, the Globetrotter's column ceased publication for a month; Gentile's murder was seen as the Communists' ferocious reply to Mussolini's attempts at conciliation. The articles stopped altogether in June, when the political groups opposing the Salò republic—organized in the Committee of National Liberation for northern Italy—moved to impose the death sentence on national traitors, meaning the Fascists and collaborators. The negotiations Mussolini had been hoping for ended before they began. Whatever the case, the Mussolini of *The Story of a Year* was anything but a resigned old man. He was a leader determined to fight to the end.

Fascist leaders continued to conduct negotiations with the Committee of National Liberation up until the Resistance's victory in April 1945, but these dealings were of no help to Mussolini since the Communist, the Socialist, and the Action parties had all agreed not to bargain with Il Duce. Moreover, the armistice agreement Badoglio signed in September 1943 contained a clause obliging Italy to turn the Fascist leaders over to the Allies to be tried in an international war crimes court. The futile negotiations resulted in Mussolini's attempt to escape to Switzerland on April 27, 1945, just before the Allied armies reached Milan, and his much described arrest by partisans on the road along Lake Como, with Claretta Petacci and other Fascist officials. During that time of Italy's liberation, history was moving too quickly to be written according to the rules of international law. Both the Fascists and the partisans understood that they were fighting to the death. Mussolini himself, under his Globetrotter byline, had prayed he would be spared "the farce of an absurd trial in Madison Square in New York" and insisted he was proud to be a protagonist in the "terrible fifth act" of the national tragedy.[52]

As Il Duce well knew, there are no sixth acts. The heads of the Resistance knew it, too, among them Leo Valiani, a leader of the Action Party, whose newspaper urged that Fascist criminals be dealt with as to do no further harm. Luigi Longo, a Communist leader, wrote that Mussolini should be "killed right away, in whatever way possible, without a trial, without theater, without any historical declamations."[53] Socialist leader Sandro Pertini invited the partisans to kill Il Duce "like a mangy dog."[54] Their conviction was widely shared by the rank and file of the Resistance. In those feverish days there were few militant anti-Fascists who believed that pardon was a republican virtue. One of the few anti-Fascists willing to look to the lessons of history was Mario Borsa, an aging journalist installed by the Committee of National Liberation as editor in chief of *Corriere della Sera*. With regard to Mussolini's fate, he quoted an intellectual of the unification period, Carlo Cattaneo, who said of an opponent, "If you execute him you will do the just thing, but if you don't you will do the sacred thing."[55] Except that justice was more in demand than sanctity.

For most of those who had fought in the Resistance, Italy had arrived at a turning point—and a new view of the body of Il Duce. In an editorial in the Socialist Party daily *Avanti!* Pietro Nenni argued on April 28 that the "dust mop of a man" who had been arrested at Dongo on Lake Como should be shot at once, before the Allies could get their hands on him and press for the mockery of a trial. Nenni was only sorry they could not "take the mop around Italy and show it off like a circus freak."[56] The Socialist leader gave vent to the same fantasy for which Fiat worker

Alfredo Colombi had been sentenced to five years of confinement. The difference was that now even the cruelest fantasies could be translated into reality.

AFTER MORE THAN half a century Italian curiosity about what happened at Dongo has still not been satisfied. The arrest of Mussolini, disguised in a German greatcoat and helmet; his brief imprisonment by the partisans; the execution of Fascist officials on the shores of the lake—there has been material enough to fill thousands of pages of books and articles and miles of film. Italians are even more fascinated, if possible, by the events at nearby Giulino di Mezzegra, where Mussolini was shot a day after his arrest. Fifty years of so-called revelations have failed to slake the thirst for the long-running drama of the deaths of Benito Mussolini and Claretta Petacci. This book gives no new version of that tale, nor does it add details to the ongoing debate as to which Communists had a hand in the execution, where it took place exactly, and the precise number of bullets fired. In fact, no new evidence has emerged since 1945 to cast doubt on the reconstruction provided in the newspapers in the days immediately after Mussolini's capture and death: Il Duce and his mistress were shot in front of the gates of Villa Belmonte at Giulino on the afternoon of April 28, 1945, by a squad of Communist partisans. They were led by a Colonel "Valerio," later identified as Walter Audisio, and by a "Guido," later confirmed as Aldo Lampredi.

Resistance leaders, especially Luigi Longo, chose the men to carry out this mission with great care. Both Valerio and Guido were experienced men whose time as partisans had been preceded by years of anti-Fascist militancy. An accountant from Alessandria, in Piedmont, Audisio began his Communist career in his early twenties when he started the local underground. Arrested in

1934, he was exiled to the island of Ponza, where he met leading Communist figures and grew more politically sophisticated. In 1939, for health and family reasons, he sent a request to Mussolini to be freed from exile. The request was granted, but it cost Audisio credibility among his comrades in Alessandria, who never fully forgave what they saw as a repudiation of his political activities. In the Resistance, though, Audisio proved himself a strong military leader at the head of the Garibaldi Brigades, and it was as such that he was recommended to Longo. Guido's political militancy was even deeper than Valerio's. Born in Florence, Lampredi was ten years older than Audisio and had been a member of the Italian Communist Party since its founding in 1921. He was arrested in 1926 and sentenced by the special tribunal for crimes against the state to ten years in prison, six of which he served. After two years of study at the party school in Moscow, Lampredi joined the International Brigades to fight in the Spanish civil war. As a captain in the republican army he gained the respect of Longo and went on to serve as a key figure in the Resistance in northeast Italy.

There are reasons to think that Lampredi, the more significant party figure, was the dominant actor in the squad that executed Mussolini, not Audisio, as has often been thought. But at the time it suited Communist strategy to portray a minor character, Valerio, as the chief decision maker. The Communists did not want to appear solely responsible for the execution of Mussolini and the other Fascist officials. Rather, they wanted it to seem like a purely military action flowing from the Committee of National Liberation and carried out in conjunction with the other Italian Resistance forces. Their concern was to emphasize the execution's legality as well as to gain legitimacy with the other parties in the Resistance as a democratic, not a revolutionary, force. To that end, on April 30, the party daily, *l'Unità,* published an account of the execution in which Valerio occupied the limelight and Guido remained in the background. Six months later Valerio published a new and more detailed version of the events leading up to the shooting of Mussolini.

To say there were propagandistic elements to these two accounts would be to put it mildly. The Communists wanted to offer a shameful portrait of Il Duce at the moment of his death, so Valerio stressed the grotesque side of Mussolini's behavior that day, his initial conviction that the mysterious colonel had come to save him and then his subsequent terror of dying. Relying on the account in *l'Unità*, the Communist review *Rinascita* expanded on the theme, reporting that "Mussolini behaved, in the final days and minutes of his life, like a dust mop of a man." Having graced Il Duce with the same description that Pietro Nenni had used in *Avanti!*, *Rinascita* went on to echo Sandro Pertini's comments, saying that Mussolini "died like a dog."[57] As far as the Communist Party was concerned, Italians should be in no doubt that at the brink of death, Il Duce showed himself a real coward.

Decades later, an account by Lampredi would lead historians to doubt two circumstances in Audisio's version. Audisio claimed to have read a death sentence to Mussolini, "in the name of the Italian people," before he faced the firing squad, thus giving the rough justice of the day the guise of a formal sentence. Audisio also reported that Mussolini had said nothing before he died. In Lampredi's account, written in 1972 exclusively for the Communist Party leadership and not published until 1996, "Audisio read no sentence; perhaps he said a few words, but of this I'm not certain."[58] As for Mussolini, according to Lampredi, Il Duce actually rose to the occasion as he faced the firing squad: widening his eyes, tugging open the collar of his coat, he shouted, "Aim for the heart!" In his memo Lampredi assured the Communist leadership that he had never spoken to anyone or written anything about Il Duce's last words, and he promised not to do so in the future. The confidential nature of his later version suggests that it is more reliable than Valerio's description provided to the party daily right after the mission.

To read a death sentence to a condemned man is to ennoble the proceedings of an execution, which would otherwise be unavoidably squalid. But it is also a way of speaking to the conscience of the condemned, a way of recognizing that he is human. Similarly, to address the executioner with challenging words implies that a summary last will and testament will be registered, thus that the hangman has some humanity left. The scene outside Villa Belmonte—the Communist partisan standing before Il Duce, Il Duce before the partisan—was not changed in its historical significance, but its symbolic significance depends on who spoke and who was silent. In reality, Audisio was probably silent and Mussolini was the one who spoke. In the legend, it was Audisio who spoke while Il Duce remained silent. Party discipline did the rest: Lampredi also kept silent, and his memo of 1972 remained secret for another twenty-four years. Thus the Communist Party succeeded in transmitting its own account of Il Duce's death to the collective memory.

Still, to Italians in 1945, no matter what happened in the last seconds of Mussolini's life, it could not have offset the actions of his last days, his desperate search for a way out, even dressing up in a German greatcoat and helmet to hide from the partisans. It was a comical show, very different from the Wagnerian pomp of Hitler's demise. By committing suicide in his bunker before the Russians arrived, Hitler seemed to control his destiny right to the end. The temptation to compare the deaths of the two dictators was strong among those steeped in Fascism's ideology of honor. The most intellectually honest of Fascist supporters saw Il Duce's shameful end as a severe judgment not only on Mussolini but on the national character of those Italians who had idolized him for so long.

Interned in a military concentration camp in Germany for refusing to enroll in the army of the Republic in Salò, Giovanni Ansaldo, a famous journalist and onetime apologist for the Fascist regime, was one of the believers who reflected on Mussolini's behavior at the end. Having learned of Il Duce's capture, Ansaldo wrote in his diary:

> Ending up like that, such a shameful, miserable end, is irrefutable proof that the man we admired, loved, and served was a grotesque, cowardly fraud. And that he and all of us who thought we were so clever to follow him were idiots. All the people laughing about Mussolini's last act haven't understood how it dishonors all of Italy, how it brands the words *Carnival Nation* on our foreheads. A truly tragic end would have been more honorable for everyone: for him, for us, and for the country.[59]

Ansaldo thought the lack of tragedy in Il Duce's end was a failing that would weigh on the country's future. "After ruining Italy, after standing in the way of Italian life for twenty years, [Mussolini] has once again thrown his body across the country's path. He is an obstacle, even if he has been defeated . . . he can still harm us." A few days later, when the news of Mussolini's fate at Piazzale Loreto reached Ansaldo's prison camp, he compared the different tragedy quotients of Italian and German history. The Führer, he said, had "died like a man," while Mussolini had proved himself "a frightful ass."[60]

From his barracks, Ansaldo was not alone in deploring the banality of the script of Mussolini's last hours. To many Italians, the events seemed all too uninspired. Mussolini trying to flee with the departing German troops; stopped at a roadblock by partisans who recognized Il Duce despite his German uniform; shot twenty-four hours later by a Communist firing squad, his body falling under a hail of bullets fired by three or four nameless partisans: what could be more banal than the scene at Giulino di Mezzegra? How could history play itself out in such an undistinguished way? Years of "revelations" purporting to solve the "mysteries" surrounding Mussolini's death suggest that the collective imagination did not easily accept so unadorned a version of events. As early as the end of April 1945, rumors were circulating that soon earned the status of legend. A tall gentleman wearing a light-colored civilian overcoat had joined Colonel Valerio on the firing squad: who was he? Around the shores of Lake Como, it was whispered that the man—in fact Aldo Lampredi—was none other than the son of Matteotti.

Historians know that false reports can be as interesting as confirmed fact. The legend that Mussolini was shot by the son of Matteotti points to a widespread need in liberated Italy to find in Il Duce's executioner a man worthy of the role granted him by history. Other rumors about the firing squad were equally telling. In one, the executioner was the most famous of Resistance fighters, the partisan commander of the Valsesia district, Cino Moscatelli. But the rumor about Matteotti's son is especially remarkable because it connects the mythical prehistory of Il Duce's corpse with its actual history. Twenty-one years after the Matteotti murder, memory of the Socialist deputy was still so strong that people could believe his son had avenged his death. Nor was it the first time that the specter of Matteotti appeared in wartime Italy. Two years earlier, the Fascist prefect of Chieti had fallen for the rumor that the city—site of the farcical trial of Matteotti's murderers in 1926—was about to be bombed by an enemy plane piloted by one of the murdered man's sons.

It had taken the partisan firing squad mere seconds to finish off Mussolini, but in fact he had begun to die two decades earlier, when his henchmen plunged their knives into the body of Giacomo Matteotti.

2

The Ox of the Nation

As Il Duce's life ended in front of the gates of Villa Belmonte at Giulino di Mezzegra, a new chapter began: the story of Mussolini's dead body. It was to be a tragedy, starting the very next day, when Colonel Valerio dumped several corpses—of Mussolini, his mistress, and some high-ranking Fascist officials—in Milan's Piazzale Loreto. After a crowd formed around the bodies and began kicking them, the partisans decided to hang the corpses—feet up, head down—from a high crossbar in front of a gas station. There they remained for hours, open to the gaze of thousands of Italians who came to stare. Thus free Italy began its new life with a celebration of death. It was hardly an edifying ritual with which to baptize the just-liberated nation.

Nevertheless, what happened at Piazzale Loreto on the morning of April 29, 1945, represented an end as well as a beginning, extreme unction as well as baptism by blood. Before looking at the impact of this episode on postwar Italy, we should therefore examine it in the light of the preceding years, in the context of

Italy's civil war raging between anti-Fascists and supporters of the Salò republic.

THE DIARY OF Corrado Alvaro, a well-known writer and journalist, offers some insight. One day in the fall of 1944, when Rome had been free for several months, Alvaro had returned from his morning walk and was enjoying the quiet of his studio. But the silence was only partial, because he kept seeing images of death pass before his eyes. "There are photographs of patriots who have been hanged posted in the streets," writes Alvaro. The anti-Fascists had put up pictures of partisans killed by the Nazis and Fascists in other areas of Italy. The crowds on their way to work had stopped to look at them. There were women shopping and "girls, having just put their makeup on, with that bored, impatient look on their faces." Alvaro does not share these young women's indifference, since in every partisan's photograph he fears he will recognize his son. At the same time he understands that he will see more than most in these pictures of Italians whom the Nazis and Fascists feel obliged not only to murder but to leave hanging in public. Of one partisan hung up on a butcher's hook he says, "It looks as if she is flying; it's incredible how the ideas of love, of seriousness, of a wedding—of flight, in short—can emerge from a young woman's picture even if she is strung up on a butcher's hook."[1] The body displayed to the public gaze is both memento mori and an example of *ars moriendi*, the art of dying; the roles played by Fascist and anti-Fascist bodies are essentially the same.

The exhibition of people who had been hanged or shot was used by the Social Republic as an extreme way of controlling the population, a silent but supremely eloquent method of social control. Butcher's hooks served an important function, degrading human beings by treating them as animals. There was nothing new in this: the Fascists had tried a similar expedient on the natives in their African colonies. But it would be wrong to credit the practice of showing off the dead only to the Fascists. Since the Spanish civil war, European anti-Fascists had also been trading in corpses. For the Republicans, displaying their adversaries' dead bodies (even digging them up) was a symbolic way of denying legitimacy to the enemy's cause. In Italy's civil war, partisans could not wait for the liberation of Milan and the capture of Mussolini to exhibit Fascist corpses like hunting trophies. There were several such episodes, among them the horrendous battle between partisans and the forces of the Social Republic in the village of Poggio Bustone in March 1944, in which the Fascists were defeated. Local farmers took the losers' bodies, stuck them on pitchforks, and hung them one by one on the trees along the main street, "lined up . . . like so many rows of straw."[2] A year later, in liberated Rome, a crowd descended on Donato Carretta, the director of the Regina Coeli prison under the Nazi occupation, threw him in the Tiber, drowned him, and dragged his body to the prison, where they strung it up from a window, then beat and kicked it for more than an hour. In the months following the Liberation other Fascists were lynched and their bodies put on public display.

Nevertheless, it was fairly uncommon for the partisans to show off their victims. When they did, the dead were more likely to be other partisans accused of theft or betrayal than the Fascist enemy. It was the Republic of Salò that considered this tactic one of its fundamental weapons. In northern and central Italy there were countless cases of Resistance fighters, killed by Social Republic forces, whose corpses were shown off for hours, sometimes days. For example, the bodies of three anti-Fascists from San Maurizio Canavese, near Turin, were put on view in the town square on

February 11, 1944. The townspeople was made to file by the corpses, "including the schoolchildren and, horrible to say, even the nursery school children."[3] Only much later, when it was dark, did the Fascists allow the families to take the bodies away for burial. That night, despite police surveillance, three small white crosses marked with "Peace to the innocent" appeared in the square after the dead had been removed. The next day, the crosses were taken away.

From one end of occupied Italy to the other, the battle to recover the bodies and bury them became a kind of extension of the partisan struggle. Often it was the parish priest, taking up his traditional role as community conscience, who would gather up the slain Resistance fighters. A number of men of the cloth paid with their lives for this service. At Marzabotto, in Emilia-Romagna, where the Germans carried out a vicious reprisal against the partisans, two priests were shot for trying to bury a few of the eighteen hundred civilians who were massacred. In these wars of the cemetery, the secular values of the Resistance bowed to popular religious belief, the conviction that a person sent to the grave with respect would be resurrected sooner. Keen to gain legitimacy with villagers in the countryside, the partisans frequently went to great risk to give the fallen a Christian burial. Each victim's sacrifice was understood to testify to the holiness of the Resistance struggle. But there was a negative side to this attention to proper burial, for the more the partisans insisted on it, the more the Fascists were determined to treat dead Resistance fighters with the maximum disrespect.

Thus, the tortured and condemned of the Resistance, in addition to knowing they would die, knew their bodies would be shown off in ways designed to frighten others. It was a fate some faced with materialist indifference. "Don't make a fuss about the corpse or anything else," wrote the Roman partisan Fabrizio Vassalli, a thirty-five-year-old economist, to his parents on the eve of his execution. "Wherever they leave me, they leave me."[4] Other partisans saw their fate with great lucidity. "They are letting me rest now until all my wounds heal," wrote Umberto Ricci, a twenty-two-year-old accounting student from Ravenna who had endured long torture sessions. "Then they are going to present me to the public tied up with a piece of rope."[5] Some were unable to conceal their distress: "My body is here by the school near Albegno, this side of the bridge," wrote eighteen-year-old Renato Magi, a Tuscan bricklayer, to his parents. "You can come right away to get me. . . . As I write, my heart pains me, dear Mother and Father, please come right away to get me."[6]

The civil war was also this: a tragedy of and about bodies. "My thoughts to my dear wife and my loved ones, my body to my faith": Giulio Casiraghi, a Communist factory worker from the outskirts of Milan, carved those words on the door of his jail cell before his fatal transfer to Milan's San Vittore prison.[7] Casiraghi could never have imagined the prophetic force of his words. His body and those of fourteen other political prisoners, shot and dumped in Piazzale Loreto on the morning of August 10, 1944, in reprisal for a suspected partisan attack, inflamed the Communist faithful as few others had. "They were one on top of the other covered with flies, lying beneath a terrible hot sun, one with his arms spread out, one all twisted up, one head down, one with his eyes wide in terror";[8] face to face with the corpses of these fifteen anti-Fascist martyrs, Communist veterans vowed to make their struggle more punishing than ever. Workers from nearby Monza and Vimercate passed by the dead, shocked at the way their

comrades were exhibited. Hundreds of Milanese citizens passed
as well. One man took a gun and shot into the heap, but there
were many women who dared to bring flowers and children who
pushed to the front to see the spectacle of death. From the murderers to the victims to the spectators, this was a wholly Italian
tragedy: August 10, 1944, was to go down in the memory of the
Resistance.

IT HAS BEEN said that Mussolini, knowing he could not avoid
reprisals for the partisans' bodies, ventured that the Fascists
would "pay a high price for the blood of Piazzale Loreto."[9] What

Fourteen political prisoners, shot and dumped in Piazzale Loreto on the
morning of August 10, 1944. (*Foto Publifoto/Olympia*)

is certain is that the ferocious executions of August 1944—ordered by an SS commando but carried out by a Fascist squad—provoked a crisis at the highest levels of the Social Republic. Piero Parini, the Fascist official governing Milan and the surrounding province, resigned, and with him went any hope for a moderate administration in the Lombard capital, which instead became the focal point of the civil war. But the symbolic consequences of the event were more important and would have the greatest bearing for the body of Il Duce, as nine months before his death Piazzale Loreto had become a place of memory for anti-Fascists, not only for Lombardy partisans but for Resistance fighters throughout northern Italy. Just as a young man from Vicenza cycled the hundred miles to Milan to honor one of the widows and pay homage at the square, many partisans saw Piazzale Loreto as a symbol of an enemy who had to be defeated and a vendetta that had to be honored.

The Nazis' and Fascists' practice of exhibiting the dead bodies of the enemy left its mark on the literature of the period. Writers and poets of the Resistance—Corrado Govoni, Salvatore Quasimodo, Franco Fortini, Elio Vittorini—filled their work with images of dead people who had not been properly buried. There were partisans whose only grave was "a long coat, stiffened with frost," mothers who raced toward sons "crucified on a telegraph pole," heads of hanged victims left on the sides of a bridge and at the market, on the ground the "fingernails of those who had been shot," and the bodies of boys "with serious faces, boys who had not died children," scattered on the sidewalk.[10] But it was the fifteen bodies thrown into the square in Milan that left the most vivid mark. In the winter of 1944–45, Alfonso Gatto's poem "For the Martyrs in Piazzale Loreto" circulated widely in clandestine anti-Fascist circles:

It was dawn, and where people worked,
where the piazzale was the lit-up jewel
of the city moving to its lights
from evening to evening, where the streetcar's very screech
of iron on iron was a salute to the morning
and to the fresh faces of the living,
they wanted a massacre, so that Milan
would have everything mingled in the same blood
on its doorstep, its proud young sons
and its strong old heart clasped together as in a fist.

Gatto's anger was the anger of a Communist, but his grief was
that of the entire city. Yet, unwittingly, the perpetrators' heartless
message, their memento mori, offered the survivors some consolation, since they were uplifted by the victims' *ars moriendi*, by their
courage in death:

I see the new day that at Loreto
above the red barricades the dead
are the first to hail, still in their work clothes
and with their hearts to the wind, still beating
with blood and their own purpose. And every day,
every hour, this fire burns eternal,
every dawn has its heart injured by that lead,
by those innocents snuffed out at the wall.[11]

Another episode of violence against the partisans took place on
the eve of liberation in Dongo near Lake Como, prior to Mussolini's capture there. On April 24, 1945, four partisans were shot
and left on a hilltop as the anti-Resistance Black Brigades of the
Social Republic went house to house on the outskirts of the town.
Two days later, some of the townspeople, mostly managers and
workers from the nearby Falck ironworks, climbed the hill to recover the four bodies. As they came back down the funeral pro-

cession grew, joined by other men and women. According to a local friar, the bodies were brought back into town by "a whole crowd of people eager to participate in this tribute of mercy and faith." When the cortege arrived at the Falck gates, the mourners stopped and recited the prayers for the dead, and a "profound and religious feeling took hold of all those present."[12] But the prayers were soon interrupted by gunshots as the Black Brigades arrived and began firing into the air.

What happened next seems almost tragicomic, taking place as it did just hours before the Liberation, as "men and women . . . bruised and bloodied" rushed through the mill gates or into nearby houses, leaving the four bodies to the Fascist militiamen. Only after friars from the local convent of the Madonna delle Lacrime intervened did the Black Brigades agree to turn the bodies over to the families and leave under cover of the nighttime curfew. The incident infuriated the townspeople, who were especially alert when they heard the next day that a column of Nazis and Fascists, possibly including Benito Mussolini, was moving along Lake Como.[13] It is likely that they told Colonel Valerio what had happened when he came up from Milan to carry out partisan justice. And it is easy to imagine that the incident gave Valerio good reason to extend his job beyond the execution of Mussolini and his men and to prolong their suffering beyond death.

BEFORE LIBERATION, PIAZZALE Loreto served as a place of memory for anti-Fascists only in their imaginations. Once the city was liberated, it immediately became a genuine site of memory, even before Colonel Valerio and his companions arrived from Dongo with their Fascist dead. On the afternoon of April 27, the day before Mussolini's execution, partisan troops from the Oltrepò Pavese district marched to Milan and into Piazzale

Loreto, where they were welcomed as heroes. The partisan brigades and the people of Milan celebrating in the square were all but paying official homage to the fifteen patriots who had been dumped there. The next afternoon they were joined by more partisan troops, who marched from the Valsesia hills. By now there were wreaths of flowers where the bodies had lain and a hand-lettered sign reading "Square of the Fifteen Martyrs."

Thus on the morning of April 29, when the truck bringing Mussolini, Claretta Petacci, and several senior Fascist officials left their bodies in Piazzale Loreto, the partisans had hardly chosen just any Milan square. Colonel Valerio/Audisio was following the first rule of partisan vendetta: that justice should be carried out where injustice had been done. The retaliation was premeditated, according to Mussolini's wife, Rachele, who told her biographer that she had received an anonymous letter in Salò in which the writer promised, "We will take them all to Piazzale Loreto."[14] It was also premeditated by Audisio, who claimed to have thought of dumping Mussolini in Piazzale Loreto back in August 1944, when he saw the fifteen patriots lying there. More likely, as Aldo Lampredi reported, the vendetta was planned at the last minute, decided during the journey from Dongo to Milan. In any case, it was a natural step given how much the partisans had suffered from the practice of the Fascist militiamen; they could scarcely resist doing the same when they had the chance.

The corpses of Mussolini, Petacci, and the other Fascists endured a two-stage trial. At first they lay on the ground in a heap, exposed to the gaze—and the blows—of the crowd. Then two of the bodies, along with those of Mussolini and his mistress, were strung up on a bar in front of the gas station in the southwest corner of the piazza—safe from the rage of the people but there to be ridiculed by all comers. The first stage of this Calvary mirrored

The corpses of Mussolini, Petacci, and the other Fascists lay on the ground in a heap, exposed to the gaze and the blows of the crowd. (*Foto Publifoto/Olympia*)

the first step in the original—the mob's demand that Jesus be killed. "Let's hear your speech now, let's hear your speech!" someone called to Il Duce's corpse, just as someone had shouted to Jesus, "Perform your miracle now, save yourself!"[15] Mussolini's theatrical skills, admired for twenty years, suddenly became the charge against him. One woman shot at the corpse, riddling it with bullets; men and women started to kick it, turning Il Duce's "iron skull" into a mass of broken bone and gray matter. So this was the great provider, the one who would save Italy from centuries of famine and starvation! The women of Milan pelted him

Piazzale Loreto, April 29, 1945.   (*Foto Publifoto/Olympia*)

with their vegetables and black bread, the rations they had eaten for the five years of the war. So this was virility incarnate, the great lover! The partisans of the Oltrepò Pavese rested Mussolini's head on Claretta Petacci's breast, in a rude simulation of the act of love.

The second stage of Mussolini's Calvary, too, mirrored the Crucifixion: like Christ on the cross flanked by the two thieves, Mussolini was strung up by his heels along with the other Fascists.

(*Foto Publifoto/Olympia*)

The fact that Mussolini was not alone showed that his fate was no different from the fate of the others; ultimately, there was nothing special about his body. They were all hung head down, which, since the Middle Ages, represented the worst possible insult. At the same time, this was a reminder of the butcher and his meat hooks; it condemned Mussolini and company to an animal destiny. And in case the crowd was unable to distinguish one criminal from another, the partisans hung the person's name in front of each pair of feet.

The privilege of the victors lay in the fact that they had survived. Mussolini and the Fascists were dead; the partisans were alive, and survival was the key to their power. They drew their force from Piazzale Loreto itself, a place of sovereign transition—sovereign being the sphere in which someone can be put to death without there being a crime. In Rome, King Victor Emanuel III and his son Umberto would continue, with some confusion, to play out the comedy of their sovereignty, but only the people who had known how to finish Mussolini off could really claim any sovereign role in the new Italy.

The public display of Mussolini's corpse also served another basic purpose: it ruled out the possibility that Il Duce was still alive. Half a century after the event this assertion might seem tautological, but in the overheated climate of April 1945 the most obvious truisms could seem inventions and the most outrageous inventions plausible. There were many false rumors about the fate of the Axis leaders. The fact that Hitler's body had disappeared, spirited away by the Soviet secret services as a weapon to use in the coming Cold War, would soon prompt whispers that the Führer had survived. By showing off Mussolini's body in a public square, the partisans wanted to prevent any Italian version of that legend.

Unintentionally, even the police who directed traffic toward Piazzale Loreto were helping to quash any such potential myth, since the more people filed into the piazza, the more witnesses observed Il Duce's demise. The shots fired at the dictator, the spectacle of the bodies hanging upside down, the placard bearing Mussolini's name: all these combined to rule out a new twist on the old European tradition of the "hidden king," in which the sovereign is forced to hide but awaits the moment to return and make his subjects happy. Only an emigrant—someone like the man identified as Guglielmo P., who remained in Ethiopia after the collapse of Italy's imperial pretensions—could imagine as late as 1951 that Mussolini was still alive and plotting his comeback. "You bring us terrible news," he told the journalist who assured him he had personally seen Il Duce's body in Piazzale Loreto.[16]

When all was said and done, there was also a strong streak of voyeurism at work that day. Decades later, witnesses still recalled the women's caustic comments about the stockings Claretta Petacci involuntarily displayed. It was said that firemen had appeared to clean the bodies, filthy with spit and urine after their exposure to the crowd. One spectator heard a comment that was then repeated in Milan like a litany: "They're nice and fat, nice and fat, nice and fat." In truth, the man admitted, "I don't remember that they were so fat."[17] As it happened, Mussolini had lost weight during the war years; he had never regained the state of florid good health that he enjoyed during his greatest popularity. But the people of Piazzale Loreto needed to see Mussolini as fat because it would prove that he had had a plot to starve them. In the "piece of butcher's meat" hanging in the square the Milanese saw a man the size of an ox.[18] However, this was not "the ox of the nation"—a description the dictator had proudly adopted— a hardworking animal, willing to pull the plow all the way to the end of the field at the urging of the people.[19] Now the crowd viewed Mussolini more as the beast in the bullfight, an animal you had to kill if you did not want to be killed yourself.

"The filthy beast has been hung up in Piazzale Loreto," wrote Carlo Emilio Gadda, a well-known Milanese novelist whose expressionist sensibility made him particularly acute at describing the world of the slaughterhouse.[20] Gadda wrote of the dictator's being "tossed into a tripe soup," again pointing to the bovine qualities of Il Duce's body. Whether animal or human, Mussolini's was a body to stare at, to consume even after the partisans—following an order by the American military command—cut him down and sent him to the city morgue. From 2:00 P.M. on April 29 until 7:30 A.M. the following day, when the coroners of the University of Milan began their autopsy, Il Duce's body continued to satisfy the morbid curiosity of all. Not content just to photograph the bodies as they lay on the morgue slabs, the U.S. Army cameramen moved the placards with the names so the corpses could be identified more easily and placed Mussolini and Claretta Petacci arm in arm for greater effect. Earlier, when the bodies were still hanging in the piazza, Italian photographers had used rifles to prop up their cameras so as to get a better shot of the dead dictator's face.

No longer an object of art as in the 1930s, Mussolini's body had been reduced to a mere thing—but a thing everyone still wanted to see. Partisans and curious onlookers who had somehow gained entry to the morgue lined up to look at Il Duce's corpse. In an autobiographical novel, Carlo Mazzantini, a Blackshirt, tells a tale, probably invented, of a young Communist prison guard who offers to take him and other Fascist prisoners to the morgue ("We could pop over this afternoon, on the late side," the guard says). "It still seemed incredible—incredible that he had existed and incredible that he was dead," Mazzantini writes, particularly successful in conveying the disorientation shared by both guards and prisoners, Communists and Fascists, facing a world without Mussolini. In his account, the more thoughtful of the anti-Fascists felt only a void in the presence of Il Duce's miserable corpse; the prison guard, "with his gun and a kerchief around his neck, seemed small and rather useless."[21] A Milanese photographer, on the other hand, captured a group of partisans at the morgue armed and smiling as they filed by the dictator's battered remains.

The crowds never stopped coming, not even during the autopsy itself. Caio M. Cattabeni, the head coroner, grasped immediately that he had been called on to operate under very difficult conditions, in a morgue where "journalists, partisans, and ordinary people" would keep bursting in.[22] Among the onlookers was a pensioner who had been brought along by his neighbor, a doctor, and who recorded what he saw during a pause in the autopsy. Although his report is probably not reliable, it is worth recounting since it shows how the body of Il Duce continued to prompt fantasies even after his death. In this account, the body lies on the marble slab, open from the forehead to the groin. On one side of the slab are the internal organs that have been removed. While everyone else is on a break, two nurses in surgical gowns begin playing Ping-Pong with Mussolini's organs. "Grinning hideously, they tossed those miserable remains back and forth—now the liver, now a lung, now the heart, now a handful of intestines."[23]

The conditions under which the coroners were working probably explain why the autopsy report lacked some crucial details, such as a description of the victim's clothes, usually essential in describing gunshot wounds to the body. Those missing details were one of the reasons hypotheses continued to circulate about Il Duce's death fifty years after his capture and execution. Still, Professor Cattabeni's report gives all the important information: Mussolini was killed by rifle fire from Colonel Valerio or another partisan, then battered by repeated postmortem violence. The report's mention of bullet wounds, bone damage, and skin lacerations with no bleeding refers to shots, kicks, and blows inflicted on a dead body.

"The corpse of an assassinated man is a terrifying accuser," the emigrant anti-Fascist Vincenzo Vacirca said of Matteotti's body; the same can be said of Mussolini's. The autopsy report reveals more than any historian could about how the Italians of Piazzale

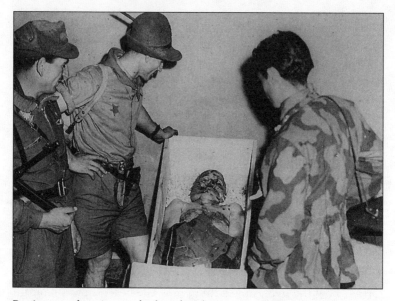

Partisans and curious onlookers lined up to see Il Duce's corpse. (*Foto Publifoto/Olympia*)

Loreto treated the body of Il Duce. Here are some of its findings: head misshapen because of destruction of the cranium; facial features rendered all but unrecognizable due to gunshot wounds and extensive contusions; eyeball lacerated, crushed due to escape of vitreous matter; upper jaw fractured with multiple lacerations of the palate; cerebellum, pons, midbrain, and part of the occipital lobes crushed; massive fracture at the base of the cranium with bone slivers forced into the sinus cavities.

THE DOCUMENT SPEAKS for itself, recounting the sad story of a body attacked with fury both equal and opposite to the passion it inspired when alive. At the same time, the autopsy report must be read in the historical context of the civil war, a context dominated by death and the dead. Faced with Mussolini's battered corpse, we must remember all the partisans who were tortured, who were dumped without proper burial, all the abused corpses that never had the benefit of an autopsy. From this perspective, the violence at Piazzale Loreto, as much as it might say anthropologically or psychologically, was an eminently political event.

In the days after Mussolini was strung up, even the newspapers representing the most moderate voices on the Committee of National Liberation—papers that might have condemned the brutality—held to this view. In a way, this was logical, for a political reading of the treatment of Il Duce allowed the Resistance forces to argue that the violence against the Fascists at Piazzale Loreto was justified by what had been done to the partisans but that any reciprocal action would be illegitimate. In Rome the paper *Risorgimento liberale* praised Il Duce's swift execution and expressed no great concern about the fate of his body after death. The Christian Democrat paper *Il Popolo* wrote that Mussolini's dead body represented a distant past, to be left behind as nightmares are forgotten. Closer to the spirit of the Resistance, the left-wing press wrote about the events with greater enthusiasm. In the pages of the party daily *l'Unità* the Communists praised the "Jacobin" justice of the execution and wasted few words on the scene at Piazzale Loreto. The Socialist daily *Avanti!* wrote that the spectacle had been barbarous but that "the people were forced to execute their tyrant to free themselves from the nightmare of an irreparable offense."[24]

Even these few examples are enough to suggest that beneath the revolutionary fervor there was uncertainty and even some contradiction within the left. Was the fate of the Fascist dictator Jacobin justice or people's justice? Was it the hegemonic gesture of a minority deciding for all or a collective decision that the leaders had merely carried out? To put it another way, had Mussolini been executed by Colonel Valerio or by the Italian people? In the chaotic days of the Liberation it was not easy for the Committee of National Liberation to admit publicly that the Resistance had been a minority movement and that in this lay its deepest ethical value. It was easier to say that the events at Lake Como and Piazzale Loreto were "the only catharsis possible."[25] At the same time, there had been tens of thousands of Italians ("20,000 is a low estimate," one newspaper said) in the piazza that day, and the Resistance leaders knew that many, many more people had been milling around Il Duce's body than had joined them in the mountains during the hard times of the civil war. Some of the more long-sighted partisans recognized a paradox, the paradox of April 29, 1945: the spectacle at Piazzale Loreto was similar in a strange way to Mussolini's rallies in Rome's Piazza Venezia.

Was the crowd that battered Il Duce's corpse perhaps the same as the one that had hailed the dictator in headier days? Leo Valiani, head of the Action Party, had the impression that it was. The possibility was disturbing, confirming as it did that the partisan fight had been a minority cause and thus that it would be difficult to build a foundation for the new Italy on the basis of the Resistance and its values. From another point of view, however, the overlap between the people at the two piazzas held a saving— if not appealing—grace: the violence could be blamed on the Milanese crowd, the "immature mob," freeing the partisans from responsibility.[26] The "disgusting" scene of the "servile" crowd attacking the bodies of Mussolini and his men, "the same crowd that cheered and trembled before them when they were alive," allowed the partisans to distance themselves from the episode—as if they had not been the ones who chose to rest Mussolini's head on Claretta Petacci's breast, to hang up the bodies by their heels, to write the placards that bore their names.

The most explicit proof of the unease felt by some in the Resistance—their sense of bad faith, one might say—appeared in the special edition of *L'Italia libera*, the Action Party paper, published in Milan on the afternoon of April 29. Anyone who has seen footage of that morning in the square—the crowds cursing, kicking, and spitting at the bodies—cannot but be astonished by the paper's interpretation. One can only imagine that *L'Italia libera*'s reporters must have been elsewhere, witnesses to some other scene:

> The crowd advances in a silent, composed line, past [the mortal remains of those responsible for Italy's ruin]. It is a crowd of men and women who have, for a moment, in the glacial atmosphere of death hanging over the Square of the Fifteen Martyrs, silenced their cries, their expressions of joy over the Liberation. It is a crowd that shows no fierce emotion before these corpses of those who have paid for their grave crimes with their deaths, a crowd that knows only that popular justice has taken its course.[27]

Ignored by Italian historians, and not by chance, the excerpt points in an obvious, even embarrassing, way to a fact that would weigh on postwar Italy. Immediately, indeed from the very day of the hanging, Piazzale Loreto constituted a taboo for the Resistance. There was no television at the time, of course, but there were also no newsreels. Beyond Milan, there was no way to know what took place in the piazza. Ingenuously—but certainly not innocently—*L'Italia libera* tried to take advantage of the circumstances to convert an orgy of violence into a respectable display of mourning.

What the newspaper had not figured on was that, in liberated Italy, photographs circulated as effortlessly as the press. The papers themselves still reproduced very few photos, but the images were printed up and passed from hand to hand. On the morning of April 29, many of Italy's best photojournalists were on hand in Piazzale Loreto, snapping thousands of shots of the extraordinary sight. Among them was Fedele Toscani, the top photographer at the Publifoto agency. "The devil Toscani" didn't miss a detail— not the moment when the partisans stuck a Fascist pennant into Il Duce's hand, making him look like a Punch figure at a carnival, nor the tableau in which Mussolini and Petacci hung head down with their arms flung out, as if in a gesture of surrender.[28] In the days that followed, Toscani's photos began to circulate throughout the country, along with images shot by other photographers. Very quickly a market for the pictures sprang up. Several were actually made into postcards, with the permission of the Liberation authorities.

In the golden days of Il Duce's reign, there had been great demand for photos of the live Mussolini, who was seen as a sort of talisman whose image should preside over every Fascist household. After the Liberation, many Italians were eager to get their hands on a photo of the dead Mussolini, and the pictures from Piazzale Loreto served that purpose admirably. At newsstands in Rome, wrote journalist Corrado Alvaro, customers clamored to buy copies. "I'm getting it for my wife," one of them said.[29] In Milan, sales were so vigorous that some anti-Fascists felt scandalized (or perhaps guilty). "Don't you think it's shameful that they're selling those horrid photos of Mussolini and his mistress in the postures that death imposed on them?" wrote attorney Giacomo Falco to his colleague Marco De Meis, secretary to the prefect of Milan. "And do they have to sell Mussolini's photo along with Matteotti's?" The shops were doing as good a business as the newsstands, Falco went on to say, "because the crowd is so eager."[30] A couple of weeks later the prefect, a member of the Action Party's national executive, ordered the immediate seizure of the photos from the shops and "any other public place." The spectacle of Piazzale Loreto was not to be allowed to continue in the streets of Milan; men would no longer be able to take Il Duce home to their wives.

It would be a mistake to see the circulation of the pictures as Grand Guignol only. The market in the photos had a political aspect as well. To the Communists, the sale of these "tragic and grotesque" images had a positive side, serving, wrote *Rinascita*, as a useful warning to anyone contemplating a revival of the dictatorship.[31] And despite the Milan prefect's order to make the photos disappear, some fellow members of the Action Party enjoyed the spectacle of Piazzale Loreto. Years later, the writer Luigi Meneghello, a member of the Action Party in 1945, wrote of his approval at seeing "the butchered Duce." It was "a just and good thing" that the corpse was strung up, because it allowed Mussolini, who had often seemed a buffoon in life, to reclaim in extremis "a more serious status"; hanging by his heels in front of a gas station was "appropriate and poetic."[32] Irony aside, Meneghello spoke as a partisan veteran with more intellectual courage than most, someone willing to recognize in all its profundity the Manichean nature of the Resistance and its ethics.

But the most striking example of how the Piazzale Loreto photos served as totemic images for a population hungry for justice may be found elsewhere, perhaps where we might not think to look: in the village of Civitella in Val di Chiana, where on June 29, 1944, the Nazis murdered the entire male population in reprisal for a partisan attack. Among the half-destroyed houses was that of Elda Morfini, a young mother who had been widowed when her husband, Dr. Gastone Paggi, was killed. Morfini was able to take very few things from her home after it was burned by the Germans along with the bodies of the murdered men. There was a nightgown stained with her husband's blood following a last embrace, a doctor's coat and stethoscope, a few letters, and a child's toy. To these precious relics Morfini later added a newspaper containing numerous photos of Il Duce's body.

EDDA, MUSSOLINI'S ELDEST and favorite child, learned of her father's fate in a terrible way. On the morning of April 29 she was on her way back to Italy from the Swiss convent where she had taken refuge after the execution of her husband, Galeazzo Ciano. Edda tuned her radio to the Free Milan frequency and heard the announcer describe the crowds heading toward Piazzale Loreto to view her father's corpse. Edda was bitter about the commentary, which sounded like a sportscaster's at a soccer match: "Mazzola passes the ball to Loik, who sends it over to Ferraris II . . ."[33] Like Edda Ciano, millions of Italians heard of Mussolini's execution from their radios, listening with trepidation as they sought to learn the fate of a son, a father, or a husband. Socialist leader Pietro Nenni heard the news while hoping to have word of his daughter Vittoria, who had been deported to Germany. A few hours later, as the party paper *Avanti!* rushed out its special edition, Nenni was gripped with conflicting emotions when the managing editor, a former Fascist, suggested they raise a glass to Mussolini's demise.

Was it a day for toasts and spontaneous national celebration? Without a full sample of reactions, the historian must be content to dig up fragments. A Turinese railway worker, owed two lire by young Mussolini for a pair of shoes, was effectively drunk with joy at the news. As he boarded a train for Milan he could hardly wait to stand before the hanging body of Il Duce and say to him, "I gave you those two lire and you never paid me back, and now there you are, so you have paid handsomely."[34] At the other end of the social scale, a distinguished university professor, historian Adolfo Omodeo, expressed delight at the fall of Mussolini in his own way: "It's easier to breathe without him in the world."[35] In the Vicenza headquarters of the Action Party, members toasted the courageous death of the "little tart of Egypt," referring to Claretta Petacci.[36] Among other anti-Fascists, the desire to get drunk was less strong than the need for self-criticism. In the pages of *Il Ponte,* a fledgling Florentine review founded by the jurist and anti-Fascist Piero Calamandrei, Il Duce was remembered through the lens of Greek poetry: "Mirsilo is dead, but no one in this restaurant has any desire to drink to that. For twenty years, sadly, we let him live."[37]

Commenting on Piazzale Loreto, one Roman daily used a reference familiar to educated Italians, Alessandro Manzoni's novel *The Betrothed,* in which the obsequious parish priest Don Abbondio speaks of the tyrannical Don Rodrigo's death from the plague. "It was a great disaster, this plague, but it was also a broom. It swept away certain people—people . . . whom, my children, we never would have seen the end of." The priest's satisfaction is the same feeling that Italians had at seeing the end of Mussolini: "Never again will we see him making his rounds with those thugs behind him, with that arrogance, with that air he had, with that rod up his back, with that way he had of looking at people that made them feel they had been put on earth just to flatter him. Now he is no longer and we are here. He won't be sending any more of his nasty messages to decent people. He gave us all a lot of trouble, you see, and now we can come out and say so."[38]

In one way or another, many Italians were like Manzoni's Don

Abbondio, trembling in cowardice before the tyrant while fortune was on his side, quick to speak ill of him when he was gone. If this was true anywhere it was in Rome, a city more attuned to worship than to resistance. The Trieste poet Umberto Saba, who was working in the capital as a reporter, described the reaction of Romans to Mussolini's death in an account he titled "Totem and Taboo." On April 30, when the newspapers and radio had erased all doubts about Il Duce's demise, there was an "unquiet air of celebration" in the working-class neighborhoods. But the next day, stopping in at the cheap restaurant where he took his meals, Saba sensed the "first symptoms of remorse." In oblique ways, both explicitly and silently, using "words that could be interpreted only by someone used to listening to the language of the uncon-scious," Saba's fellow diners expressed the uneasiness of turning anti-Fascist in the post-Fascist era, of being survivors who had no shame but could claim no merit.[39]

Outside Rome, outside Italy, reactions to Il Duce's death ranged from joy to shame. In the Gross-Hesepe prisoner of war camp in Germany, the onetime apologist for Mussolini Giovanni Ansaldo saw anti-Fascism flower overnight. Word of Il Duce's end provoked joy among men who, only a couple of years earlier, "would have walked with their heads down and their heels up" to be received by the dictator at Palazzo Venezia.[40] The display of Mussolini's body, which Ansaldo thought abominable, dismayed his fellow prisoners only on behalf of the worms that had to eat the corpse's "rotten meat." But in a camp near Atlanta, Georgia, the Italian POWs baptized the rations of pork trotters they re-ceived as "Mussolini foot."[41] Italian officers freed by the Red Army near Dresden the day after Hitler died were astounded to see houses flying Nazi flags at half-mast, walls covered with pledges to Hitler's immortality in the German soul, soldiers in uniform playing a Wagnerian requiem for the Führer in a church tower. In shop windows there were no photos of the dictator disgraced, as in Italy, but rather portraits of Hitler wreathed in mourning and decorated with flowers. "Could anyone be more idiotic?" wondered a shocked Italian officer.[42]

If any such Italian idiots were to be found, it was in a British POW camp in Kashmir. While the guards were distracted, the more nostalgic of the prisoners collected images of Il Duce hidden away in their baggage. The photos were pasted on a board in the camp sitting room, reconstructing Mussolini's biography from boyhood to Piazzale Loreto. In the same room, a plaster bust of Il Duce was mounted on the wall and an artist among the prisoners sketched a crowd of admirers on a screen. The bust, flanked by a pair of prisoners standing at attention, was lit by an oil lamp and, if we can believe one account, was saluted by hundreds who filed past "like a long thread through the eye of a needle."[43] All night pilgrims in this camp paid homage to their Duce, much as the pro-Nazi citizens of Dresden had to Hitler. But there was also some soul-searching. In a book recounting his experiences in a POW camp in Texas, officer Gaetano Tumiati disapproved of the about-face that had taken place after Piazzale Loreto, accusing Italians of opportunism.

To the less superficial of foreign observers, Italy's rapid switch after Il Duce's death was evidence that its people were not serious: the American press, in particular, devoted a great deal of coverage to Mussolini's execution and to Piazzale Loreto, and on the whole the reports were not very flattering. An army officer imprisoned in the United States sent a bitter letter to the Italian government after his release, deploring the image of Italy as it appeared on the front pages of several American newspapers in April 1945. Photos of Mussolini hanging by his heels in Piazzale

Loreto were shown side by side with pictures of President Roosevelt, who had just died. Banner headlines compared "Italian civilization" with American, unfavorably.

The reaction of foreigners to the end of a dictatorship does not necessarily correspond to the reactions of the people who lived under the dictator. It would be worth taking a closer look at the foreign press coverage of Mussolini's death, perhaps comparing it with the reactions to Hitler's demise. The press summaries that the Italian Foreign Ministry received after Mussolini's execution offer a quick first impression. In neutral countries such as Sweden and Spain, newspapers judged his death inevitable but expressed uneasiness about the macabre scene in Piazzale Loreto. In Paris, the Italian ambassador, Giuseppe Saragat, a Socialist, quoted *Le Monde*, which strongly condemned the "rabble" that had "stepped on the beaten body and covered it in filth" after having admired it for twenty years.[44] But the most significant comments came from Britain. It was perfectly right to carry out a summary execution of Mussolini and the others, argued the British papers: "But the subsequent sensational scenes, brutally evident in the chilling photographs that appeared in the newspapers, provoked disgust, especially because they came hard on the heels of the chilling revelations, documented in film footage as well as in print, about the atrocities in the German concentration camps."[45]

So Il Duce was to have the unlikely destiny of being compared to the Jews, whom he had failed to rescue from their fate in the Holocaust.

3

An Unquiet Grave

The body of Il Duce displayed in Piazzale Loreto, the bodies of the Jews exterminated in the death camps—it was not only a few British journalists who thought of the two images side by side. Freed from the Gusen concentration camp, Aldo Carpi, an artist, returned to Milan with a vision that he rendered in an oil painting. Set in an urban square, the painting's foreground showed ghostly figures engaged in a *danse macabre*; the figures looked much like the people Carpi had secretly sketched during his internment—prisoners selected for the crematorium. In the painting's background, another dance took place; this time the figures were alive and dressed, and behind them were several corpses that had been strung up, one of which was more prominent than the rest. *Sarabanda*, Carpi titled the painting: mad dance.

Indeed, there was much dancing in the streets in the summer of 1945, celebration of a joy that was as great as the grief and suffering had been sharp and painful. On July 14, Bastille Day, Giorgio Strehler, a young anti-Fascist and later Italy's best-known theater director, returned from exile and organized a Festival of Fraternity in Milan. Seven dance floors were laid down in the public gardens, and the mayor, Antonio Greppi, who had lost a son in the Resistance, was to be seen among the crowd in his shirtsleeves. *Liberté, Egalité, Fraternité* was emblazoned on three hot-air balloons high above the gardens. At every street corner the people of Milan were invited to dance as the Parisians were dancing, and they needed little encouragement. On the outskirts of the city, working-class Milanese descended on Monza and Lambro parks, where they celebrated the entire night. Loudspeakers atop the trucks delivering the next day's papers broadcast the refrain "Dance, citizens of Milan, it is your day, for Hitler and Mussolini are dead."[1]

A few weeks earlier, several dozen anti-Fascists had danced to the death of Mussolini in an even more literal way. They had assembled at section 16 of the Musocco cemetery in Milan, where Mussolini, Claretta Petacci, and the Fascists strung up in Piazzale Loreto had been buried in unmarked graves. There the anti-Fascists did a slow dance on the packed earth to the measured cadence of an accordion. Then a woman stood with her legs apart and urinated on one of the unmarked graves, to the general applause of her companions. Throughout northern Italy in the year of the Liberation, occasions were found to celebrate the victory with dance. In November 1945, the Communists of Novara, in Piedmont, held a festival to commemorate the Bolshevik revolution that would be a model for the annual party festival held all over Italy. First there were speeches, then a soccer match, then a party meeting, then dancing. But at that first festival, the dancing did not begin until a huge paper head depicting Mussolini had been put to the torch.

Even among those who didn't dance, there were leaders of the Resistance who made it clear that they considered Piazzale Loreto a high point in the battle for the Liberation, a moment of catharsis in the civil war. Although the Socialist Sandro Pertini had disapproved of the way Mussolini and the others had been strung up in Milan, speaking in Rome two weeks after Piazzale Loreto he announced that "in the north we cleared the slate" because "in Milan there was Piazzale Loreto."[2] Pertini, who liked to tell how he had once tried to assassinate Prince Umberto of Savoy, embodied the contrast between northern Italy and the center-south—between the territory of the Resistance and the territory loyal to the monarchy. He also embodied the contrasts at the heart of the Committee of National Liberation. Pertini's incendiary speech in Rome, condemned as thuggish by the moderate press, was light-years away from the thinking of Christian Democratic leader Alcide De Gasperi. While Pertini saw democratic politics as the extension of armed struggle, De Gasperi saw the fight against revolutionary tactics as part of the "permanent method" of democracy.[3] To the moderate press of the center-south, Pertini was hardly the only Jacobin in the Resistance. When Ferruccio Parri, leader of the Action Party and a man of the north, was named prime minister, the satirical magazine *Il Cantachiaro* depicted him in a cartoon in which he tells King Victor Emanuel III: "Your Majesty, I bring you the Italy of Piazzale Loreto."[4]

Piazzale Loreto remained a place of memory in the postwar years, but only for part of the population. Beginning in December 1945, when De Gasperi replaced Parri as prime minister, the legacy of the piazza passed to the ranks of the opposition. From then on, it was kept alive by the most radical of the anti-Fascists. "In Milan there was Piazzale Loreto": for at least thirty years, various versions of Pertini's remark served as the rallying cry of left-wing militants, scrawled on walls and chanted in demonstrations by would-be revolutionaries. Indeed, the Milan piazza entered the political language of the new Italy immediately. Antimonarchy posters in Milan read, "Piazzale Loreto instructs us and awaits us."[5] One of the many angry letters the De Gasperi government received after pardoning a long list of Fascists who had been charged with a variety of crimes also came from Milan. It admonished "the most foolish prime minister in the world" for his servile obedience to orders from Washington (the left accused De Gasperi of being a tool of the Americans) and warned that "there is already talk of hanging you up in Piazzale Loreto."[6] When the field hands or metalworkers in the Po Valley demonstrated against the government, they often hanged an effigy of the prime minister. When the demonstrations took place in Milan, they were able to hang the effigy on the crossbar in front of the most famous gas station in Italy.

In the bitter view of Orio Vergani, a journalist and sworn Fascist supporter back when the pro-Mussolini rallies were held in Rome's Piazza Venezia, "the spirit of Piazzale Loreto" hovered over all of postwar Italy.[7] Indeed, in the heat of the victory over Fascism in 1945–46, there were traces of the Milanese piazza in the most unexpected places. *Oggi,* a conservative family magazine, published comments of a sort that in only a few years would be unthinkable. Thus the following excerpt, striking in its outright cruelty:

> Mussolini was a madman who thought he was Mussolini: that was already clear the morning of Piazzale Loreto. Among the bodies tossed in the piazza to sleep for all eternity, Mussolini lay on his back with his head tilted away, with the golden eagle Fascist pennant in his fist and a flash of the whites of his eyes against his yellow face, visible beneath lowered eyelids. He seemed still to be dreaming a crazy and distant dream: of cities to conquer, seas to dominate, battles to win. . . . Perhaps in the

dream he really was the man of the legends that had held sway for twenty years.[8]

With the Resistance still a vivid memory, Italians in the north considered themselves patriots and wondered if the same could be said for Italians in the south, who had escaped the rigors of the civil war. Meanwhile, Italians in the south, unashamed that they had been liberated without having to pay the price of war, questioned how civilized their fellow citizens in the north had been during the insurrection. Small skirmishes in the press reflected the deep political and social contrasts. Had not a Communist daily published a photo of Guido Buffarini Guidi, a minister of the Social Republic, looking on in terror as he was sentenced to death? The new right-wing populist magazine *Uomo qualunque* ("Everyman," or "The Cynic") lit into the Communist journalists, not the Fascist minister, portraying them as the equivalents of Polynesian cannibals. The *qualunquista* movement, which disavowed political engagement, generally expressed the spirit of the center-south, which rejected the Resistance's rhetoric and criticized its supposed excesses. Besides *Uomo qualunque,* which sold widely in the center-south, there was another new paper along the same lines, *Il Tempo,* published by Renato Angiolillo.

Crude as its journalism could be, the *qualunquista* press must be taken seriously by the historian. Their publishers understood the mentality of a country that was too worn out by war to regret the passing of Fascism but too extraneous to the Resistance struggle to believe in the battle of liberation as an ideal. Even before the north began to produce mass-market magazines reflecting a conservative line, the press in the center-south was giving voice to an anti-Fascist but non-Resistance Italy. This voice was more than just reactionary journalism offered in consolation to Italians who had not fought in the North. It posed a challenge to the idea that the Resistance had been fought exclusively by partisan brigades and anti-Fascist politicians. In its confused and sometimes vulgar way, the *qualunquista* line represented certain perspectives that historiographers would arrive at fifty years later. Today, various historians have recognized other contributions to the Resistance against the German occupation besides those of the armed struggle. There were the farmers who hid and fed Allied soldiers, ordinary citizens who helped Italian Jews fleeing from persecution, and people in the cities who took care of their neighbors after the bombing raids. Then there were all the Italian soldiers imprisoned in Germany, tens of thousands of officers and hundreds of thousands of rank-and-file soldiers (many from the center-south) who refused to support the Republic of Salò's army—today no one would dismiss their resistance as merely passive.

From 1947 on, after the broad wartime political front of the Committee of National Liberation split apart, the Christian Democrats stepped into the breach occupied by the *qualunquisti* to represent the political and antipolitical moods of the center-south on a national level. But in 1945 the disagreement over how to interpret Piazzale Loreto was still taking place at the local level, inside the Milan office of the Turin publishing house Einaudi, for example. In the summer of 1945 the Sicilian Communist writer Elio Vittorini sent out an outline of *Il Politecnico,* a forthcoming weekly, to other consultants at Einaudi. Vittorini's letter included the draft of an editorial evoking "Piazzale Loreto, with the figures of writers hanging upside down." His memo asked, "Who should be hanging in Piazzale Loreto? . . . Who are the monsters of the contemporary literary scene?"[9] Keen as Vittorini was on this question, it seems to have appealed little to his colleagues, for there was no mention of the events of April 29, 1945, in the first edition of *Il Politecnico.* That does not mean, though, that the magazine did not reflect the radical impulses then widespread in the intellectual left.

In his celebrated inaugural editorial Vittorini did in fact provide a list of literary monsters. Benedetto Croce was the only Italian mentioned, flanked by Thomas Mann, André Gide, Johan Huizinga, John Dewey, and other foreign intellectuals. According to Vittorini, their culture—moralistic rather than socialist, consolatory rather than radical, defenseless rather than armed—had not halted the horrors of Fascism, including the supreme horror of the extermination of children in concentration camps. *Il Politecnico*'s art director, Albe Steiner, who invented the review's extraordinary graphic style, accompanied Vittorini's article not with a photo of bodies hung up by their heels but with a picture of a nameless dead partisan—an image of the "good" Italian rather than the evil one, but nevertheless an image depicting death.

Good and evil are also sharply distinguished in Vittorini's Resistance novel, *Men and Not Men*. Here, the corpses of anti-Fascists are human bodies, and they transmit their dignity to whoever happens to look at them. The corpses of Fascists are not human and thus elicit no mercy from the Resistance fighters. "Dogs," says one worker. "Carrion by now," another character replies. Not that the distinction between corpses and carrion was made only by the Communist Vittorini in his Resistance novel. In liberated Italy Fascists and anti-Fascists continued the battle over decent burial begun in the civil war. But now the power of burial was in the hands of veterans of the Resistance and it was the survivors of Salò who had to struggle to give their companions proper graves.

During the German occupation of Rome, workers at the Verano city cemetery carried out a courageous act of civil disobedience. Opening the caskets of Italians shot by the Nazis and condemned to burial in unmarked graves, they noted the features,

the clothes, the wounds, and anything else that would help identify the bodies. After the Liberation, whole villages took part in
the work to identify fallen partisans, digging up mass graves
where they had been thrown and transporting the bodies to
proper cemeteries. In Castelnuovo al Volturno, in Molise, the
farmers, women, and children of the town turned out as undertakers for a renowned Resistance fighter, the anti-Fascist intellectual Giaime Pintor. The bodies of veterans of the Republic of
Salò did not receive the same kind of spontaneous mercy, in part
because the authorities tended to apply different standards to the
Resistance and the Social Republic dead. Because of postwar lo-
gistical problems—mainly a shortage of railway transportation—
it was forbidden to transfer bodies from military cemeteries to
their places of origin. In practice, with the help of Resistance-
aligned town councils, partisan organizations, and even the pre-
fectures themselves, many families were able to bring home their
fallen Resistance fighters. But the authorities were not disposed to
bend the rules for supporters of the Social Republic. According to
the caustic comment of one observer, there was more interest in
"the national cadaver industry" in democratic Italy than there was
respect for the dead.[10]

In the case of the Social Republic dead, there was often no one
to exhume the bodies, particularly those of the numerous Fascists
and collaborators who were killed in the "triangle of death," part
of Emilia-Romagna. At the beginning of 1946, for example, mass
graves of Fascists were discovered in the towns of Casina, Cam-
pagnola, and Poviglio, in the province of Reggio Emilia. But according to the prefect, the exhumation order was met with
resistance by the local population, which included many partisans. Nor were people willing to work as grave diggers, despite the
high level of unemployment in the area. The local authorities
themselves refused to cooperate with the Carabinieri and the pre-

fecture in the search for other suspected mass graves nearby. Not until 1947, when the local partisan resistance softened, were officials able to exhume the bodies and proceed with burial.

In the letters they were allowed to write before being killed, some partisans expressed concern that their bodies would be put on display after their death. Writing to their families for the last time, some of the condemned of the Social Republic also imagined in detail the unpleasant fate awaiting their corpses. Eighteen-year-old Giulio Bianchini of the Second Light Infantry Regiment of Salò, shot in Piedmont on May 6, 1945, an only son, wrote a letter to his parents four days before he died that illustrates how the civil war tragically continued into the postwar period:

> Don't come to search for my body, for not everyone in the world is like our people, and seeing you here there would be those who would laugh at you. They would be the ones who wanted me dead, who condemned me, killed me, perhaps even the mothers of those here who have died. I know you would not behave like this, Mother, but the people here would, for they don't understand the meaning of forgiveness. But you will be capable of pardon, my dear parents, won't you? I am sure you will. You will do it for me, and so that your feelings don't sink to the level of a vendetta.[11]

A letter like this reminds us that Mussolini was not the only Fascist denied a proper burial, nor was his the only case in which personal grief and collective mourning came together. Postwar Italy conducted a no-holds-barred battle over the bodies of Resistance fighters and Salò veterans, a battle to have a monopoly over memory and the civil war.

A tragicomic chapter of this battle took place in Barlassina, near Milan, in November 1946. During the German occupation the five bells of the local church had been confiscated and melted down. When the war was over, the townspeople took up a collection so that the priest could cast five new bells. The smallest of these, weighing a respectable six hundred kilos, was dedicated "To the dead of 1915–18 and 1940–45." The cost of casting this bronze bell, seventy thousand lire, was paid in its entirety by a local notable, Mario Roncoroni, who was able to get the priest to agree to inscribe the bell with the name of his eighteen-year-old son, who had died fighting for the Social Republic. The bishop came to consecrate the new bells and then they were ready to be hung in the bell tower, which had been restored for the occasion. At this point some Socialist and Communist ex-partisans, scandalized by the inscription of the name of a Fascist soldier, threatened to destroy the bell, and teams of young Catholics organized a night watch to protect it. The mayor of Barlassina, a Christian Democrat, sided with the priest and the donor. The Socialists and Communists seized the occasion to accuse him of trading in war goods abandoned by the Germans. The controversy was finally resolved when the Carabinieri intervened and the partisans decided to desist. The bell with its inscription to the dead Fascist soldier was finally hung in the tower with the others.[12]

This was one of many clashes over inscriptions, if not on church bells then on monuments to the war dead. Socialist and Communist militants wanted only partisans to be honored, while Catholics insisted on commemorating all "the fallen in all the wars." While the left sought to impose a religion of republicanism, the Church in the early postwar period put itself forward as the nation's chaplain, encouraging a blanket pardon for sins that tended to conflate individual responsibility with collective guilt. Millions of Italians—many of whom had been committed Fascists from World War I—were profoundly eager to see the distinction between Fascism and anti-Fascism disappear, while some non-Catholic moderates were inclined toward a conciliatory approach like that of the Christian Democrats. One of them was Indro Montanelli, a journalist known to Italian readers first as a Mussolini apologist, then as a war correspondent, and finally as an opponent of the Republic of Salò.

In the fall of 1945 Montanelli published a slim volume, *Here They Do Not Rest*, dedicated to "all the Italians who died in this war," whether in prison, in the trenches, in the mountains, or in their cellars.[13] The book was composed of three ostensibly autobiographical texts that Montanelli pretended had been left him by an elderly priest as the spiritual last testaments of three victims of the civil war. All invented, one of the victims was an anti-Fascist, one a critical Fascist (much like Montanelli himself), and one a complete agnostic regarding the Fascist /anti-Fascist divide. Montanelli's purpose was to present a case for what he thought of as the "gray zone," those Italians who took no obvious side.[14] He was writing for all the people too polite to be involved in politics, to convince them to "remain bystanders" and not be swayed by the "professional anti-Fascists."[15] Guglielmo Giannini, publisher of *Uomo qualunque*, was not mistaken when he praised the book as the gospel of the *qualunquista*. In the early postwar years, Montanelli was a key figure in persuading Italians that the conflict over Fascism and anti-Fascism should end with the death of Mussolini.

Here They Do Not Rest: what better formulation of the troubled postmortem destiny of certain victims of the civil war? After the Liberation of Milan, the bodies of Blackshirts who had been executed were dumped by the wall of the Musocco cemetery, and there, under the hostile gaze of the partisan guards, mothers, wives, and girlfriends searched for familiar signs in the heap—the color of an item of clothing, the shape of a shoe—in order to identify their men. As for Mussolini, Claretta Petacci, and company, their bodies were buried in great haste and secrecy in section 16 of the cemetery in unmarked graves. In February 1946, when a false rumor began to circulate that Mussolini's and Petacci's bodies had been dug up by the British and taken to England, not even the Carabinieri were able to get cemetery officials to tell them which bodies were buried exactly where.

ON APRIL 11, 1946, the prefect of Milan received an anonymous letter on the letterhead of the Partito Fascista Democratico, or Democratic Fascist Party, proposing that the prefect himself, a stern man of the Resistance, agree to a political accord as well as to an ultimatum. The anonymous writer invited the "Communist democracy" of postwar Milan, as he called it, to "walk the path between Fascism and anti-Fascism" that the Fascist Party was ready to lay down. But this accord, said the letter, depended on the prefect's willingness to release the Fascist prisoners being held in the San Vittore prison and allow a mass to be held in a church in Milan to honor the Blackshirt victims of April 1945. The prefect had a week to make up his mind and issue a press release; failing that, the Democratic Fascist Party would begin a battle, to be fought with "terrible means and methods" in the name of the Fascist martyrs.[16]

The prefect, Ettore Troilo, gave no indication that he was overly worried; he limited himself to forwarding the anonymous letter to the minister of the interior, the Socialist Giuseppe Romita. Just the previous month, Troilo, in a monthly report, had denied that there was any risk that Fascism could be revived in the Lombardy region and suggested that Fascists—legally forced to operate in secret and living on the margins—were more likely to become common criminals. The prefect had not changed his opinion, not even when copies of *Lotta fascista*, the Democratic Fascist Party's newspaper, were circulated at a political meeting at the end of March. Yet *Lotta fascista* was a violent publication, full of virulent appeals to punish the "cannibals" of Piazzale Loreto and strike the preachers of the "vile word of the Jew of Trier" (Karl Marx), as well as demands that Mussolini's remains be reinterred at the Altar of the Nation in Rome's Piazza Venezia.[17] But in Rome, Minister of the Interior Romita expressed some alarm about the appearance of the Fascist paper and sent a "very urgent" message to Troilo urging him to find the activists responsible as quickly as possible.

Thus, political and law enforcement officials had trouble evaluating whether clandestine neo-Fascism represented a real danger. Were the Democratic Fascist Party's threats merely words or did they reflect actual plans of action? In Rome, Romita was taking no chances: with just fifty days until the June 2 referendum on whether to abolish the monarchy in favor of a republic, he wanted to rule out any neo-Fascist attacks or blackmail. And, despite Troilo's lack of concern, there were many in Milan who were worried, especially about an ongoing conflict between police regulars, who served under the crown, and auxiliary police forces, made up of ex-partisans who had refused to work under the regulars' command. After the Liberation, the police had spent more time pursuing ex-Resistance fighters than veterans of the Republic of Salò, according to an April 11, 1946, report given to the Ministry of the Interior. This state of affairs had allowed the "rebirth of neo-Fascism."[18] But it was a small rebirth, if we are to judge by the numbers of clandestine neo-Fascists operating in the region between 1945 and 1946. The Mussolini Action Squads, which specialized in bombing the Committee of National Liberation's headquarters and distributing portraits of Mussolini, counted fewer than 300 members in all of northern Italy, while the Democratic Fascist Party had no more than 250.

Historians have not yet studied the clandestine neo-Fascist demimonde, and until they do we must rely on the scant available accounts of militants. One, written by a former member of a Mussolini Action Squad, shows the movement faithful divided into three categories: the "desperadoes," those who were "burned," and the "creatives." The desperadoes had lost brothers or fathers in the civil war and saw the goal of neo-Fascism as personal vendetta. The burned were people who could not return home because they would be condemned to death by the partisans. The creatives were the liveliest and most vital element of the movement, the writer says: men old enough to have fought in the war but still young enough to believe in politics, men distanced enough from the bloody side of the civil war not to see everything in terms of an eye for an eye.

One such member, Domenico Leccisi, is key to the next phase in the odyssey of the body of Il Duce. Leccisi was young in 1946, just twenty-six years old. He was hardworking and bold, having written most of the first issue of *Lotta fascista* and the letter of ultimatum to the prefect of Milan. He understood political symbolism, having begun his career as an insurgent burning posters for *Open City* (*Roma, città aperta*), a film dear to the Resistance. And he knew how to use his imagination, at least with regard to Mussolini: he came up with the idea and the plan to steal the body from its grave in the Musocco cemetery.

Leccisi began his political life in 1943, after fighting as a soldier on the French and Yugoslav fronts. Not long after the Italian armistice and Mussolini's escape from prison at Gran Sasso, Leccisi, who worked for a metallurgical company near Como, distributed a leaflet in which he urged Italians to support Germany against the English Leviathan. "With the Duce of our youth on our side, no one can stop us," the leaflet exhorted, and as the slogan suggested, Leccisi had come of age in the Fascist youth groups during the 1930s.[19] Born in 1920, the son of a railway station chief, he was too young to recall the origins of the Fascist movement. He had lived through Mussolini's reign as a child and adolescent and become an adult only with the beginning of war, when the regime was already waning. So Leccisi was exposed to the last gasp of Fascist propaganda, which was steeped in anti-bourgeois sentiment, fervent on social equality, and unforgiving on the matter of revolutionary justice. Young people like Leccisi had felt moral outrage in July 1943 when Mussolini was removed from office by the king. They felt he had been betrayed by the Fascist leadership and by the rank and file's indifference; they were appalled by the founding fathers' "suicide," as they saw it. With the surrender to the Allies and the dissolution of the Fascist state, they were all the more convinced that Italy needed young idealists. The fact that Mussolini owed his political resurrection at Salò to the Germans made Leccisi and the others certain that the alliance with Hitler was the only way to realize the absolute truths of the totalitarian religion.

Leccisi would have imbibed the cult of Il Duce from his schoolbooks as a Fascist adolescent. But he also had the special good fortune, at sixteen, to see Mussolini in person, to get so close he could almost touch him. At Forlì in 1936, in the company of twenty thousand members of the Fascist youth league assembled from all over Italy, he had proudly received a magnificent diploma as "Chief Centurion." Sixty years later his eyes still misted over when he recalled the words Mussolini had addressed to the valiant young crowd: "You are the springtime of life, you are the regime's heartbeat." But soon after the assembly at Forlì, Leccisi's admiration for Mussolini began to waver on the battle-fields of France and the Balkans. Was it possible that the Fascist leadership was responsible for Italy's military disasters and that Mussolini himself was blameless? Like many other young soldiers raised to believe in Italy's invincibility and chastened by the de-feats of war, Leccisi decided that Il Duce had been "Petaccified," that the aging dictator had become foolish in his pursuit of Clara Petacci. The Republic of Salò was Mussolini's chance to redeem himself, to return to the ideals of early Fascism, especially in the social sphere. The Social Republic would limit bourgeois prop-erty rights and give the working class some control of the fac-tories: it would take from the rich and give to the poor. This was the last possible opportunity to bring protest to the halls of government. During the civil war, Leccisi was a true believer— anticapitalist, anti-Semitic, in favor of the so-called socialization of the economy.

Socialization, meaning the participation of workers in man-agement, was the most important measure Mussolini tried to in-stall as head of the Social Republic. Against the explicit opposition of the Nazi authorities but in the spirit of the Repub-lic of Salò (it was not called "social" for nothing), Il Duce sought to let the state manage companies deemed necessary to the na-tional interest. From early 1944, when the socialization policy was formally inaugurated, Domenico Leccisi expressed his support in a series of articles in the Fascist press, gaining the notice of Giuseppe Spinelli, head of the organization of Milanese indus-trial workers. In June 1944, Spinelli asked Leccisi to head a new office overseeing public canteens and refectories and policing food supplies and prices. It was a thankless job in some ways, not only because people were angry about tight rationing but because the big agricultural and industrial suppliers had a great deal of power and resisted his interference. But it was exciting for Leccisi, who considered himself a Fascist revolutionary, because controlling supplies and prices was a key element in the economic redistribution integral to the socialization policy.

The energy with which Leccisi went at the job—seizing goods hidden in stores' back rooms, filing charges against merchants selling rationed goods illegally, closing down dozens of shops, directing the rounds made by inspectors, most of them factory workers—did not endear him to the German police or to the Milanese notables of the Social Republic, to whom these methods seemed decidedly Bolshevik. But Leccisi's position was strengthened when Spinelli was named mayor of Milan. For a brief period Leccisi served as chief of the political section of the local Fascist Party, returning in the fall of 1944 to his job supervising food supplies, a job that rumor had it Mussolini himself said was being done well. However, when several of Leccisi's inspectors were caught trading goods they had seized from merchants, the head of the province ordered the immediate shutdown of the inspection operations. Leccisi reacted with a protest, leading three hundred workers past the prefect's office and then under the windows of the Fascist federation in Piazza San Sepolcro. That evening Radio Bari, representing the Badoglio government, announced that the workers of Milan had finally rebelled against the Fascists. But the German authorities were none too happy, and neither was the Republic of Salò's minister of the interior, Guido Buffarini Guidi, who ordered Leccisi arrested. Thanks to the intervention of Spinelli, the young hothead saw his arrest order canceled.

Just a few weeks later, back in Piazza San Sepolcro, Leccisi had the greatest satisfaction of his young political career. As a journalist for *Brigata Nera Aldo Resega*, the Fascist federation's Milan weekly, he was presented to Mussolini, who was making an official visit to the city. Il Duce had apparently been informed of Leccisi's exploits and gave him special treatment—not the Fascist salute but a warm handshake. Surprised by the gesture, Leccisi felt the need to respond in kind. He held out a copy of the magazine and succeeded in croaking, "Duce, with this paper we have stepped on the corns of quite a lot of people."

"Very good," came Mussolini's reply. "People who have corns need to know there is someone who can step on them."[20] It was Leccisi's second meeting with Il Duce; the third would take place after the dictator was dead, on Easter night 1946.

During the final months of the Social Republic, Leccisi was mostly busy with journalism. He wrote on economic policy for, among others, the Fascist daily *La Repubblica fascista*; the last of his articles was published the day Milan was liberated. Leccisi, like some other young journalists working in the twilight days of the Social Republic, always signed his articles, near-masochistic proof of his unfailing faith. In writing, Leccisi found solace for the sorry turn events had taken. How else to explain that on the very day the regime came to an end he was writing about the Social Republic's iron will to make good on its promise of "a new era of distributive and social justice"?[21]

Like many other journalists writing for the Salò press, Leccisi never referred to the German occupation, remaining silent about the Third Reich's support of the Social Republic. On April 7, 1945, when he wrote the latest of many articles in favor of socialization, another, anonymous columnist on the same page urged that the property of Italian Jews be seized and sold and argued that "any position of moral . . . hesitation" was criminal.[22] Leccisi never seemed to understand that being a Social Republic militant meant defending the Italy of the Risiera di San Sabba concentration camp, which in turn meant defending the Germany of Auschwitz.

IN A CELEBRATED passage that Italo Calvino thought one of the most telling in modern Italian literature, the novelist Elio Vittorini describes the restless days of early postwar Italy as an unending railway journey—a country where life was conducted on a train, traveling from one end of the peninsula to the other without actually stopping. It is on one of those trains that we find Domenico Leccisi, who between 1945 and 1946 traversed northern Italy daily, traveling from the countryside near Cuneo, in Piedmont, where he lived with his wife and daughter, to Milan, where he kept in touch with his neo-Fascist friends. According to his memoir, published decades later, he was on a train when he first hatched the plan to steal Mussolini's body. The Turin-Milan route that he traveled every day passed right by the Musocco cemetery walls. Looking out the window, seeing the cypresses growing among the tombs and the large cross that stood above the main gate, Leccisi found himself continually thinking about the mortal remains of Mussolini lying there. Il Duce's last resting place, Leccisi thought, an anonymous grave, was not worthy of him. "One sleepless night" after the usual trip, Leccisi decided to move the body. "To force Italians to think about the need to have closure on the past, the cover had to come off of that tomb."[23]

Opening up a grave to induce historical closure? The reasoning is too tortured to sound convincing. The truth, in fact, was very different: far from wanting to bring the story to a conclusion, Leccisi wanted to start a new narrative, one about Il Duce's body, buried without so much as a marker but still alive in the memories of Italians. This story was to commence on the eve of the first anniversary of Mussolini's execution, just as Italy was preparing for the referendum to abolish the monarchy in favor of a republic, just as the government was about to pass an amnesty for many of the Fascists accused of crimes. The theft of Il Duce's body was supposed to send a message that Fascist ideology was thriving. With regard to the referendum, the act would announce that the Fascist vote had to be taken into account for either side to win the ballot. Furthermore, the message would proclaim that the far right was capable of pursuing its own ends, should the amnesty for Fascists fail to bring them into the legitimate political arena. In short, the theft of Mussolini's body over Easter 1946 was not intended as a mere act of daring. As Leccisi saw it, this was a way to transform clandestine neo-Fascism into a legitimate political force.

With the help of two young neo-Fascists, Leccisi went into action in the early hours of April 23. The choice of Easter might have been symbolic—Il Duce's resurrection—but in fact the neo-Fascists decided to act that night because a riot was under way at Milan's San Vittore prison. With most of the city's police busy trying to put down the rebellion, Leccisi and his companions would have an easy time. They did not even have to worry about the two cemetery guards, who, it turned out, were highly negligent. One was taking a nap in the guard's shed while the other had gone home, where he spent the whole night "having his dinner," as he would later explain.

Leccisi and the others climbed over the cemetery fence and found section 16. According to Leccisi's memoirs, they located Mussolini's tomb without trouble, thanks to careful investigation ahead of time and because "the grave's identity was an open secret."[24] The three were also easily able to dig up Mussolini's casket because, as the deputy police chief later reported, it had been carelessly buried just in earth rather than set in cement or reinforced concrete. Leccisi pried off the top and found himself looking at the remains of Il Duce. He had his companions wrap the body in a piece of canvas they had brought for that purpose and lay it on a grave digger's cart they found on the site. Before they left the grave they tossed in a statement giving the Democratic Fascist Party credit for the theft. As dawn was breaking, the three young men headed for the gates of the cemetery as solemnly as if they were a funeral cortege. A few hours later, when the guards appeared and sounded the alarm, there was nothing for the authorities to do but admit that Mussolini's body had been stolen. Photographs of the empty grave—a huge crater in the lunar landscape of section 16— quickly made their way around Italy and the rest of the world.

The empty grave, a huge crater in the lunar landscape of section 16: the Musocco cemetery, April 23, 1946.   (*Foto Publifoto/Olympia*)

For the next hundred days (until the police succeeded in arresting Leccisi and recovering the body), the real and imagined misadventures of Mussolini's corpse occupied the papers' front pages. Il Duce's body seemed to be as ubiquitous as the dictator had been in life, keeping Italians occupied even as the country was counting down to the June 2 referendum. Phone calls kept coming, some from Leccisi and his companions, reporting sightings of Mussolini's body in one place or another. On April 24, on the eve of the first anniversary of the Liberation, the police set up roadblocks on the main access roads to Rome, pursuing a rumor that the corpse was being marched to the capital to be put on show at Palazzo Venezia or perhaps at the Altar of the Nation. In the following weeks Il Duce's body was spotted in a hundred places: on a barge on the Po near Caorso, in an airplane heading toward Rome's Ciampino airport, being ferried across the English Channel on Churchill's orders, in the hull of a ship departing from Genoa, at Brissago on the Lake of Lugano, even in the basket of a balloon being carried westward by the wind. Well-informed sources maintained that after the disinterment the body had been cremated to make it easier to move. Perhaps influenced by such rumors, the Como police questioned the parish priest of Giulino di Mezzegra about reports that an urn containing Il Duce's ashes had been carried around the town in a procession on the first anniversary of his execution.

More than any other, one newspaper, the *Corriere lombardo*, founded by the monarchist Resistance veteran Edgardo Sogno, took the trouble to follow the adventures of Mussolini's stolen corpse and the police investigation. The attention given to the matter by this paper—whose circulation in the greater Milan area was second only to that of the *Corriere della Sera*—reflects its readers' all-too-human curiosity to know what had become of the corpse of a famous dead person. They welcomed the type of detail that the *Corriere lombardo* liberally divulged, drawn from unofficial police reports: the fact that "traces of decomposing human matter" had been found near the fountain of section 16 and along the Musocco cemetery wall, the discovery of "two segments of a human finger" outside the wall, where Mussolini's corpse had been loaded into a car.[25] At the same time, someone, perhaps Sogno himself, had a weak spot for Leccisi's escapades. And possibly Sogno found the adventures of Mussolini's corpse—so embarrassing to Romita, the minister of the interior, an ardent republican—politically congenial. In any case, Leccisi and his companions could hardly have found a better mouthpiece for their efforts than the *Corriere lombardo,* one far more effective than the clandestine *Lotta fascista.*

Even before Il Duce's body was spirited away from the Musocco cemetery, Sogno had written an indulgent editorial about the Democratic Fascist Party, claiming that the neo-Fascists were victims of Communist persecution. Some moderate and right-wing publications agreed after the body disappeared. Why get so alarmed about a handful of Fascist grave robbers when platoons of Communist assassins were circulating freely? Why not demand that the Rome police investigate the many killings of Fascists and collaborators in Emilia-Romagna, rather than spend their time chasing down one lost corpse? Writing in the right-wing paper *Candido,* journalist and humorist Giovanni Guareschi called on Interior Minister Romita to devote less energy to the bones of one dead man and more to the bones of the living in the Communist-dominated Emilia region. But these were the perhaps predictable comments of the most hardened anti-Communists. What did the independent press have to say about the disappearance of Mussolini's body? Here, beyond discussion of the political implications, attention was given to the superstitious aspect, what some saw as the "survival of bar-

barism," the toll that archaic Italy, which for centuries had worshipped the bones of saints, continued to exact of the modern
nation.[26]

This approach implied unspoken questions: Did not an archaic act like the theft of Il Duce's remains prove that this was a
very unusual body? Did it not highlight the charismatic nature of
the Fascist regime at a time when Italians preferred to forget it?
Thus the shrewder journalists used the story of Mussolini's disap-
pearing remains as an occasion for a sermon about the immaterial
nature of mourning: "Memory has little to do with physical remains. The corpse displayed in Piazzale Loreto that drew hatred
and vengeance from the same crowd that had once applauded
him—this was not Mussolini. The corpse the Fascists took from
the sacred ground of Musocco and hid who knows where—this
was not Mussolini either. Mussolini is a memory—a memory of
disaster, of error, of suffering for most and illusory grandeur for a
few. The body has nothing to do with that memory, for good or
for evil."[27]

Il Duce was no longer a body, merely a memory—an easy assertion to make in postwar Italy but difficult to believe. Hence the
Communists' sense of disturbance when the corpse disappeared.
On May 1, Labor Day, an unsigned editorial in the party daily,
l'Unità, linked the theft of Il Duce's body to negotiations for a
peace treaty that Prime Minister De Gasperi was conducting in
Paris. Fascism was not dead, warned the Communist paper, and
the world should be aware. For *l'Unità* the theft was "doubly
criminal" because it betrayed Italy's national interests.[28] At the
same time the editorial was published, the Communist Party was
engaged in secret negotiations with clandestine neo-Fascists, hoping to gain consensus for the republican cause prior to the referendum and perhaps even to enroll new party members. But these
overtures to the "Blackshirt brothers" posed no contradiction to

the party's condemnation of the grave robbers. Both derived from the party's fear of the subversive power of the right. The efforts at reconciliation were part of the same political calculation that resulted in an amnesty for former Fascists granted by Justice Minister Palmiro Togliatti, secretary of the Communist Party. The Communist executive, aware that the Resistance creed had limited appeal and that the republican ideal was not universally shared, was afraid of Fascists, even when they came in the guise of undertakers.

IN THE SEARCH for Mussolini's body, Interior Minister Romita appointed several of the highest-ranking police officials. The investigation was headed by a Dr. Marrocco, chief of Rome police units, assisted by Dr. Emilio Santillo, deputy inspector, who would later oversee the capital's most crime-ridden districts. Dr. Ugo Sorrentino, director of Rome's Special Investigations Unit, produced the report on the actual theft, while Dr. Mario De Cesare, deputy chief of police, presented a report on the concurrent events in Milan (the riot at San Vittore prison). At first, the investigation results seemed to justify deployment of top police officers. Sorrentino affirmed that the body had been stolen by "several people accustomed to contact with corpses—undertakers or technicians from the coroner's staff." He based his judgment, which we know was flawed, on the inherent difficulties in extracting a body from a casket and a grave, not to mention the skill required to handle a body "in an advanced state of putrefaction." The presence of "small slivers of organic matter" on the cemetery wall over which the body was pushed, as well as the discovery in the cart that was used to transport the body of two small bones that appeared to be from fingers, failed to persuade Sorrentino that the perpetrators were amateurs. On the contrary, he concluded that the crime had required "significant expenditures," enough to warrant a search for clandestine financial backers.[29]

A week or so after this first report, Deputy Police Chief De Cesare gave Interior Minister Romita a considerably less alarming assessment, concluding that in any case, the Mussolini family had not been involved and that the theft of the body appeared to have had little impact on public opinion in Milan. "The word . . . is that the corpse 'isn't even good for soap,'" he reported.[30] Such was the cruel popular view of Mussolini's remains, evidence that people had a lively memory of making soap at home during the war and of the "soapmaker of Correggio," a famous female serial killer at the time. De Cesare believed that the persons responsible for the theft were officials of the old Fascist regime, not underground neo-Fascists. Their aim, he thought, was to push the new government into passing the widest possible amnesty. Some small-time veterans of the Social Republic were probably working for them, people who had been fired after the Liberation and were reduced to criminality to survive. "I would rule out any concern they represent even the least danger," the deputy chief of police summed up his report.[31]

The view that secret neo-Fascism was a world of petty criminals motivated by economic necessity as much as by politics was shared by others besides the police investigators. The left-wing press portrayed the Democratic Fascist Party alternately as a group of bloodthirsty bomb throwers and as mere pamphlet distributors, men who would rob people's apartments but also scrawl slogans on walls, who traded in black market Swiss francs but also begged for handouts. Neorealist literature, ideologically inspired by the Communist Party, also portrayed the neo-Fascists in minor hues—not as dangerous counterrevolutionaries but as petty crooks engaged in negligible exploits. Sandrino, the main character in Vasco Pratolini's novel *A Hero of Our Time,* the orphan son of a Fascist soldier killed in Abyssinia, takes advantage of the mad passion of a middle-aged widow, Virginia, to extract money from her. But far from a mere gigolo, Sandrino intends to use the money to buy arms for a neo-Fascist insurrection and give meaning to the sacrifice of his father's generation. Unfortunately, Sandrino falls victim to three Milanese comrades who gain his trust by pretending to be the thieves who stole Mussolini's body. After pocketing the money, the three neo-Fascists disappear. As Sandrino travels to Milan to take his revenge, he is more pathetic than evil:

> They had told him to show up that evening, at a house where he was supposed to meet his assistants, 34 Noname Street. But was there really a Noname Street? Even the widow would never have believed those three had stolen Mussolini's body. In exchange for the 300,000 lire, they'd given him a small black rag: a piece of the shirt Mussolini had worn on the day of his martyrdom! There it was, the little black rag he was going to stuff down the throat of thief number one, after he had flattened him.[32]

For the real thieves, problems began just a few days after their adventure. By April 29, the police had arrested Mauro Rana, one of Leccisi's two assistants in the theft. On May 17, the Carabinieri broke up an executive committee meeting of the Democratic Fascist Party, rounding up twelve men and four women, who quickly confessed to involvement in the crime. The group was a representative sample of clandestine neo-Fascism: young, with an average age of just over thirty and a background of military experience in the Republic of Salò. All the men had served in the Republican National Guard or other military branches of the Nazi-Fascist regime, and one of the women had served in the auxiliary. There were five white-collar workers, two unemployed people, one factory owner, one teacher, one barman, one political science graduate, one landlord, one woman who made a living ironing. The party's activities ranged from providing economic aid to comrades in difficulty to organizing armed attacks on left-wing parties to minting 200 million lire in counterfeit banknotes. The archives don't tell us whether this roundup was connected to an anonymous letter sent to the authorities a few days earlier that identified the apartment that served as the Democratic Fascist Party's usual meeting place. The letter also contained information about the theft of Il Duce's body that would turn out to be very close to the facts. The perpetrators, it said, were "three young individuals" and the body had been hidden "about 50 kilometers from Milan."[33]

As the weeks went by the papers reported the arrest of dozens of neo-Fascists in Milan, Turin, and Rome. Each report suggested a link between the arrests and the corpse's disappearance. In the meantime, Italy had turned an important page in its history, having voted in the referendum to abolish the monarchy and establish a republic. The change of system did not, however, lessen people's appetite for news of Mussolini's body. At the end of July, the investigative noose began to tighten. A police inspector posing as a factory owner interested in financing the neo-Fascists succeeded in arresting Fausto Gasparini and Giorgio Muggiani, two men close to Leccisi who had helped him with the theft. Gasparini was already sought by the police, following an arrest warrant issued for crimes perpetrated in 1944 as commander of the local Republican National Guard. Muggiani was an art student who the police thought was involved in the Democratic Fascist Party "more for love of novelty and in a spirit of adventure than out of political conviction."[34] Muggiani did not wait long to tell the police everything he knew. He told them, among other things, that his first meeting with Leccisi and his initiation into neo-Fascism had been arranged by a Franciscan friar well known in Milan, Enrico Zucca, abbot of the convent of Sant'Angelo. Gasparini gave the police the address of Leccisi's wife and mother-in-law.

A search of their apartment proved fruitful. The police found counterfeit banknotes left to dry after being soaked in coffee to enrich their color. More important, they found a key to a bank safety-deposit box where trousers and boots taken from Mussolini's casket had been stored. Now a hunted man, Leccisi did not even have time to get out of Milan. He was arrested on July 31 as he was leaving a neo-Fascist meeting. The next day the police also arrested Leccisi's second assistant, twenty-year-old Antonio Parozzi, a member of the Muti, a ferocious militia band active during the Social Republic. Still, their capture did not lead the authorities to Mussolini's body. Leccisi took an approach the police described as "boastful and provocative," refusing to admit any involvement. It would be up to Parozzi and Gasparini to recount the adventures of Il Duce's corpse. After taking the body from the cemetery, Leccisi, Parozzi, and Rana had hidden it in the village of Madesimo, in the Valtellina mountains, in a house that belonged to Rana. When Rana was arrested, Leccisi and Gasparini, concerned that he might reveal the location under police questioning, took the body from Madesimo and brought it to Milan, where Father Zucca concealed it in Sant'Angelo.

Not content to have confessed enough, Gasparini and Parozzi also told police about several other offenses they had committed in Milan in the weeks following the theft. The most serious of these involved hurling a bomb at the Communist federation building in Piazza Garibaldi and setting off dynamite on the eve of the referendum at the presses where the Socialist *Avanti!* and Communist *l'Unità* were printed. The Leccisi gang was also charged with hiding a genuine arsenal: four munitions cases containing numerous hand grenades, both Italian and foreign, fourteen tubes of explosives, three boxes of dynamite, dozens of detonators and fuses, a land mine, six automatic pistols, and an American machine gun with ammunition. In addition, the band was accused of minting and possessing counterfeit banknotes worth 200,000 lire. Gasparini and Parozzi insisted that the fake money came from Father Zucca, a point the police were inclined to believe because the two were interrogated separately. Leccisi, confronted with the other confessions, explained that the counterfeit notes were used to support unemployed Fascists. But the authorities found little evidence of such "criminal charity" among the documents they seized, which showed only a few payments of several hundred lire to some of Leccisi's closest associates.[35]

Still, the evidence the Milan police supplied to the prosecution to initiate criminal proceedings depicted the offenders as petty crooks rather than dangerous subversives. The group had engaged in action merely "to prove a point," the police chief wrote, adding that the gang lacked "seriousness, a doctrinal basis, and the principles of honesty and organization that characterize a movement."[36]

BEFORE WE LOOK more closely at Police Chief Vincenzo Agnesina, we will follow the steps of the police as they pursued Mussolini's corpse, which some of the Fascist detainees insisted was hidden inside Sant'Angelo. On the basis of the confessions, the police suspected not only Father Zucca but also Father Alberto Parini, the brother of Piero Parini, mayor and prefect of Milan under the Social Republic. On August 11, Zucca and Parini went voluntarily to the police for questioning, but they denied knowing Leccisi, Gasparini, and Parozzi. In a direct confrontation with the prisoners, the Franciscan friars stuck to their version of the facts. But slowly the investigators came closer to the truth. Father Parini, exculpating Father Zucca, insisted that he alone had conducted negotiations with the neo-Fascists. He said he had received Leccisi at Sant'Angelo, where he had given him spiritual counsel according to the rules of the order. He claimed to know the precise location of Mussolini's body but would reveal it only if his conditions were met. Once the body was recovered, he insisted, the state must guarantee a Christian burial, with the proviso that no one, not even the Mussolini family, be told where the new burial place was.

After consulting with the Rome chief of police, Agnesina agreed to the friar's demands. And so the following day, the travels of Mussolini's corpse came to an end. Father Parini led Agnesina to the Certosa di Pavia, a well-known fifteenth-century monastery outside the city of Pavia where the Franciscans had taken the body after the neo-Fascists were arrested. According to the statement issued by the Milan police, Il Duce's body had been sealed in a trunk, wrapped in two rubberized sacks, and placed in a closet in one of the monks' cells on the ground floor. Along with Mussolini's mortal remains ("no longer a corpse," according to one newspaper, "but a skeleton falling to pieces") the authorities found a declaration by the Democratic Fascist Party that spoke of the day when the august body would have the distinction of being buried on Rome's Capitoline Hill.[37] But these were feeble words, given to Agnesina's success. After months of investigation, the government had triumphed over the ghosts of the past.

Journalists and photographers were summoned. What better occasion for political show than the public exhibition, if not of the body of Il Duce, of the receptacle that had held it? Years later, a reporter would recall the atmosphere that day in a little room on the third floor of the police headquarters: the brown trunk, with its black buckles encrusted with mud—a trunk so small that those present could only wonder how the body, even bent in two, had fit in it; the heat of the room, gradually filling with a pungent smell; the silence, broken only by the sound of cameras clicking. The scene was altogether surreal: "Everyone was looking down, looking at the trunk, and the magnesium flashes made the shoes of all those people standing in a circle seem enormous, all those dusty shoes of the police officers, the reporters, and the photographers."[38]

The receptacle that held the body of Il Duce—a trunk so small those present could only wonder how the body had fit in it. (*Foto Publifoto/Olympia*)

Among the journalists covering Mussolini's postmortem adventures was a reporter for *l'Unità*, Tommaso Giglio. Barely past adolescence, he had the ethical certainty of so many young people who had become Communists during the war. "To show indulgence means to pile hate onto hate," he wrote in a poem published in *Il Politecnico* around this time.[39] His articles avoided the pitfall of indulgence. Giglio described Father Parini and Father Zucca as favorites of a large circle of wealthy, idle Milanese ladies who hoped to get to heaven by aiding outlaw Fascists. This well-informed reporter named a number of such outlaws who had been protected in the Sant'Angelo convent. Besides Leccisi and his sidekicks, they included Vanni Teodorani, Mussolini's right-hand man at Salò. According to Giglio, Father Parini was closely tied to Guglielmo Giannini, head of the *qualunquista* movement, and to the former king, Umberto of Savoy, while Father Zucca was dealing counterfeit money, if not actually drugs, to ex-Fascists and ex-Nazis who had taken refuge in the Alto Adige region, bordering Austria. The right-wing *Corriere lombardo* replied to *l'Unità*'s charges blow for blow. Its rebuttal relied heavily on the attorney for the two friars, who had been incarcerated on charges of aiding and abetting Leccisi and the others. According to him, the monastic order of the convent required the friars to be compassionate and forgiving. The right of asylum, he argued, was as valid for corpses as for human beings.

In a country with Italy's churchgoing tradition, few wished to challenge the Church's long-standing claim to the handling of corpses and commemoration of the dead. But in Mussolini's case, the issue was not as simple as his body's right to "return to legality" under the "great wing" of Christian mercy, as Father Parini argued.[40] Behind the skirmishes in the press, the lawyer's resonant pronouncements, and the friar's pious statements lay the political question of where the Church stood on the epuration of Fascist officials from public office after the war. From 1943 on, following the Italian armistice, the ecclesiastical hierarchy had kept its distance from anti-Fascism as a political movement, embracing it only as a moral option. Father Parini made implicit reference to that position when he said, of the theft of Il Duce's body, that "the act was, just as it seemed to the great majority of Italians, moral and not political."[41] Upholding the distinction between morality and politics, the Milan branch of the Pontifical Committee on Welfare was so active in helping veterans of the Republic of Salò that police reports began to refer to it as "ill-reputed."[42] On the whole, a large segment of the Church made little of what was a major transition from dictatorship to democracy. As for Father Parini, who claimed to be anti-Fascist, his actions were to prove more revealing, for the friar of Sant'Angelo eventually gave his public backing to a group of neo-Fascists called the Italian Liberation Army.

In the summer of 1946, Father Parini and Father Zucca were well known in Milan, and their trouble with the justice system threatened to cast the entire Church in a bad light. They were also respected and well liked, however, so any harshness against them risked casting the justice system in an even worse light. The interests of church and state thus came together, resulting in the friars' release and the dropping of the charges against them. Domenico Leccisi counted for nothing and had no reputation. Thus there was no Machiavellian calculation nor were there any reasons of state to prevent Police Chief Agnesina from coming down hard on Leccisi in his report to the state prosecutor. In Agnesina's view, the Democratic Fascist Party was as absurd as its name, a pretext, "a means of profit that never worked out," Agnesina wrote. Leccisi was an ex-Blackshirt nostalgic for the "comfortable Fascist feeding trough" to which he had long been attached, a political zero, a parasite, a clever do-nothing. As for the theft of Mussolini's corpse, Agnesina called it a tragic farce. While *Lotta fascista* boasted "with the usual upstart Fascist language" that Il Duce's body had been safely guarded by the movement faithful, the corpse, "folded up for four long months," had in fact been tossed around Lombardy inside a steamer trunk.[43] Four months after Agnesina wrote his report, the courts confirmed the spirit of his version of events: Leccisi was sentenced not as a political criminal but as a common delinquent, receiving a six-year sentence for the phony banknotes and nothing for the theft of the body. *Avanti!* was then able to run the headline "Thieves of Supercorpse Bag Sentences as Counterfeiters."[44]

We have seen enough of Leccisi to know that the Milan police chief's judgment was not only politically mistaken but humanly unfair. The graveyard thief was certainly a fairly disreputable figure, a thug and a bomb thrower, but he was also a genuine believer, sincerely dedicated to the cult of Il Duce and the cause of neo-Fascism, not the petty crook with no principles whom Agnesina described. It is rather the Milan police chief who warrants closer examination because he is in many ways an example of what historian Claudio Pavone had in mind when he wrote of the long-term "continuity of the state"—the persistence of old Fascist officials in the new democratic republic.[45] A series of snapshots of Agnesina, taken during his career as an exemplary civil servant, are revealing. In 1931, at the height of the Fascist system, Agnesina, as chief of the political section of the Naples police, sought to prevent the young Communist Giorgio Amendola from leaving the country (Amendola's father, Giovanni, shared Matteotti's posthumous role as a symbol of anti-Fascist martyrdom). A few years later, his repressive tactics were such that the Naples police earned the admiration of no less a Nazi figure than Heinrich Himmler. On July 25, 1943, when Mussolini was overthrown, Agnesina worked directly for the dictator as chief of personal security. He did nothing, however, to prevent Il Duce from being arrested. In 1947, as Milan police chief, Agnesina was secretly appointed by the Ministry of the Interior as an anti-Communist superprefect with broad powers. Finally, years later, in 1962, as deputy national police commissioner, he led a brutal repression of strikers in Turin. The evidence prompts the question whether, in 1946, Agnesina had any right to present himself as an anti-Fascist chasing down the thieves of the Musocco cemetery.

At the end of that year, Leccisi was in prison when an aboveground neo-Fascist party, the Movimento Sociale Italiano, or Italian Social Movement, was founded. The party received the blessing of the Vatican and the approval of the Ministry of the Interior, both of which were eager to prevent the radical neo-Fascists—firm believers in "socialization"—from swelling the ranks of the Communists. Incarcerated though he was, Domenico Leccisi deserved a place among the founding fathers of the Italian Social Movement as the mastermind of the theft of Mussolini's body; no other act had done as much to lift neo-Fascism from the private realm of self-pity to the public sphere. In fact, the first step taken by the new party showed that Leccisi's investment in Il Duce's body was neither madness nor folly to the fledgling political organization. On the contrary, his act helped define the neo-Fascists' identity and ensure their future. According to the party's unofficial gospel, the abbreviation of its name in Italian, MSI, also stood for "Mussolini Sempre Immortale"—Mussolini ever immortal. And in the party symbol, a flame sits atop a trapezoidal base—the shape of the casket Leccisi had the nerve to uncover, so that the body of Il Duce would continue as a historical actor.

4

MUSSOLINI, DEAR DEPARTED

Rescued from its posthumous embrace with Domenico Leccisi, the body of Il Duce was hidden away between 1946 and 1957 for reasons of state. On orders from the prime minister and with the agreement of Cardinal Ildefonso Schuster, archbishop of Milan, Mussolini's remains were kept in the chapel of the convent of Cerro Maggiore, near Milan, honoring the commitment that Police Chief Agnesina had made with Father Parini to give Mussolini a Christian yet secret resting place. For that eleven-year period, only a very small group of politicians, religious figures, and civil servants knew the exact location of the tomb.

By declining to return the body to the Mussolini family, the Italian government wanted to prevent Il Duce's grave from becoming, for better or worse, a shrine. The authorities did not want the cemetery at Predappio, Mussolini's birthplace, to turn into a pilgrimage destination for neo-Fascists, nor did they want any of the vandalism inflicted on the Musocco cemetery while the body was buried there. The secret resting place did not, however, stop Italians from wondering about the fate of Il Duce's corpse. On the contrary, the fact that nobody knew where the body was stimulated the popular imagination. Italians were free to fantasize about the most likely places the dictator's remains might be hidden. The physical absence of the body guaranteed it would be everywhere, in the imagination.

Mussolini's posthumous legacy was hardly limited to his corpse. The legends of Il Duce's ghostly peregrinations were not the only means through which Italians grappled with his symbolic afterlife. In the early postwar years, Mussolini's posthumous vitality was perpetuated by a great deal of journalism and literature, by no means all banal. Distinguished writers, not just obscure Fascist nostalgics, wrote about the body of Il Duce. Mussolini's life after death went beyond remaindered copies of books by passionate neo-Fascists. It is found in some of the classics of modern Italian literature.

In the first decade of the Italian republic, anti-Fascists preferred not to dwell on the "sad figure" of Mussolini, as they saw it. So the word on Il Duce was left to writers who stood aloof from the ideals of the Resistance. In various genres, at various levels of quality, this literary production was remarkably consistent in what it had to say, since its necrology was informed by ideology.

LENIN, MUSSOLINI, HITLER, MAO: when leaders who have had large followings die, posterity asks whether they left a political last will and testament. The question differs depending on whether the death marks the end of a regime, as in Italy and Germany in 1945, or whether the system survives its founder, as in the Soviet Union in 1924 and in China in 1976. In the two Communist systems, the deceased leaders' intentions posed a lively political problem, since the fate of the country rested on how well the candidates for succession were able to interpret them. For the two Fascist regimes, the dictators' last wishes represented more of a symbolic legacy. To Germany, in ruins after the war, Hitler's testament was a melodramatic final assertion of the Nibelungian ties the Führer felt linked him to his people. In Italy, determining the last wishes of Mussolini did not seem very urgent because Il Duce had repeatedly insisted that he would never leave a final testament.

But with the passage of time, many Italians began to wonder whether Il Duce had indeed left any parting wishes. The question had little political weight in the republic born of the Resistance, because Prime Minister De Gasperi showed no interest in courting Mussolini's political heirs, even after the birth of the neo-Fascist Italian Social Movement. The concern with Mussolini's will for the future emerged not from the political arena, but from the collective imagination. Italy of the late 1940s was a country that looked forward to the ethos of consumerism and, at the same time, backward to the rituals of Fascism. Like the characters who live in Italo Calvino's Laudomia, in *Invisible Cities,* early postwar Italians felt the need to turn to the cemetery to find explanations for themselves. Above all, they needed to understand the reasons for their recent Fascist past. But after the trials of Mussolini's body in 1946, there was no cemetery—not even a metaphorical one— where Italians could ask their questions at the tomb of the leader. If conversation with the dead Mussolini was impossible, perhaps the live Duce's last words could provide some enlightenment.

For ten years after Mussolini's death, the debate over the dictator's parting vision—whether this or that document qualified— periodically occupied the popular press. There was one statement, though, that was so evidently an invention that nobody wasted time arguing its legitimacy. *My Good Man Mussolini,* as it was called, was published in 1947 by journalist Indro Montanelli, who in his postliberation novel *Here They Do Not Rest* (1945) had established himself as an able interpreter of post-Fascist sentiment.

In 1946 he and writer Leo Longanesi coauthored *Memoirs of Mussolini's Manservant,* in which they imagined the life of Il Duce's doorman in the days when the dictator held court at Palazzo Venezia. This retrospective keyhole view allowed them to show Fascism not as a totalitarian regime but as a bonfire of the vanities in which Mussolini was not a terrible tyrant but merely the most fatuous of Italians. Now, in *My Good Man Mussolini,* Montanelli was ready to speak for Il Duce himself.

My Good Man Mussolini pretends to be the dying wishes that Il Duce entrusted to a faithful priest at Lake Como and that the priest then passed on to Montanelli in his role as journalist for the *Corriere della Sera.* The hundred-page text was immediately taken up by the popular weeklies. "All of us," the book's prologue asserts, "have felt the need for a will left by Mussolini." This was true both of his Fascist defenders, who sought reasons for self-justification, and of anti-Fascists, who looked for new cause to attack the regime. "Well, here it is," Montanelli proclaims—Mussolini's long-awaited final testament.[1]

Montanelli's audacity was matched by that of one other distinguished journalist of the regime, Curzio Malaparte.[2] Montanelli's book and Malaparte's novel *The Skin*—a best seller of higher literary quality, published in 1949—shared the same paradoxical message. In *My Good Man Mussolini,* Il Duce declares that he meant for Italy to lose in World War II because Italians show greatness not in victory but in defeat. In Malaparte's work on defeated Italy, he too depicts the losers as superior to the winners. Among the country's most influential commentators, "young" Montanelli, who was thirty-eight when he published his book, and "old" Malaparte, fifty-one when he published *The Skin,* were united in playing the contrarian. But they also shared a desire to give voice to "Italy's bad conscience," writing in the service of an ideology that might be called anti-anti-Fascism. Their efforts represented a glossy bourgeois version of the more vulgar, plebeian *qualunquista* protest; they were a rebellion against the ideals of the Resistance and the system's desire to punish those who had served under the Fascists. What were they so guilty of, anyway, Italians who had believed in Il Duce? And what was Mussolini himself so guilty of? Paradoxical, part-serious, theatrical, or *qualunquista*—whatever they intended, with their polemics, the two journalists helped push the ghost of Mussolini onto the new republic's stage.

Leaving Malaparte aside for the moment, let us look at Montanelli's invocation of Mussolini. His short book concentrates all the historical and political arguments that for half a century after the Liberation constituted the anti-Resistance arsenal. Mussolini's defeat on July 25, 1943? The Fascist Grand Council's decision that day to oppose Mussolini was courageous—perhaps the only act of courage against Fascism in the history of the regime. The anti-Fascist celebrations of the following day? They didn't amount to much, says Montanelli-Mussolini. And why should Italians hate Il Duce, anyway? After all, "the worst thing about him was the faces he made." For over twenty years the Mussolini government was marked by its "mildness," having only punished a few hundred opponents with internal exile.[3] It was significant that all the victims of the antiregime marches after Mussolini's fall were symbolic— monuments, plaques, busts. In a gentle dictatorship, these were the objects of hate. As for the epilogue of his political career, Montanelli's Mussolini speculates as to what might have become of him had the Nazis not rescued him from his prison at Gran Sasso. Perhaps he would have gone on to be a Hollywood actor (as the great Neapolitan actor and playwright Eduardo De Filippo once said of Il Duce). Perhaps he would have found himself the defendant in a war crimes trial at the United Nations. "More likely, though, the commander of a partisan band, like so many of my officials."

Montanelli's Mussolini justifies his choice to head the Republic of Salò with the same line of reasoning later used by Salò apologists: he made a personal sacrifice "to save what could be saved in occupied Italy."⁴ He knew the vengeful fury of the Germans and the cruelty they could have unleashed after the monarchy embraced the Allies, and so he had positioned himself as a fender between the Nazis and the Italians. For six hundred interminably long days Il Duce had sought to soften the blows the Wehrmacht and the SS delivered to the nation's body and soul. Like Pétain in Vichy France, Mussolini bowed to the moral law that obliges the true statesman to choose the most difficult option available. He elected to walk the path of death to spare countless fellow citizens the same fate. His decision was all the more tragic, says Montanelli's Mussolini, because he expected to be finished off "by the people's fury." At the end of April 1945, he left Lake Garda for Milan so that the circle of Fascism would close where it had opened in 1919, so that the city of his defeat would be the same as the city of his victory.

In the concluding pages of Mussolini's "last words," Montanelli has Il Duce attack the same idol the journalist himself tirelessly attacked over the next decade—the idol of anti-Fascism. Postwar Italy, says Montanelli-Mussolini, can progress only by ending the "melancholy back and forth" of Fascism versus anti-Fascism.⁵ Rather than worship at the tattered images of Fascism's political exiles, better to be wary of such heroes because "any choice was preferable to exile."⁶ Italians had no reason to be ashamed of their history in the years before the Resistance. Above all, there was no reason to be ashamed of their past as Fascists; from the start, Fascism served to block the spread of Bolshevism in Europe. If Mussolini was guilty of any crime, Montanelli suggests, it was not that he deployed the Fascist terror but that he declined to deploy it. During the late 1930s, Il Duce had staged an "operetta" while Stalin's henchmen in Italy were busy with full-blown tragedies. Anyone who thought that Italian democracy had begun with the Liberation was mistaken; they had been blinded by the Communists, who had been cleansed of their crimes by the Committee of National Liberation.

Thus the Fascist March on Rome became the logical reaction to the Bolshevik victory in St. Petersburg, the Resistance a cabal of turncoat Fascists, Mussolini at Salò a martyr with stigmata. That is how Montanelli, writing in 1947, outlined the strategy for future revisionists. From the point of view of those under attack, Montanelli's revisionism was all the more insidious because he was no mere neo-Fascist but an influential journalist in the new republic—a top reporter for the *Corriere della Sera*, whose byline appeared frequently in the popular weeklies and the right-wing intellectual magazine *Il Borghese*. Montanelli's widespread success owed much to his ability, as "Italy's bad conscience," to address the consciences of those Italians who had been Fascists but were no longer and did not want to be made to feel guilty for the past. So *My Good Man Mussolini*, read by a broad audience, probably did greater harm to the anti-Fascist cause than one other, more explicitly Fascist book, published a year later. Read mostly by neo-Fascists, *Mussolini's Political Testament* arguably gave a better representation of Il Duce's last will, had there been one.

Mussolini's Political Testament had all the characteristics of a religious relic, being a photographic reproduction of the typed copy of Il Duce's final interview, which he gave to a reporter for a small paper in Piedmont, the *Popolo d'Alessandria*. The text was "dictated, corrected, and signed by Him," according to the book's title page. Apart from anything else, the book reveals how vacuous an article from the Salò era might look in postwar republican Italy. The author, Gian Gaetano Cabella, a journalist possessed of dubious professional abilities, seems to have coped with the challenge of meeting Il Duce one on one by oscillating between

Fascist clichés and homoerotic appreciation. Mussolini's voice had the "metallic tones" of the human machine Italians had come to admire at Piazza Venezia. His "white hand, a little plump," lay so close to Cabella's that the journalist had to "exercise restraint not to caress it."[7] As for the interview itself, Mussolini embraces the role of ox of the nation, the leader who is ready to sacrifice himself for the good of the Italian people. Countering the infamous charges of the anti-Fascist press of the center-south—that Mussolini was a puppet of the Germans, that the only thing that moves Il Duce anymore is his mistress, that the dictator has his bags packed, ready to flee—the interviewer reveals a Mussolini who says he would never budge from his "place of work," where whoever won the struggle would inevitably find him.

It is impossible not to read these words (from April 22, 1945, three days before the Liberation) against the reality of what happened the following week, when Mussolini, wearing a German greatcoat, took flight with Claretta Petacci at his side and Bank of Italy gold in his suitcase. But Cabella saw no reason, after the war, to let that embarrassment stop him from publishing the interview. Just three years after the events, when *Mussolini's Political Testament* appeared in 1948, the memory of Il Duce's shameful flight was too vivid for the book to appeal to any readers who were not neo-Fascists. The image of a leader who stood, irremovable, awaiting the arrival of the Allies and the Resistance forces, could only have seemed a lie to the great majority of Italians. More convincing—especially in 1948, when the electoral campaign was marked by priestly interventions against the Communists and on behalf of the Catholic party, the Christian Democrats—was the story that Mussolini had converted to Catholicism in extremis. The rumor complemented the image of Il Duce in his final days as the victim of circumstance, a man dragged along by other high-ranking Fascists rather than a leader, resigned rather than resolute, peace-loving rather than bellicose—in short, a humble Christian rather than a pillar of Fascism.

Just two weeks before the elections, the legend of Mussolini's conversion got a boost when it was recounted in the popular weekly *Oggi*. The article, written by Alberto Giovannini, a reporter who had worked in the Republic of Salò, depicted Il Duce in the edifying guise of a man preparing himself for baptism: "As the years passed, perhaps pressed by the blows of destiny, Mussolini had become a believer." He held frequent talks, Giovannini said, with Father Eusebio, the Franciscan who headed the Black Brigades' Spiritual Assistance Office, talks during which Mussolini "liked to discuss God at length." Then, sometime around mid-April 1945, Mussolini asked Father Eusebio to absolve his sins, said Giovannini. Taken by surprise, the priest initially refused, but seeing Mussolini before him with his famous jaw humbly resting on his chest, Father Eusebio relented and raised his hand, repeating the words of the rite, "*Ego te absolvo . . .*"[8] It was a scene of high repentance, conceded to Mussolini by an undistinguished journalist on the eve of an important election. Before long, Mussolini's "return to God" was postdated by another priest to his imprisonment in 1943 on the island of Ponza. And some years later, in the 1950s, the legend of Mussolini's conversion was revived with the publication of a purported spiritual last testament of Il Duce, dated April 27, 1945, Dongo, on Lake Como.

Even today, a visitor to the Mussolini family tomb in Predappio will be handed a brochure quoting this document in full—a text of some twenty lines. As early as 1946, brief excerpts were published in the Rome weekly *Il Pubblico*. In 1947, it appeared in a neo-Fascist paper in Buenos Aires, *Il Risorgimento,* and in 1951, the document made the rounds at a secret mass celebrated for Mussolini in the Sant'Agostino church in Rome. Then, two years later, Duilio Susmel, the editor of Mussolini's complete works, prompted a public discussion about the veracity of the "spiritual will"; priests, graphologists, historians, and Salò veterans all leaped to the fore to express their opinions. In June 1953, the weekly *Epoca* declared the document an "absolute falsehood," while Susmel, who also wrote for *Epoca*, maintained that Mussolini had "rejoined himself to God in the moment of his defeat," quoting the "spiritual will" as evidence of Il Duce's conversion.[9] Since then, the document has generally been considered legitimate by amateur historians while professionals believe it a fake.

In this "spiritual will" Mussolini declared that he could face death reassured by the supreme comfort of religious faith. "I believed in the victory of our military forces as I believe in God, our Lord," the text reads. Il Duce's faith in the other world had been bolstered by Italy's military losses, because it was in defeat, he thought, that the Italian strength of character and moral grandeur became most visible. "So if today is therefore the last day of my life," the will says, "I give my forgiveness even to those who abandoned me and have betrayed me."[10] Thus, from one phony testament to another, the vigorous, living Mussolini had been transformed into the ethereal, dead Mussolini. The good man of Montanelli's title had instead become Mussolini, dear departed.

AMONG THE SURVIVORS of Fascism's defeat, there was at least one who genuinely converted to Catholicism—the intellectual and ex-minister Giuseppe Bottai. He converted without waiting until the very last minute, having found consolation in the Christian faith in the early 1940s, during intense conversations with a priest, Don Giuseppe De Luca, who was accustomed to dealing with nonbelievers. After Mussolini's unexpected resurrection as head of the Republic of Salò, Bottai, who had withdrawn his support for the dictator in July 1943, risked serious repercussions for his disloyalty. Only the intervention of the Holy See protected him from Mussolini's revenge. But Bottai had no desire to remain hidden in the shadow of Vatican power. In the fall of 1944 he undertook to expiate his sins by enrolling in the French Foreign Legion and going off to fight in France and Germany. For three years after the end of the war, Bottai served as a legionnaire in North Africa, waiting for the right conditions—both judicial and political—to return to Italy. He did not want to go to prison for his past as a high-ranking Fascist, nor did he consider his public career necessarily closed, perhaps the only leading ex-Fascist in that position.

Bottai's diary from his period as a legionnaire suggests the conflicts of a post-Fascist. He expresses pride at having been a Fascist and having consciously obeyed history's command. Yet he registers disapproval of neo-Fascism, which he sees as a sterile imitation of the original model. From his African exile, Bottai reads the news about cemetery plundering and Domenico Leccisi with great indifference. "This neo-Fascism, scratching around between tombs and epitaphs, . . . it smacks of cadavers and tarnished crowns," he writes.[11] The ex-Fascist has no intention of repudiating Mussolini, who had been the guiding influence of his youth, his compass in maturity, even the inspiration for his betrayal in 1943, with him playing the role of disillusioned lover. But he refuses to follow the Italian Social Movement in its absurd cult of "Il Duce resurrected," and few developments on the political scene seem to him more pernicious than the reborn Mussolini.

At the heart of the diary entries lay a criticism Bottai had voiced from the earliest days of the March on Rome and repeated through two decades of Fascism. He believed that the regime was too closely tied to the figure—and thus the mortal existence—of Il Duce. As the cult of Mussolini grew, Bottai had warned of the danger that Fascism would become a theatrical display. In private, Bottai conceded the time-honored anti-Fascist cliché that Il Duce was above all

Playing the farmer, miner, athlete, soldier, man of the world, or worker, Mussolini was "the great universalist." (*Istituto Luce*)

a great actor: in notes from 1940, he wrote that the multiple Mussolinis on offer to the people had turned Il Duce into a politician "of the stage." Playing the farmer, miner, athlete, soldier, man of the world, or worker, Mussolini was "the great universalist . . . in the style of an actor."[12] At the same time, the regime's collapse after Mussolini's ouster in 1943 was yet more proof of the man's charisma. How to imagine, then, a Fascism that did not depend so much on Mussolini? In the monasteries outside Rome where he hid in 1943 and 1944, on the battlefields of Alsace and Lorraine where he fought in 1944–45, in the Maghreb battalions where he took refuge between 1945 and 1948, Bottai mulled over the problem that intense charisma did not translate into stability of power.

Some of the most telling pages of Bottai's diaries were written in Algeria in 1946 and published in 1949 as *Twenty Years and a Day*, a memoir. Bottai thought of the book as notes toward the phenomenology of Fascism "in corpore Mussolini."[13] Bottai praised that body, "not too large," that nonetheless conveyed an impression of enormousness; he praised the inexplicable grandeur, "a grandeur beyond the physical, of those limbs," the eyes "normally sized" that still projected an "immense, limitless" gaze. The voice was "not so powerful" yet vibrant with "infinite echoes."[14] In more ways than one, the legionnaire Bottai's declaration of love for the deceased Mussolini formed the first chapter in his phenomenology of Fascism. While early anti-Fascist historians of Fascism ignored the extraordinary qualities of the body of Il Duce, Bottai understood perfectly the corporal nature of the Fascist regime.

From 1922, Bottai said, the entire plan for the future society had rested on the shoulders of Mussolini—strong shoulders, but human nonetheless; unlike Atlas, Il Duce was subject to fatigue. The Fascist state had been incarnated in the body of Il Duce, turning the political order upside down. "No longer is the state man writ large," argued Bottai. "Man is now the state writ small." But Fascism did not fail because of this; the regime faltered when its theatricality overtook its corporeality, less because Mussolini wanted it so than because the Italian people did. Italians saw Il Duce as a character more than a person and pressed the reluctant regime to take to the stage. The Fascist crowds, said Bottai, had transformed the puppeteer into the puppet. "Alone before the mirror," Il Duce was "forced to admire himself, to contemplate himself, and to posture."[15] Mussolini had merely followed a script written by forty million faithful followers. This conclusion that Bottai reached in exile emerges from his diary as hard-earned and sincere. But it is also lenient, for it exonerates both Mussolini and the Italian people from any moral responsibility for Fascism's failure. If everyone was guilty, then no one was guilty.

Formed during his lonely years as a legionnaire, Bottai's interpretation nevertheless mirrored the many other memoirs by ex-Fascists—part autobiography, part amateur history—that crowded the bookstores after the war. One of them was *Roma 1943,* by the journalist Paolo Monelli, a book that, despite its narrative and historical merit, ultimately lacked intellectual honesty. Like Bottai, Monelli blamed Italians for Fascism's focus on the person of Mussolini, for the atrophy of the founding ideals, and for the excessive growth of the physical cult of Il Duce—in sum, for the Fascist revolution's degeneration. He considered "theatricality" a distinctive characteristic not only of Mussolini but of Italians in general and believed Il Duce was a "typical representative of a large part of us."[16] The love of uniforms, medals, and honorary titles; the tendency to change one's behavior when observed, particularly by a woman; the need to let others know immediately who one was and what one did; the desire to be at the center of things—these were all characteristics Mussolini shared with legions of his followers.

This revised version of what Fascism had been—pantomime—was tempting to many in the first years after the war. But again, the idea that Il Duce had been "sent by destiny to act as our mirror" served as much to absolve Italians of responsibility as to incriminate them.[17] In *Three Unconquered Empires*, a book published in 1946, Aldo Palazzeschi sought to indict all Italians:

> "Il Duce" does not exist and never existed; there is only an image that is a mirror in which we must study ourselves. We are the ones who, day after day, gave him those hands and that voice, those eyes and that jaw; "Il Duce" is our creation, flesh of our flesh and blood of our blood. We created him at a moment of vanity, vacuity, and ecstasy. So you must look as carefully at this image as into a mirror; otherwise you will create not a new society but only a new image, vain and foolish. Not a society but the mystification of one.[18]

One reviewer, Vittore Branca, certainly no Fascist sympathizer, responded to Palazzeschi's book with unease, asking several tough questions. Could Fascism really be reduced to a play acted by Mussolini and written by the people, his playwright? Was Italian support for Fascism really motivated exclusively by the body of Il Duce—the "massive chest rising above short, spindly legs, the criminal tilt of the eye, the outsize jaw"?[19] Writing in 1946, Branca responded as a veteran of the Resistance, his career as a literature professor still ahead of him. His questions implied another, more subtle, more burning problem: was there really a difference between collective incrimination and general absolution?

"If you read Monelli's *Roma 1943* or Palazzeschi's *Three*

Unconquered Empires, you may find them interesting, even amusing," wrote the novelist Carlo Emilio Gadda, one of twentieth-century Italy's most original writers, to a friend in 1946. Gadda, a thoroughgoing misogynist, certainly enjoyed Monelli's allusions to a state of imperial decline in the waning days of Fascism, when Mussolini, at the mercy of Claretta Petacci, permitted national policy to be dictated by the moods and caprices of the "busty, curly-haired brunette (just his type)."[20] And Gadda surely appreciated Palazzeschi's discussion of the "strange itch" that afflicted Italian women in the presence of Il Duce's powerful virility. "Normal" men and women held little interest for these writers, whose sensibility made them scathing toward the presumed greatness of those considered "grand" and gentle toward the "fools," people who had somehow failed to make the grade or had fallen by the wayside.[21] Unless this mercy for the victims of history is taken into account, it is difficult to understand why Gadda, in his own writing, treated Mussolini as he did.

No history of Mussolini's dead body would be complete without Gadda, whose depiction of Mussolini could not be further from the figure of Il Duce, the dear departed. Beginning in the winter of 1944, Gadda turned on the head of Salò and the corpse of Piazzale Loreto with a ferocious outpouring of deadly invective. From *That Awful Mess on the Via Merulana,* first serialized in 1946, then published in a best-selling version in 1957, to the *First Book of Fairy Tales* of 1952, to *Eros and Priapus* of 1955, Gadda worked like no other writer in the 1950s to examine the physical implications of the cult of Mussolini—even, one might say, the genital implications. Focusing on Mussolini's body to study the Fascist regime, Gadda employed a surprisingly innovative historiographic approach, something close to what today might be called "body history." In practice, though, Gadda's approach was original in form but conventional in substance. Damned and pelted with insults, Gadda's posthumous Mussolini nonetheless paved the way for an all-too-indulgent representation of Fascist Italy. The names Gadda dubbed Mussolini were near inexhaustible, each one adding meaning to the last and the sum of them amounting to an elephantine corpus of features that constituted the body of Il Duce: Dearly Beloved, Plague-Ridden Plague, Toad, Bowler Hat, Caciocavallo (a round, hard cheese), Cowardly Ass, Our Gloomy One, Maternal Piece of Shit, Emir with Fez, Megalomaniac, Old Bomb, Nastyface, Tool, Broken Tool, Rotten Scoundrel, Farting Genius, Smelly One, Dumb Knee, Judas in a Bowler, Vainglorious, Boneless Boaster, Big Imago, Big Fart, Big Donkey of a Captain, Big Drum Signifying Nothing, Big Bull, Pigface Badblood, Big Puffed-Up Artist's Model, Blasted Big-Mouth from Predappio, Marquis of the Marches, Jaw of a Jackass, Schizophrenic Jawbone, Crap, Crapola, Little Prick, Great Chief Asshole, Great Big Show-Off, Braying One, Napoleon the Big Ass, Bad Lot, Empty-Headed One, Puffed-Up Paphlagonian, Miles Gloriosus, Idle Threat, Predappio, Predappio Judas, Predappio Crap, Phallus-Obsessed, First Garbage-Collector Loudmouth and Spitter, Small-Town Prophet, Provolone, Punch Playing Caesar, Puppet, Senile Romulus, Fourth-Rate Warmonger, Punched-Up Blowhard, Ass, King of the Seed Spillers, Booted One, Super Penis, Impotent Bully, Death's Head, Thresher, Triple-Heeled Dwarf, Big-Assed Braggart Optimus Maximus, Ferocious, Big Tuber, Empty-Worded One, Cop of Destinies. . . .

The torrent of vituperation fails to mask a bad conscience, for, like Bottai, Gadda wrote of Mussolini with the intensity of a lover betrayed. A member of the National Fascist Party from 1921, a moralist who had believed in Fascism as a necessary means to strengthen the nation, Gadda witnessed the miserable end of the regime with a sense of unworthiness at having survived it. He was too profound a spirit and had been too marked by the Great War to have backed Fascism in any superficial way. As little as he liked the roughness of the Blackshirts, Gadda, a middle-class Italian who had been on the battlefield when Italy suffered its historic defeat at Caporetto, sympathized with the regime's nationalistic passion, its demand for order, its xenophobia. His disenchantment began at the end of the 1930s, after the bloody military campaigns Mussolini undertook in East Africa. Defeat in World War II did the rest, triggering his visceral, all-consuming, paranoid hatred of Il Duce. The sentiment went hand in hand with Gadda's sexual immaturity; a repressed homosexual, he was obsessed by the story of Mussolini's syphilis, which was rumored to be a consequence of sexual hyperactivity. Gadda's writings do not, however, require psychoanalysis to be understood. A powerful portrait of Il Duce emerges from his postwar production; unrivaled in its irreverence, the portrait still provides a moral and historical interpretation.

In Gadda's rendering, Mussolini's bald head is like a provolone or a cabbage, but always empty, since Il Duce lacked brains. His piggish face is the sort that says, "born stupid." His eyes are possessed, the eyes of a man in the final stages of syphilis. His donkey's face has not one jaw but two, more like a mule's. His "oral sphincter" is ringed by lips set in an idiot's pout. His tongue is "red, black, then red and black, the tongue of an ass licker." At the end of two very short arms, the arms of a toad, his hands stick out oddly, like the hands of a dead man or a scarecrow. "Ten fat fingers . . . rest on his hips like two bunches of bananas," showing off his "very shitty fingernails." His chest, which Mussolini frequently liked to bare naked, sports "just two hairs (where others boast a forest) clustered around his nipples." His stomach is puffy and sagging, barely held in by the belt of his uniform. His genitalia are "leprous," his penis covered with syphilitic ulcers. Finally, Il Duce's locked knees, his "legs crossed in an X," and the triple heels on his shoes conspire to make the globe of his backside "unappealing to all."

This hideous portrait cannot be attributed wholly to a lover's sense of betrayal. Nor can it be dismissed as an attempt to show off literary creativity and expressiveness. Gadda uses Il Duce's body to teach an ethical lesson that consoles him for the national tragedy: Mussolini's boast notwithstanding, his spirit was not stronger than his material reality. In Il Duce's grotesque appearance and his Lucifer-like fall, Gadda sees the retribution brought on a false idol. In a section of the *First Book of Fairy Tales* dealing with "the Great Ass's Funeral," Mussolini is subject to the most degrading bodily functions: he is a dead dictator compelled to replicate his living exploits in an excremental hell.[22] In fable III, Gadda has the ghost of Mussolini foolishly haranguing a covey of bats, his hands on his belt to push in his swelling gut, his feet splayed in a way that makes his backside look especially round. But the bats, who couldn't care less about Il Duce's oration, are "pissing on the nape of his neck and shitting over his bare head." And finally, as Mussolini falls silent, from his backside, "by something like divine decree, [comes] a trumpet blast." In another fable, Gadda writes of Il Duce's trysts with Death. Mussolini favors the most bestial of sexual positions and refers to the old witch Death as "like Clara" preparing herself "for her marelike duties."[23]

There is a well-developed Italian literary tradition of dead men who recount tales from beyond the tomb. But Gadda did not play on that tradition, preferring to rely not on flights of imagination but on the material of history. He was particularly struck by Mussolini's last hours on the shores of Lake Como as he fled with his lover in one hand and gold from the central bank in the other. Along with millions of other Italians, Gadda saw this last act as evidence of Mussolini's cowardice, thievery, and infidelity to his wife. Gadda spares the coward Mussolini, about to die at the gates of Villa Belmonte, the attack of diarrhea that he visits on the dictator as he is driven away to prison after his arrest in July 1943. However, faced with the executioner Valerio's machine gun, Gadda's chief of the Italian Social Republic has nothing better to say than "But, Colonel!" before he grasps "that these were bullets."[24] The gold Mussolini carries with him is the second capital sin of his final act: he has run away with state money after having repeatedly promised to face death with empty pockets: "They found gold sovereigns in his hollow Fascist purse."[25] Finally, Claretta Petacci's presence at the execution, rather than Mussolini's wife, Rachele, gave Gadda telling proof of the hypocrisy of the Fascist propaganda about the sanctity of the family. But he was not content merely to follow Mussolini to the shores of Lake Como or even to Piazzale Loreto; he also alluded—cryptically but earnestly—to the posthumous adventures of Il Duce's body. "God willing, they have strung him up on a more worthy lamppost. And now he is scattering decomposed thumbs all over the ground," he wrote in 1946.[26] Apparently he had heard enough about the theft of the body from the Musocco cemetery to know that it had cost Mussolini's corpse a couple of bits of his fingers.

Indirectly in *That Awful Mess on the Via Merulana* and more systematically in *Eros and Priapus,* Gadda relates the story of Il Duce's body to a broader history of the Fascist period. His interpretation is based on several core truths, and they are very clear. Mussolini's "first crime" was his erotic narcissism, his "phallic arrogance."[27] He infected Italian men with the same syndrome, an absurd pride in their sexual prowess, even more than in their political skills. Worse, he infected Italian women with a bottomless sexual appetite: from menarche to menopause, they lived in hope of experiencing the exaggerated virility of Mussolini. The desire for that "ricket-ridden big head," which *That Awful Mess* claims began in 1927, grew only more powerful with the years:

They began to go crazy about him as soon as they had their first communion, all the Maria Barbisas of Italy began to invulvatize him on the way down from the altar, all the Madgas, the Milenas, the Filomenas of Italy, wearing their white veils and smelling of orange blossom, captured by the photographer as they left church, dreamed of unforgettable, rotating performances of educational nightsticks. The ladies, whether at Maiano or Cernobbio, went crazy with venereal sighs over the big member of Italy.[28]

Pathological misogyny partly but not entirely accounts for the virulence of Gadda's polemics against Italian women. There was an idea in postwar culture that Fascism could be explained, among other things, by women's passion for the body of Il Duce. More precisely, Fascism was the place where female ignorance and Mussolini's cult of the phallus met. When *That Awful Mess* was published in 1957, very few voices on the left refused to join the chorus of praise or pointed out the novel's reactionary ideological implications. Anti-Fascist culture sought to link Gadda to its own traditions. Giulio Cattaneo, writing in the left-wing literary magazine *Belfagor,* extravagantly seconded the book's insults to the dead dictator, while several Communist reviewers suggested that the unsolved murder at the center of *That Awful Mess* was committed by Il Duce himself.

The singular enthusiasm of the left intelligentsia for the novel's political philosophy says much about the troubles of anti-Fascist culture in the 1950s. In a period when the dear departed soul of Mussolini enjoyed much favor, even Gadda's outburst seemed to some a "salutary antidote" to a mere "farcical nostalgia."[29] But Gadda's interpretation of Fascism was misleading and ultimately not very critical. Il Duce's main crime was not, as Gadda suggested, that he doused the crowds in Piazza Venezia with the sperm of his rhetoric. Nor was Fascist Italy nothing more than a big pond into which millions of Latin lovers gazed, checking the reflected size of their masculine attributes. Fascist Italy was even less a giant brothel where millions of sighing women awaited Mussolini's visits. By reducing the Fascist period to the "era of the prick," Gadda obscured the historical significance of dictatorship with a sea of seminal fluid.[30] Beyond the pond and the brothel, were there no intellectual circles, no libraries, no prisons? Beyond the insatiable bodies, were there no ideas, no books, no weapons? Gadda's genital history of Fascism rendered any history of anti-Fascism futile. At the same time, Gadda never concealed his dislike for the priestly voices of the opposition, for Resistance worthies who righted all wrongs, for the idealists of the republic.

Deep in his North African exile, Bottai the legionnaire saw traces of "necrotic cowardice" in the anti-Mussolini stance of many writers with an expansive Fascist past.[31] But when read with care, Gadda, the non-Catholic, with his invective of the corpse, offered an interpretation of the Fascist period that was not so different from the Catholic Bottai's more pious memoirs. Mussolini and Fascism added up to a display of bodies: the puffed-up body of the chief and the beautiful young bodies of the Fascist youth league, whose multiple perfection Il Duce treated as if it were his own. Like Bottai, Gadda viewed the dictatorship from the deceptive perspective of the stage. Mussolini was a histrionic character and Italians imitated him. The Fascist regime had been an optical and acoustical phenomenon. Through the sting of his vituperative prose, Gadda even managed to dismiss the cult of the knife, a weapon the Blackshirts liked to hang off their belts like a silvery male member. For Gadda, this was one of the many "theatrical myths" of Fascism—as if the Blackshirts never stuck their knives into living Italian flesh.[32]

* * *

LONG AFTER 1945, Gadda insisted that Mussolini had been afflicted with syphilis, "the scarlet plague that eroded his prick."[33] This was an enduring legend, one that Il Duce's published autopsy report did nothing to dispel. Indeed, the story gained renewed credibility when the U.S. Fifth Army decided to send a sample of Mussolini's brain tissue to Washington for further study. The American authorities were bound not to reveal the results, but that did not prevent numerous gossipy articles about Mussolini's brain from appearing in the Italian press for more than a decade.

The legend of Il Duce's advanced case of syphilis was so widely known that neo-Fascists could not ignore it; they could not allow the notion that Mussolini had descended into madness during the last chapter of Fascism. Various officials bore witness to the contrary: there was the Salò ambassador to the Third Reich, who declared that Mussolini was in full possession of his faculties, and a minister of the Social Republic who said the rumors about syphilis were "clichés of bad taste." But where the pathologists did not succeed in banishing the legend, neither did the neo-Fascists. Many Italians remained convinced that toward the end Mussolini had been mentally disturbed because of syphilis.

The story of Il Duce's syphilis was typical of what happens when a totalitarian system collapses, when people become disenchanted with the leader's superhuman qualities. When the leader dies, the myths so vital in his lifetime are turned upside down; the charisma is transformed into a deep flaw. In the century of Freud, was there any context more congenial in which to situate the leader's physical (and mental) flaws than in his sexuality? In post-Nazi Germany, there were those who sought to explain the extermination of the Jews by claiming that Hitler had contracted syphilis from a Jewish prostitute. Others made much of the connection between Nazi policy and the fact—confirmed by the Führer's autopsy—that Hitler lacked a left testicle. In the journalist Corrado

Alvaro's diary, we find echoes of such obsessions in postwar Rome. "C. asserts that Il Duce had an undeveloped male member," writes Alvaro, adding, "B. replies that he took the trouble of measuring it when he saw the corpse and says that the entire genitalia were of normal size."[34] Mussolini's supporters also had their say in the matter, as in *The Handsome Priest*, an ironic novel by Goffredo Parise published in the 1950s. In it, Esposito, a retired jailer and widower with four daughters to marry off, is convinced that Il Duce was well endowed. "He had studied him attentively, Il Duce, on more than one occasion, in order to be sure. . . . You could see it perfectly, even without special equipment."[35]

Mussolini's life after death thus relied on diagnoses dredged from memory or created out of whole cloth. They were perpetuated not only by Il Duce's doctors but by prominent officials of the defunct regime, by journalists, many of them well known, as well as by ordinary Italians. In a memoir written after the war, Georg Zachariae, a German who was his doctor during the Salò period, recalled a Mussolini in dire physical condition, with low blood pressure, anemia, dry, taut skin, an enlarged liver, stomach cramps, a shrunken lower abdomen, poor peristalsis, and acute constipation. At that stage Mussolini was "a ruin of a man," Zachariae wrote, suggesting that it was very likely overwhelming pain that caused him to make wrong decisions.[36] According to Guido Leto, the former chief of OVRA, the secret police, Mussolini's physical decline was the real reason for his ejection on July 25, 1943. That is, Fascism died of fatigue rather than as a result of conflict. Cesare Rossi, a Fascist notable in the early years, gave further details in *Mussolini Remembered: X-rays of the Former Dictator*, advancing the idea that Il Duce's mental decline was due to the use of aphrodisiacs. To meet Clara Petacci's voracious sexual needs, Mussolini was reduced to consuming a preparation called Hormovir in large quantities. "This habit," Rossi explains, "accounts for Il Duce's personal tragedy, which was the tragedy of Italians." Fascism was a bodily tragedy, even down to the measures taken by an aging, impotent man.[37]

Posthumous indiscretions about Mussolini's medical condition merit the historian's attention in inverse proportion to their reliability. In fact, when criticism of the Fascist period is reduced to assessments of Mussolini's health, the result is indulgence, since the victim of a medical syndrome is still a victim of something. It was left to intellectuals, to the students of Benedetto Croce and Gaetano Salvemini, to weigh whether Fascism was a moral disease of the ruling class or a structural disease of the whole society. Middle-brow thinkers had something better on their minds. The way they saw it, the idea that the body of the regime was sick was less compelling than the idea that the body of Il Duce was sick— and this approach was one that many Italians could subscribe to.

The most highly developed version of it was published in 1968 by Antonino Trizzino, a retired admiral and militant member of the Italian Social Movement, who wrote several best sellers. Trizzino attributed the entire experience of Fascism to syphilis, including Il Duce's disastrous military campaigns in World War II, when the dictator was "on the brink of madness."[38] But as early as 1950, the journalist Paolo Monelli had already taken the larger ramifications of Il Duce's frailties to their logical conclusion. In *Mussolini, Petit Bourgeois,* Monelli traced Il Duce's uncertainty, frustration, and perpetual doubts to a duodenal ulcer and his megalomania, extreme vanity, and vengefulness to syphilis. Thus, wrote Monelli, "It is pointless to look to heredity, degrees earned, books read, or a man's environment to understand his character. These two illnesses, one of them due to an encounter with a woman, are all we need to explain everything about him— virtues and defects, triumphs and defeats, decline and fall."[39]

We do not know whether Gadda liked *Mussolini, Petit*

Bourgeois as much as *Roma 1943,* Monelli's previous book. What is certain is that the interpretations of both writers were excessively physical. By going deep into the recesses of Il Duce's body, they remained on the surface of Fascist Italy.

AT RAI, THE state broadcast network where Gadda worked as an editor in the 1950s, Giovanni Guareschi, a writer far more familiar to the average reader, launched a radio program called *Ladies and Gentlemen, the Court Is in Session.* Every Sunday afternoon Guareschi, assisted by actors from the Radio Milano theater company, broadcast a "radio trial with a jury." The cases were fictional, but they were believable enough that listeners often responded as if they were based on fact. The success of Guareschi's show can only be explained by Italians' strong interest in crime reporting and court proceedings after twenty years of half-truths and silence. The program did not, however, touch on the moral problems connected to Benito Mussolini; in the postwar years of De Gasperi, state radio preferred to keep its distance from the Fascist period. Here Guareschi's radio trial is of interest because the popular interest in court cases extended to a book published in the same period, a book that dealt directly with Mussolini's posthumous destiny.

Il Duce's summary execution on the shores of Lake Como deprived Italians not only of his final testament but of a trial—the international trial for war crimes that he feared facing in the hellish confusion of New York's Madison Square Garden, the trial Allied prosecutors eventually convened against Nazi war criminals in Nuremberg. Anti-Fascists and neo-Fascists experienced the absence of a due process differently. Few anti-Fascists, at least immediately after 1945, publicly deplored the fact that Mussolini's execution had robbed the country of court proceedings. In their view, Il Duce's had been a hasty but necessary affair, even if Italians were denied the satisfaction of unmasking their "cardboard Caesar" in public.⁴⁰ Neo-Fascists held the conviction that the Communist partisan squad had prevented a trial whose outcome was by no means certain—Mussolini might well have shown the world that he had acted in good faith. Once again, imagination sought to fill the void left by reality. In the absence of an Italian Nuremberg, several writers produced reports of an imaginary trial.

The one conceived by Yvon De Begnac, a writer with an open passion for Il Duce, is a pro-Fascist version of an ancient classic. With Il Duce as his protagonist, De Begnac, Mussolini's "official" biographer during the 1930s, wrote a *Trial of Socrates on the Banks of Lake Como.* It is hard not to laugh at the idea of placing the Athenian master next to the man from Predappio; the comparison refers to the story that in his waning years Mussolini became an assiduous reader of Plato, both in Italian translation and in the original. De Begnac's Mussolini claims credit for building the dam of Italian Fascism to contain the powerful river of Soviet Communism. He criticizes himself for not having assumed the powers of a dictator in full. He did not commit suicide after the Italian armistice with the Allies, he explains, because he wished to defend Italian lives from Salò. The democratic forces that sought to condemn him were a macabre farce, Mussolini–De Begnac goes on. It is his hope that he will be remembered by his fellow Italians as a man above politics.

These arguments follow the anti-Resistance gospel of the immediate postwar years. They differ little, in essence, from Mussolini's last wishes as expressed by Indro Montanelli in *My Good Man Mussolini.* But the open neo-Fascism of De Begnac limited the impact of his *Trial.* Although an anti-Fascist publication like *Il Ponte* called De Begnac's tale scandalous, the anti-Fascist cause had little to fear from such a book, which at best demonstrated the ability of neo-Fascists to write fiction. Il Duce's imagined trial needed to be written by someone outside the demimonde of neo-Fascist journalism, if it was to have any ideological impact. All the better if it appeared in a controversial best seller. Curzio Malaparte's *The Skin* was such a work—indeed, it was among the most widely read and discussed books in postwar Italy.

Malaparte was a man obsessed by corpses. He was also obsessed by fantasies about Il Duce's body. The diary he kept in Paris from 1947 to 1949 during the writing of *The Skin* makes this evident. Having once admired Mussolini the tough guy, he had come to see him as a human monster. In Malaparte's description, Mussolini is a beast whose veins flow with thin blood, or perhaps just whey. He is "a goose, an enormous goose," worthy of Bosch, Brueghel, or Rousseau, a swollen, slow, lazy beast, "a body on the verge of decomposing." Thus Malaparte depicts not the ox but the goose of the nation, whose head, always large in relation to his body, has over the years grown gigantic, deformed. When he speaks, Il Duce's large, dark, disturbing eyes roll, so the irises float in a sea of white, "like the eyes of a gazelle in its death throes or of certain women enjoying sexual pleasure." His skin has "the smell of a wet chicken" or "the odor of a corpse."[41]

These quotations from Malaparte's diary do not appear in *The Skin*. But the imaginary trial of Il Duce in one of its chapters is just as morbidly expressionistic. Malaparte explains that he had taken a break from his work as a journalist following the Allied troops during Italy's bitter civil war and was staying in the tiny house of an obstetrician friend in Rome. Because space was cramped, he slept on a sofa in the doctor's studio, which was crowded with books, obstetrical instruments, and a row of jars filled with yellowish liquid, each one containing a human fetus. Understandably, Malaparte found the company disturbing, "because a fetus is a cadaver, a monstrous cadaver that was never born and never died."[42] One night, his studio companions came too close for comfort. The fetuses climbed out of their jars and began to move around the room, scaling the desk, the chairs, and even the bed of the feverish writer. Then they drew back to the middle of the room and sat on the floor in a semicircle, "almost like an assembly of judges," and fixed Malaparte with their round, dull eyes. Suddenly the fetus chief, a three-headed female specimen, turned to several little monsters standing off to one side and ordered them to bring in the accused.

So Malaparte, in a nightmarish place between life and death—or between nonlife and nondeath—has Mussolini enter the scene:

> Slowly an enormous fetus with a loose stomach and two legs covered with shiny, whitish hair came forward between the two guards. . . . Two huge watery yellow eyes, eyes like a blind dog's, shone in the large, white, swollen head. The fetus's expression was proud yet fearful, as if traditional pride were doing battle with a new fear of something unknown, neither winning, so they combined to produce an expression at once cowardly and heroic.
>
> The face was made of flesh (the flesh of a fetus yet also of an old man, the flesh of an old fetus); it was a mirror in which the grandeur, poverty, superiority, and cowardice of humans shone in all their stupid glory. . . . And for the first time I saw the ugliness of the human face, the disgusting matter of which we are made.[43]

Beyond the bravura writing, there is a message in Malaparte's text, a message to be decoded. *The Skin* is not just literary prose to be admired; through his trial of Mussolini, Malaparte—a Fascist true believer in the 1920s who fell into disgrace in the 1930s and then improvised a new anti-Fascist identity in the 1940s—has something to tell Italians. He confesses that he despised Il Duce, his chest puffed out triumphantly, at the apex of his glory in Piazza Venezia. But now, in an obstetrician's humble studio, with

Mussolini reduced to a "bare, repellent fetus," Malaparte refuses to laugh at him. No, the more he looks, the more Malaparte feels "affectionate compassion" for Mussolini. His compassion extends to Fascists and anti-Fascists, to the Republic of Salò and to the Resistance—all joined by the wonderful fatal destiny of defeat. Before the council of fetus judges, Malaparte assumes the role of Mussolini's lawyer and the Italian people's defender. "A man, a people, beaten, humiliated, reduced to a bit of rotten flesh. What in this world is more beautiful, more noble?"[44]

Malaparte's political message is not so very different from Montanelli's in *My Good Man Mussolini:* the Resistance was a Grand Guignolesque bloodbath from which the defeated paradoxically emerged the victors. Furthermore, Malaparte explicitly rejects any reading of the civil war as a tragic but salutary rite of passage toward Italian maturity. "The dead, I hated them. All the dead," he writes in *The Skin.* What made Malaparte, writing in 1949, different from both the left and the right was that he embraced an ethic of survival, while the ex-Resistance fighters and neo-Fascists cultivated an ethic of sacrifice. It was precisely that ethic of survival that helped explain *The Skin*'s extraordinary success, all the more notable in the light of the critics' negative reviews and the absence of backing by a major publishing house. The book sold seventy thousand copies in its first eight months, or twenty times the average novel's sales in that period. It seems unlikely that all of its readers shared the narrator's voyeuristic interest in the dead and unborn; more likely, *The Skin* attracted readers drawn to anti-anti-Fascism. The book was calculated to appeal to Italians in the gray area—all those who, after the collapse of Mussolini, were still not won over to the ideals of the Resistance.

After Malaparte makes his case in *The Skin,* he ends the trial without reaching a verdict. Before leaving the courthouse, the fetus Mussolini recalls, "in the sweetest of voices," the final days of his incarnation as a man: "They slaughtered me, hung me up by my feet on a butcher's hook, spat on me." Then two fetuses who look like police take Il Duce out of the hall as he "cries quietly." This lachrymose nonending must have pleased the profoundly Catholic Italians whom Malaparte considered his audience. At a time when a certain segment of post-Fascist Italy shrank from the stark Calvinist reality of the Nuremberg trials, there was an alternative to the brutal choice between blessed and damned, an alternative deeply rooted in the Italian tradition, at once terrifying and consoling. Was Mussolini destined for hell? Or was he headed to paradise? Neither: Mussolini was sent to purgatory.

IN THE EARLY postwar years, his followers prayed for Mussolini as if he really were a soul in purgatory. Each year on the anniversary of his death, pious and enterprising neo-Fascists organized secret memorial masses to be said in the absence of the body. At times the assembled crowds were large enough to draw the attention of the authorities: in Rome in 1947, the police estimated there were hundreds of participants at the masses. When, not content with intercession for the dear departed's soul, the faithful extended the Catholic liturgy to include the Fascist salute, the police proceeded to make arrests. But in general, the forces of order avoided interfering with the neo-Fascist services, a fact that earned the praise of the independent press. In his column in the illustrated weekly *Tempo*, onetime Fascist enthusiast Vitaliano Brancati applauded the police for standing back as the "best way to show that 'weak' democracy feared Mussolini's soul a thousand times less than 'powerful' Fascism feared Matteotti's soul."[45] During the Fascist period, said Brancati, anyone even suggesting a mass for Matteotti would have found himself in prison, along with his card-playing friends.

In an article about the masses offered in three Roman churches on the second anniversary of Il Duce's death, the popular weekly *Oggi* provided an intriguing detail. On the same evening as the masses, a number of Romans gathered at the office of a "famous" lawyer for a séance to make contact with Mussolini's spirit. A session held in Palermo a few years later gives some sense of what may have transpired that evening. A group of people from various social backgrounds assembled at the house of a man who described himself as the Professor, according to the local neo-Fascist paper, *I Vespri d'Italia*. First, the Professor had each participant fill out a questionnaire. What was their overall judgment of Mussolini? Was the conquest of Ethiopia a heroic venture or an error? Was it opportune or mistaken for Italy to join the war in 1940? Was the Italian Social Republic legal or illegal? Then the group was conducted to a darkened room where, next to the only lamp, stood a giant photo of Mussolini on the balcony at Palazzo Venezia. From next door a gramophone played the most celebrated of Il Duce's speeches as the assembled attempted to commune with his spirit: "Each person's gaze was nailed to the huge photograph. In the holy silence Mussolini's words cut into the flesh like slivers of glass."[46] When the recording ended, the Professor handed out the same questionnaire as before. Inevitably, the answers were more pro-Fascist this time around.

One should not overemphasize the importance of such sessions in Il Duce's posthumous life. Attendees amounted to no more than a few dozen Italians, perhaps a few hundred, drawn as much by a dictator who died in ignominy as by a fascination with the paranormal. It seems that even Mussolini's wife, in her modest home on the island of Ischia, where she lived in compulsory residence after the war, had the ability to commune with the spirit world. At least once, in the fall of 1947, Rachele Mussolini called together her children and several trusted friends and asked the table legs to indicate the secret place where the prefect of Milan had buried Il Duce's body. According to Giorgio Pini, a founder of the Italian Social Movement as well as the ghostwriter of Rachele's memoirs, who was present at the session, the reply, although wrong, was clear: P–A–V–I–A. Spiritualism and table levitation say a lot about postwar neo-Fascism, which was more ingenuous than rational, more pathetic than insidious, as much sentimental as political.

Along with the thrills of spiritualism, Rachele Mussolini had dreams, image sequences that she fed to the hungry readers of the illustrated weeklies. In one such dream, Mussolini, young and smiling, appeared from on high to tell her, "There are no bad feelings here, Rachele, not about anyone."[47] Yet Il Duce occupied other dream landscapes beside his widow's. Carlo Levi, a painter and writer, had a landlady, Jolanda, who also encountered Il Duce. "You should have seen him, pale, sad, and suffering," she told Levi. "He said they had wronged him, they had betrayed him, but up there it is a better world, and from there he would protect us."[48] Levi himself could hardly have better conjured up the bizarre world of neo-Fascism in the late 1940s and early 1950s, a world turned upside down. Author of the classic *Christ Stopped at Eboli,* with its sharp yet tolerant vision of the Italian south, Levi was well equipped to re-create the atmosphere of early postwar neo-Fascism, its hoped-for phony miracles, spiritualism, cult of the saints, and invocations of the dead.

As we know, the neo-Fascist world was not entirely apolitical. When Il Duce's body disappeared from view, his followers were given the chance to revive the Fascist mystique through its absence. One such initiative was the Buried in Italy campaign of the autumn of 1950. The idea was to find, in every city and town, a small but visible place—a street corner, a chapel wall, the base of an abandoned monument—to decorate with flowers, candles, photographs of Mussolini, and sacred images. In short, to create a substitute tomb for Il Duce, an altar for his devoted followers to tend or to rebuild in the event that it was destroyed. Thanks to the neo-Fascists' efforts, Mussolini would have countless graves around the country. "His tomb is Italy," explained the newspaper that launched the initiative.[49] Thus Mussolini's life after death grew ever more intense so long as his real burial place remained a secret. Making a virtue of necessity, the dialogue with Il Duce eluded the strict relationship with the corpse imposed by a tomb. By reviving age-old traditions of talking dead men and messages from the Great Beyond, the neo-Fascists were able to bring Il Duce's formidable profile to life against the gray backdrop of De Gasperi's Italy and give voice to his big baritone. Like the Führer, the dead Mussolini got his share of posthumous literary attention, effusions somewhere between yellow journalism and pulp fiction, more fanciful epitaph than coherent political statement.

The most original of these creations was *Benito Mussolini without Fascism: 12 Conversations from the Other Side*, published in Milan in 1952 by Piero Caliandro (possibly a pseudonym). The book opens with a declaration addressed by Il Duce to the coroner who did his autopsy: "Oh, anatomist, these are not the imaginings of someone who is dead. I here am in possession of the truth; you, instead, examine putrefying matter or that which has hardened in formaldehyde or alcohol." Why, Mussolini wonders, was Professor Cattabeni, the coroner, melancholy and irascible, in the days after the autopsy? In part because working on such a corpse inevitably affected one. In part because he was annoyed at failing to find an ulcer that had turned cancerous, a brain tumor, or a case of tertiary syphilis—in short, "something big" to describe to the scientific world and earn himself academic titles and to offer to the public as cytological proof of the biological basis of Mussolini's politics. People should stop, then, spreading the legend of a Mussolini "sick in the head," suggests Caliandro's Mussolini. They should accept the evidence that Fascism is still alive and promises Italy a new season. "You, anatomist, along with the executioners, you have not extinguished Mussolini; rather, you have blown on a flame that was going out," says Il Duce. Dozens of incoherent pages follow, concluding with an appeal for Italians to solve their problems by forming a National Patriotic Party, a party that will replace the decrepit pyramid of the state with a "scientific arboreal construction" that will be the nation.[50]

More remarks from the Great Beyond were published by Marco Ramperti, a journalist who was a theater critic before becoming an official spokesman for the Republic of Salò and who was sentenced to prison after the war for anti-Semitic propaganda. In *Benito I, Emperor* Ramperti imagines the Axis partners winning the war, thanks to the timely use of the atomic bomb, and Mussolini returning to Rome to be triumphantly crowned as emperor. The book is thus a monologue by a Mussolini "victorious and imperial rather than defeated and hanged."[51] It is also a torrential assault on anti-Fascism—the rotten fruit of the betrayal of the monarchy on September 8, 1943—and on the false flag behind which a band of assassins hid. But the shadow of Il Duce fell over writings more cultivated and sophisticated than Ramperti's *Benito I, Emperor*. *Il Borghese*, a magazine of culture and politics founded by Leo Longanesi in 1950, used every pretext to contrast the volcanic master of Predappio with "boring old Aunt" Democracy. That the Fascist period had been one of illusions was acknowledged, but they were illusions of the sort that made life nobler or at least gave meaning to the young, dreams of transforming the country or of winning a war. For while Longanesi hated Fascism for the damage it did to Italy, he saw Il Duce as the only statesman in modern times who had asked something serious of the Italians.

Longanesi's main contribution to the theme of Mussolini, dear departed, came with a book entitled *A Dead Man among Us*, which he published in 1952. It expresses a philosophy that he shared with his many affectionate readers, the cynical philosophy of every man for himself, the skeptical philosophy of "let he who is without sin cast the first stone." It is the kind of history writing that Longanesi thought the Fascist period deserved, fundamentally merciful and eager to preserve all the little details of a past that had been shared by all Italians. In the closing pages of the book, Longanesi tells how he recently rediscovered his enthusiasm for painting, which he had not indulged for many years. And how he painted a picture of an ancient castle clinging to a hard spur of rock. Imagine his surprise when, several nights later, he looked at the picture and saw a lit window in the castle. Longanesi was sure he had never even painted that window, because he was certain that no one lived in the castle. The following night, when it was dark, the artist returned to look at his painting and found the window once again lit up. There was surely someone in the room—the scene was reminiscent of Il Duce's insomniac nights in Palazzo Venezia. "Then," wrote Longanesi, "I heard, far off, some dogs howling." The wind blew across the rock, under the squalid light of a moon that Longanesi said he had not painted. Finally, dawn broke over that troubled landscape. "Then I heard a cry, a terrible cry, that came from the window. The light went out and from the crevices of the rocks I saw rivulets of blood streaming down."[52] Longanesi's ghost of Mussolini, it seems, had been torn apart by the dogs.

5

THE EXECUTIONER

With their invented last words, imagined autopsies, and fantasized trials, the writers who put Mussolini's case to the people swelled the ideological arsenal of anti-anti-Fascism and kept the dictator vividly present. But the history of Il Duce's posthumous life requires mention of a third party, one that stood between the dicator and the country: the executioner. To reconstruct Il Duce's existence beyond the grave during 1946–57, when his body was hidden from public view, we need to look sideways, at the man who shot him.

The story of Il Duce's body was shaped by living men, and the first to have made his mark was the executioner, Colonel Valerio. When Italians thought of Colonel Valerio, they thought of Mussolini. Grateful to him or not, they inevitably saw the dead man embodied in the live one.

WHO SHOT MUSSOLINI? In Italy in 1947, few people could have answered the question. Immediately after Il Duce's execution, the Communist daily *l'Unità* reported the role of a certain Colonel Valerio, a Communist partisan. But just who stood behind the nom de guerre remained a mystery. What did he look like, the man who had erased Mussolini from the face of the earth? As we have seen, rumors had emerged from the shores of Lake Como that the executioner was as charismatic a figure as the one executed, that the action had been carried out by Cino Moscatelli, a famous partisan. When the rumor proved false, there was no further word on the man responsible.

In Rome, the Communist Party leaders did nothing to solve the question. A young party member who worked at the headquarters recalled that "a special air of admiration and mystery" surrounded two functionaries in the party executive, Walter Audisio and Aldo Lampredi.[1] It was whispered that they had taken part in the action on Lake Como, but no one dared to ask direct questions. The ability to keep secrets seemed to be an essential requisite for an organization that was just emerging from twenty years of clandestine activity. But neither the economic and social imperatives of rebuilding the country nor the important postwar political issues kept Italians from being curious about the executioner. On the contrary, as Resistance momentum declined and the removal of former Fascists from office slowed, many ex-Resistance fighters were tempted to see Mussolini's executioner as the sole winner in a civil war that had otherwise been lost. At the first Socialist Party congress following the Liberation, held in Florence in the spring of 1946, party leader Pietro Nenni was applauded when he said that only one man had really been successful in eliminating Fascists from public life—Colonel Valerio.

A few months later, after the ballot to establish the constituent assembly, in which the Christian Democrats received more votes than parties of the left, ex-partisans felt less than enthusiastic about how the vote had gone. The amnesty for Fascists promoted by Justice Minister Palmiro Togliatti, Communist Party secretary, was also a source of rancor. To make matters worse, the Fascists were back on the scene with stunts like the theft of Mussolini's remains. Perhaps it was no surprise that on the left, too, there was a desire for political action. So at the end of August 1946, a few dozen ex-partisans from Asti, in Piedmont, declared the "rebellion of Santa Libera," after the village in the Langhe district where they barricaded themselves in. They called for the expulsion of Fascist functionaries from office and for Togliatti's amnesty to be overturned. The prestige of Cino Moscatelli, acting as mediator, was required to persuade the rebels to back down.

At this point, nobody still believed that Moscatelli had been Il Duce's executioner, yet a year and a half after his death only a handful Communist leaders knew Colonel Valerio's real identity. The habits of secrecy adopted during the underground years were not enough to explain why the party hid Walter Audisio from public view. Nor were reasons of security, especially considering that the party never assigned Audisio bodyguards, even after his name was revealed. There were other motives for the silence surrounding Colonel Valerio's identity, and these were ideological.

As far back as 1925–26, during the first wave of attempts on Mussolini's life, and especially in 1931–32, after a second, the Communists had condemned any focus on individual targets, preferring a broad battle against an entire class of enemies. In opposition to other Resistance forces, among them Emilio Lussu and leaders of Justice and Liberty, the Communists argued that killing Mussolini was the crudest of political expedients. After 1945, when Communist partisans formed Il Duce's execution squad, it no longer made any sense for the party to dismiss the "exemplary gesture" as futile. Nevertheless, the fact that Il Duce's execution had occurred not at the beginning but at the end of a movement of national insurrection made the Communists cautious regarding the presentation of Mussolini's death. The party's strategy under Togliatti was to legitimize itself as a democratic force, and that meant casting the Resistance as a war of the people rather than a revolt of a minority and the Liberation as a season of brotherhood, not of violence. The terrible tableau of two or three partisans shooting an old, unarmed man and his young lover did not fit easily into this frame.

In 1947, the unity of the Committee of National Liberation came to an end when the parties of the left were excluded from the government. Thus the first months of that year marked an important turning point in modern Italy's political history. At the same time, Italians learned something new about the death of Il Duce—hardly an insignificant coincidence. In March 1947, Italians discovered the name and the face of the man who had shot Mussolini. But Colonel Valerio's identity—that he was Walter Audisio, an accountant from Alessandria, a Communist militant since 1931, leader of the Garibaldi Brigades, secretary of the high command of the Liberty Volunteers Corps—was not revealed to the world by the Communists, those who had suffered the highest casualties in the fight against Fascism. Audisio's name was instead made public by a neo-Fascist publication in Milan, by his enemies rather than his comrades. Naturally they presented him not as a man carrying out justice but as an assassin. It was only later, making the best of a bad situation, that Communist leaders decided to treat Audisio as a political asset, taking him around Italy in triumph.

The propaganda battle surrounding Colonel Valerio's identity was part of a larger war that in Milan, at least, pitched indomitable veterans of the Republic of Salò against the most pugnacious ex-partisans. At the same time, this localized recrudescence of the

civil war was set in the context of the early Cold War and the attendant conflict regarding Italian Communism. Thus, the skirmishes
in the press over a crucial episode in Italy's past—Mussolini's
execution—were a way of fighting a conflict in the present as well
as one for the future. In this way, Mussolini's dead body continued to write history.

The clash between the two most active militant groups in the
province—adherents of *Lotta fascista,* familiar to us through the
activities of Domenico Leccisi, and Volante Rosso, a band of
Communist ex-partisans based in one of the party's clubs—
began in 1946 and was by no means confined to warring over
the memory of Piazzale Loreto. On October 9 that year, the
neo-Fascists threw a bomb at a Communist Party club in the
Porta Genova neighborhood, killing a five-year-old child. Then,
on January 17, 1947, the Communists shot two neo-Fascist activists, one from the Democratic Fascist Party and another from
the Mussolini Action Squad. While the bullets were flying, the
Milanese neo-Fascist paper *Il Meridiano d'Italia,* which under
editor Franco De Agazio took a critical approach to the Resistance, decided to reconstruct the precise movements of the
Communist partisans at Dongo following their capture of Mussolini. In the course of its breathless account, the paper revealed
documents that made it possible to name Walter Audisio. On
March 3, Audisio gave an interview to a Swiss radio station in
which he admitted to having shot Mussolini. Eleven days later
followers of Volante Rosso killed De Agazio, firing four bullets
at close range.

De Agazio was an unusual Fascist journalist in that his political roots lay in Italian liberalism. His paper's representation of the
Resistance as caricature cost him his life. But in effect, the articles
published in *Il Meridiano d'Italia* were the first of thousands on
the "mysteries of Dongo" that the popular press turned out over

the next fifty years. Somewhere between detective mysteries and bodice rippers, they offered a mixture of hasty executions and private vendettas, hidden treasure and lusty passions. "In America they would have made a couple of movies by now" about Il Duce's end, one weekly observed of *Il Meridiano d'Italia*'s scandalizing.[2] The approach was quickly picked up by the establishment press. What could be more interesting than to populate the scene where Mussolini and Claretta were shot with attractive partisan women and undercover Communist agents?

Before De Agazio died, he did more than launch the "mysteries of Dongo" scandal sheet formula; he was enlisted by Giorgio Almirante, leader of the Italian Social Movement, to work with the cardinal of Turin to form anti-Communist squads in the Piedmont region. Meanwhile, the cardinal of Milan was meeting with another neo-Fascist, General Leone Zingales, who had been chosen by the military to investigate possible crimes by partisan forces at Lake Como after the Liberation.

These clandestine encounters organized by neo-Fascists and the Vatican did not escape the notice of U.S. intelligence, which was convinced that Yugoslav spies had a role in De Agazio's death. In the Cold War climate, U.S. agents in Italy wanted to exploit the murder of the neo-Fascist journalist to gather American support for the Italian Christian Democrats and other parties of the center right. Thus, in the weeks following De Agazio's assassination, Communist leaders had more urgent things to worry about than the public identification of Walter Audisio. They were facing a combined front of Christian Democrats, the Vatican, and the Truman administration in its efforts to eliminate the Communist Party altogether. Still, the labored way the Communist executive dealt with the revelation of Audisio's identity seems to reflect more than just the leaders' preoccupation.

For weeks after *Il Meridiano d'Italia* published its revelation, the

Communists downplayed the matter, criticizing the "yellow press" and insisting that Il Duce's execution was a routine affair ordered by the Committee of National Liberation. Some two weeks later party secretary Togliatti was still telling an Italian news agency that Mussolini's execution had been "one of the greatest, perhaps the greatest contribution that the movement of national liberation made to the nation."[3] It was not until March 21, eighteen days after Audisio himself acknowledged his role in the execution, that Togliatti officially confirmed that Colonel Valerio and Audisio were indeed one and the same. At the end of March, Audisio was formally presented at a Communist Party rally in Rome. The Communists reluctantly unveiled their role in Mussolini's execution, and only because it had already been revealed in the neo-Fascist press. Accordingly, the party also decided, reluctantly, to display the body—very much alive—of the man who had executed Il Duce.

THE WARY UNMASKING of Colonel Valerio revealed the Communists' great caution about taking responsibility for the most radical aspect of the Resistance struggle, the tragic exit from twenty years of Fascism. At the same time, the party's secretiveness underscored a determination to portray the Resistance as a people's uprising. Two weeks after Audisio confirmed his identity on Swiss radio, Communist leader Luigi Longo still maintained that "it is best . . . that comrade Valerio remain simply comrade Valerio, the representative of justice for all the people."[4] Even after the party acknowledged Audisio's role, it still sought to play it down. *L'Unità* presented him as an ordinary person, not a figure of history, sketching his working-class childhood, his studies at a technical school, his military service, marriage, work as an accountant, and sentence to internal exile for anti-Fascist activity. There were countless young people who would "recognize in

Walter Audisio's life the traces of their own," wrote *l'Unità*.[5] Even as the party launched a campaign to award Colonel Valerio a gold medal for bravery in action, the party press was depicting him as just an average Italian.

In fact, the description fit Walter Audisio rather well. Corpulent, jovial, good at telling jokes, he had what one journalist describes as "more the air of a traveling salesman than of a partisan hero."[6] For this reason, the young women at the Communist Party headquarters thought he was less interesting than the elegant, discreet Aldo Lampredi. Unlike Lampredi, Audisio did not have the rock-hard faith of the model Communist. He also had a black mark on his record, the letter he had written abjuring his anti-Fascist past to gain release from internal exile in 1939, although this was unknown to the great majority of Communist militants. Still, in a period when faith in the Resistance seemed to be giving way to "desistance" (a word coined by the anti-Fascist Piero Calamandrei to describe the changing climate in 1947), the Communist rank and file wanted nothing more than a comrade to venerate as the living incarnation of the partisan creed. What better symbol of the Resistance ethos than Il Duce's executioner?

L'Unità opened its pages to Colonel Valerio—for the first time as Walter Audisio—so he could tell the story of his fateful mission. Not surprisingly, the ex-partisan took advantage of his monopoly on information to give a rather black-and-white version of events. He painted the scene as a one-on-one contest between himself and Il Duce. Faced with the Resistance in person, he said, Mussolini showed himself to be "less than an average man," his eyes wide with fear, his mouth half open, his arms hanging limp: cowardice personified.

On March 30, 1947, when Walter Audisio was presented to the public at the Basilica di Massenzio in Rome, forty thousand people showed up for the rally. So large was the crowd that it made the Palm Sunday faithful at St. Peter's look like a handful. As preparations for the rally were in progress, the Vatican was in fact calling Colonel Valerio to the attention of Western diplomats and secret service organizations. On the eve of the rally, the Vatican secretary of state, Monsignor Giovanni Battista Montini (later Pope Paul VI), alerted the American embassy, which in turn alerted the State Department, that the Communist Party had give out Carabinieri uniforms to special gangs of provocateurs who were supposed to mingle with the crowd. When Audisio appeared, he would be shot, while the false Carabinieri would fire into the gathering, inciting panic. Afterward, according to Vatican officials, the Communist press would accuse neo-Fascists and the Carabinieri of killing Audisio.

Although the information sounded "somewhat doubtful" to the Americans, the embassy duly told Washington that word had been passed on to the British secret service and the counterintelligence corps. On April 1, however, U.S. ambassador James C. Dunn telegraphed the State Department in Washington to say that the rally had taken place without incident.[7] Nonetheless, Dunn aired the suspicion that a Communist plot lay behind the De Agazio murder and Audisio's unveiling, cleverly manipulated by the Soviet Union.

Within just a few months of the rally, Audisio became a charismatic figure to Communist followers—even a mythic character. There was an especially memorable event on September 7, 1947, in Modena, when Communists came together for the annual Festa dell'Unità. It was celebrated in the way these things were done in the years just after the war: whole families came loaded down with their lunch preparations—men, women, and children with only a few lire in their pockets but enough to buy flags sporting the hammer and sickle. People streamed into town from the countryside to see the allegorical floats, the sack races, and the bookstands, and the chance to see the party leaders up close—Palmiro Togliatti, Luigi Longo, Pietro Secchia, Cino Moscatelli, Giancarlo Pajetta. According to the press, however, it was Walter Audisio who got the most enthusiastic reception. "Va-le-rio, Va-le-rio, Va-le-rio," the crowd chanted, as if at a football stadium.

When Longo began to hand out gold medals, the crowd would not quiet down until Audisio received one. "Valerio, there's still a lot of work to do," yelled one man. A tiny woman with a red flag pinned in her gray hair managed to climb up on the stage and grab Audisio's hand. She would never again wash the hand that had touched Colonel Valerio, she declared as she came down, not even if she lived a hundred years. It is hard not to compare these moments to the clichéd vignettes of Mussolini's rule, to Il Duce embracing workers and the lucky ones pledging not to wash their faces for a month. The Communists appeared to feel the same excitement from contact with Il Duce's executioner as the Fascist loyal got in the presence of the dictator.

In 1948, the party national congress gave Audisio his official political investiture. Photographs show Colonel Valerio on the platform of Milan's Teatro Lirico in highly select company. Beside him are Palmiro Togliatti, and direct from Moscow, Delio and Giuliano Gramsci, sons of Antonio Gramsci, a founder of the party who had died a Communist martyr after being imprisoned by the Fascists. Another guest from Moscow, Vagan G. Grigorian, noted the enthusiasm for Il Duce's executioner. According to this important member of the Soviet delegation, Audisio "serves as the party's interior minister." In his memo to Moscow on the activities of the party congress's political committee, Grigorian conveyed a unique version of what had happened at Piazzale Loreto, which he attributed to Audisio:

Colonel Valerio Audisio [sic] . . . says that some partisans had been hanged in Piazzale Loreto in Milan with a notice saying that they were supposed to remain there until there were no partisans left in Italy. They brought Mussolini's corpse and some of his men, and overnight took the partisans down from the scaffold and put up Mussolini and the others. So the next morning, the Milanese found Mussolini hanging there instead of the partisans.[8]

Whether this account emerged from a linguistic misunderstanding or from Audisio's penchant for telling tales, the fact is that three years after the event, the Soviet leadership was spreading a completely imaginary version of what had happened.

Meanwhile, the anti-Communist press did not hesitate to target Audisio with its sarcasm. A vignette in *Candido* depicted a tall, proud Audisio at the party congress wearing his ever-present beret, standing next to a tiny Togliatti, who looked very timid behind his glasses. "In honor of the foreign delegation," Togliatti is saying, "the famed executioner comrade Walter Audisio will sing 'How I Executed Benito.' "[9] Colonel Valerio was subjected not only to the press's irony but also to accusations. An article in *Il Tempo* claimed Audisio was in possession of lists of people who would be outlawed when the Communists mounted their uprising. Accompanying the article was a photograph of an apartment building that belonged to the party. "In this house at Via Pavia 4 in Rome," read the caption, "Audisio is said to be hiding weapons and a plan to take the capital."[10]

Fanciful suspicions notwithstanding, Mussolini's executioner did play an important role in more clandestine activities of the Communist Party, a role that brought him obsessive police surveillance. The critical attention in the anti-Communist press must also have enhanced Audisio's charisma. Certainly, as national elections—scheduled for April 18, 1948—approached, the pro-government press waved the threatening image of Colonel Valerio before good Italians, as if to say, The man who killed Il Duce could kill any of you. In early postwar Italy, Audisio was also infamous, a negative model.

All the ghosts of the past hovered over the election. The Italian Social Movement, for one, offered policies and candidates with the definite stamp of the Republic of Salò. At the opposite end of the political spectrum, Il Duce's executioner, Walter Audisio, a candidate for the united Socialists and Communists, ran against Tito Zaniboni, the Socialist Unity candidate for the vot-

The executioner, Walter Audisio.   (*Foto Publifoto/Olympia*)

ing district of Cuneo-Alessandria-Asti in Piedmont, a man who had once tried to shoot Mussolini. The Christian Democrats, somewhat more cautious about evoking historical ghosts, had based their campaign on the theme of "turning the page." But that did not stop Mario Scelba, the Christian Democrat interior minister, from stepping into the historical fray by disbanding the partisan units that had flanked the police since the Liberation. Eager to ingratiate himself, Vincenzo Agnesina, police chief of Milan, went so far as to arrest police officers sympathetic to the Communists. The election campaign in Milan took place in a climate poisoned by memories of the civil war. There wasn't a rally of the Socialist-Communist front that didn't have a placard extolling the memory of Piazzale Loreto.

In Milan, as election day approached, celebrations of the third anniversary of the Liberation turned into a clash between anti-Fascists and the police. The anti-Fascists had wanted to hold a ceremony in Piazzale Loreto honoring the martyrs of August 10, 1944. Angry that the police chief barred them from entering the piazza, demonstrators pushed past the barriers and moved in. The police then charged the crowd, and in the scuffle that followed one Carabinieri officer was killed. The Resistance veterans succeeded in taking the piazza but it was a Pyrrhic victory, since the Christian Democrats' triumph at the polls ushered in a long period that would leave them out in the cold. Only a month or so after the election, Jesuit priest Riccardo Lombardi—the foremost interpreter of the Christian Democrat line—announced at the Ara Coeli in Rome that the Lord would punish those responsible for Mussolini's "assassination."

Less apocalyptically, the popular illustrated weeklies targeted Audisio. Now an elected deputy, Audisio had not yet taken his seat in the chamber before a parliamentary reporter described him as "ever-present and belligerent," the captain of the "Communist

boxing team."[11] As the elections receded into the past, the polemics failed to die down: throughout the entire legislature of
1948–53, the weeklies lambasted Walter Audisio and Cino Moscatelli as the incarnation of Communist perversity, superficially
democratic but bloodthirsty at heart. In the cartoonish prose of
the pro-government press, the Resistance heroes became the "ju-
nior officers in an army of death."[12]

The more sophisticated anti-Communist journalists depicted
the infamous Colonel Valerio as an instrument—in his infinite
moral and physical degradation, the partisan hero was the personification of evil, and therefore as necessary to the designs of Providence as the terrible Sanson immortalized by Joseph de Maistre
in *The St. Petersburg Dialogues.* Nantas Salvalaggio, a young journalist writing for *Il Borghese*, cast Mussolini's executioner as a
scapegoat, condemned to suffer for the gap between his personal
mediocrity and the grave historical role he had been assigned. Salvalaggio's Audisio was a man who returned to his filthy apartment in Via Pavia in the dead of night, a fretful insomniac,
haunting rooms where no crucifix hung. In the mornings, he had
to skirt the newsstands to avoid the covers of the illustrated weeklies, red as they were with the blood he had spilled on the shores
of Lake Como. In vain he tried to take out life insurance. When
Audisio's friends dragged him to the amusement park he was unable to hit the bull's-eye because he always saw himself back at
the Villa Belmonte aiming at Mussolini, and the gun would fall
from his hand.

Salvalaggio wrote about Audisio with a pathos absent from the
illustrated weeklies, but the popular press's inclination to caricature what was made their depiction so successful. The parliamentary reporter for *Oggi*, Ugo Zatterin, worked harder than any
other writer to spread the cliché of Audisio as a silly man, certainly as silly as he was dangerous. Mussolini's executioner was

not merely an expert on the use of the machine gun, wrote Zatterin, he was also the party's "wine expert," surprisingly knowledgeable about the differences between Freisa and Grignolino. He was a man so foolishly taken with his role as Il Duce's executioner that he gleefully accepted the gift of a little golden gun sparkling with diamonds from some Tuscan Communists. Thus even the more measured portraits of Audisio in the anti-Communist press took on laughable outlines, as damning as outright sensationalism. In the Thermidor era of the French Revolution, the anti-Jacobin press had depicted their targets in the same way: at once frivolous and bloodthirsty, murderers who would drink the wine from their victims' cellars and polish off roast chickens they had slaughtered with tiny guillotines.

In May 1949, one illustrated weekly, *Settimana Incom,* explicitly wrote of the "Thermidor butchery of Piazzale Loreto" when it seemed that the debate over Colonel Valerio's misdeeds might be the prelude to a trial against Audisio. Nevertheless, the article warned of the danger of criminalizing the Resistance. The hanging of Mussolini and company in Piazzale Loreto showed what kind of society the Socialists, Communists, and Action Party had in mind: a world where habeas corpus was superseded by habeas cadaver, *Settimana Incom* said. But putting Mussolini's executioner on trial would mean putting four years of Italian history on trial, including, of course, Prime Minister Alcide De Gasperi.

This article marked the limits of the pro-government press's campaign against Audisio. It was one thing to take verbal aim at Colonel Valerio, another to assemble the evidence to drag him into court. To accuse Audisio formally of inflicting Mussolini's mortal and postmortem wounds would put in question all that had come after, including the role played by centrist politicians. A trial against Audisio risked becoming a trial against Italy's republican institutions.

* * *

"SEND HIM TO prison," urges the schoolteacher in Cesare Pavese's *The Moon and the Bonfires*. "Hang that Valerio." In reality rather than in fiction, there was a shortage of people ready to kill Walter Audisio. But deep in the rough circles of neo-Fascism, in the Italian Social Movement party section in the Colle Oppio neighborhood of Rome, during the spring of 1953, one such assassin dreamed of Audisio's death.

The candidate, Giulio Salierno, was a serious bully, so capable of violence that he had been promoted—at just eighteen—to political leader of several districts in the capital. Too busy beating up Communists to indulge much in theory, Salierno was convinced of one thing: the true path of neo-Fascism was the radical one preached by members like Giorgio Almirante and Giorgio Pini, not the conservative line taken by such leaders as Augusto De Marsanich and Arturo Michelini. Unfortunately, though, since the Chamber of Deputies had outlawed much of the neo-Fascist program, the moderate line had prevailed in the Italian Social Movement. So the radical neo-Fascist youth decided to dedicate themselves to terrorism, to demonstrate that the party really was subversive and to embarrass the leadership in double-breasted suits. With that in mind, what better target than Audisio? The Social Movement's leaders could hardly deplore the murder of Mussolini's murderer without losing face with the party base. But nor could they greet Audisio's death with joy without losing face with their Christian Democrat interlocutors.

To Giulio Salierno, these thoughts were more than a mere political program—they were his life's vocation. "The activists had no alternative but to pursue violence, and I Audisio," Salierno wrote in his memoirs twenty years later. For the young Roman neo-Fascist, Communist deputy Audisio's murder would be a rite of passage into adulthood and a chance to put into practice Mussolini's precept about making ideas come to life:

> The killing of Audisio represented a goal I had dreamed of for years, the instrument through which I would leave my childhood behind and break into the adult world. . . . The other actions, the battles with the Reds and the police didn't mean anything; they were just routine, without glory. Audisio was different. It would mean leaving my mark, giving substance to my ideas. . . . It would transform that substance into life, consciously making me not just a number or a thing but a person.[13]

Salierno's memoirs offer a vivid picture of the context in which his criminal plan evolved—and then foundered. In the weeks before the 1953 elections, the neo-Fascist thug who was still too young to vote saw Audisio's murder as an electoral mission. "His corpse," wrote Salierno, "would bring the Communists no votes." From a practical point of view, the killing did not seem very difficult. At the time, Audisio lived in Rome at Largo Brandano, between the Via Nomentana and the Via Salaria. It was a quiet neighborhood, an easy place to carry out the murder. Audisio came and went at regular hours and he had no bodyguards. There was really no choice when it came to the weapon: it had to be an automatic rifle—that is, a weapon of war—to confer the maximum political significance. To practice his aim, Salierno took his gun apart and went to the countryside. He returned to his practice range again and again as he prepared to strike, with a photograph of Audisio glued to a wooden target and the target fixed to a tree. "With his mustache and his beret, 'Colonel Valerio' looked like a peasant dressed up for a party," wrote Salierno.[14] He drilled into that peasant until he had become a sieve and the "head had exploded," using bullets with a cross carved into the lead.

A few days before the elections, everything seemed ready. All of a sudden, though, Salierno's plans unraveled. One June night, in an outlying district of Rome, he murdered a young man about whom he knew nothing, "for no reason." He then fled to France and joined the Foreign Legion but was recognized, identified by the police, and sent back to Italy. Tried for murder, he was sentenced to thirty years in prison. So much for Salierno's dream of going down in history as the executioner of Mussolini's murderer. Like other neo-Fascist *squadristi*, he was fairly self-destructive: among the members of his Rome party section in the years after Salierno's arrest, one committed suicide, two died in the Foreign Legion, another two died while performing stunts with an airplane and motorcycle, and yet another with his throat slashed in Africa.

While Audisio's would-be killer went to his destiny as a condemned neo-Fascist, Mussolini's executioner—reelected with the Communist slate for the city of Alessandria—returned to the Chamber of Deputies in the second legislature. At the far end of the chamber sat the man who had stolen Mussolini's body, Domenico Leccisi, a newly elected deputy for the Italian Social Movement. "Contrary to expectations, his arrival provoked not the slightest incident, not even when his path crossed with Walter Audisio's," noted one illustrated weekly, under a picture of Leccisi entering the sanctuary of Italian democracy.[15]

6

THE QUALITY OF MERCY

For reasons of state, Mussolini's corpse remained hidden in the convent of Cerro Maggiore from 1946 to 1957, a decade and more, during which there were periodic rumors about Il Duce's burial place. Sometimes the rumors evaporated with the same rapidity with which they had brewed. One brief assertion, resulting from a deathbed confession by a chauffeur from Verona, had Mussolini's grave in the northern Italian city of Bressanone. The whispers that Il Duce lay in a grave at Nettuno, south of Rome, proved just as evanescent, as did the suggestion that his remains could be found under the altar at the Milanese church of Sant'Angelo.

At other times, the rumors seemed more convincing. When the press chose to delve into them, the public responded with fascination. Two Milanese photojournalists—who spread the word that Mussolini was buried under the altar at the Monte Paolo sanctuary, only a few kilometers from Predappio, his birthplace— were rewarded for their troubles with seven-month sentences for damages to a religious order. Faced with what they thought was the biggest scoop of their lives, the two had drilled a hole in the stairs leading up to the altar to search for a casket. The friars of Monte Paolo had to face some angry left-wingers armed with machine guns who accused them of encouraging neo-Fascists to make pilgrimages to the site.

Among all the rumors about Mussolini's last resting place, the most curious circulated for a few days in late October 1949. A mysterious story published in the Milan paper *Corriere lombardo* claimed that the body of Il Duce had recently been buried, under a false name, in section 37 of the Verano cemetery in Rome. The reporters who then rushed to the cemetery were convinced when they located a tomb marked "Bruno Misèfari" that they had found the right grave. Not only did the initials of the man's name correspond to those of Il Duce, but the words inscribed on his tomb were suggestive:

Eternal Night is far less grave to me
Than the day I witnessed the cowardice of the strong
And the way the lowly slaves behaved like sheep.
Do not weep for me: I am glad to lie with the dead.[1]

Was there, the reporters asked, a more fitting epitaph to the tragedy at Piazzale Loreto? Although some dates appeared on the tombstone—Reggio Calabria, 1892–Rome 1936—the journalists dismissed them as irrelevant. The minister of the interior and Mussolini's family issued denials, but the press remained unconvinced. Many neo-Fascists in the capital, moreover, were willing to entertain the *Corriere lombardo*'s hypothesis and so, with All Hallow's Day at hand, crowds poured into the Verano cemetery to pay their respects at the tomb of Bruno Misèfari. A young man who stood guard by the grave was mistakenly identified as Mussolini's son and the crowd paid tribute to him, too. This collective fantasy continued until November 3, when even the scandal sheets had to admit that Bruno Misèfari was not Mussolini. The name of the deceased was not the invention of some Interior Ministry functionary, nor was the epitaph a reference to Piazzale Loreto. The real Bruno Misèfari, it turned out, had been an engineer from Calabria who had been repeatedly jailed during the Fascist years as an opponent of the regime. After his death his widow had ordered the inscription, too hastily identified with the sentiments of a Fascist.

In 1950s Italy, as the fantasies about Il Duce's body ran wild, they found their most able interpreter in Roberto De Monticelli, a journalist. The son of theater actors, he had begun his career writing for *L'Italia libera,* the Action Party paper. Eventually he made his way to a job at *Epoca,* an ambitious new weekly founded by the publisher Alberto Mondadori on the model of *Life.* A successful magazine, *Epoca* sold as many as 500,000 copies soon after it was launched. De Monticelli began a brilliant career there as a theater critic, but he was also assigned to cover the trail of Il Duce's dead body, the odyssey of some bones said to belong to Mussolini, the pilgrimages made to monasteries and sanctuaries by the faithful, the intrepid activism of some parish priests. In De Monticelli's description, Mussolini's afterlife took an intensity that could probably only have been conjured up by a man steeped in the theater. "To die, therefore to wander": it took a writer familiar with Shakespeare to find so apt a depiction of Il Duce's posthumous fate in the collective memory.[2]

In the autumn of 1951 De Monticelli was invited to visit the Certosa di Pavia. He wanted to investigate why large crowds were converging on the sanctuary during the mild October weekends—many more visitors than normal. A few weeks earlier, Father Enrico Zucca, who had played a role in the theft of Mussolini's body from the Musocco cemetery, had told a newspaper that Il Duce was buried in the Certosa di Pavia's little cemetery, just where the Franciscan brothers had relinquished the corpse to the Milan police in August 1946. Father Zucca, now in Brazil, had given this information to a French weekly and it immediately struck a chord in the Italian papers, which explained the crowds flocking to the convent.

Once on the scene, Di Monticelli found it impossible to extract any information from Father Casimiro, priest of the Discalced Carmelites, who went so far as to pretend to have lost the key to the door behind the altar where the relics were stored. But another informant turned out to be more forthcoming: this was Dr. Maddalena, the owner of the pharmacy that sold the liqueurs distilled in the convent. Maddalena knew nothing about Mussolini's burial place; still, he was happy to share his memories. He had been the *podestà* of the little town at the gates of the Certosa for fifteen years. It was he—sporting a blue scarf around his neck and a dagger in his belt—who had received Mussolini when he made an official visit on October 31, 1932, and asked the prior to pray for him. Could anyone deny that request twenty years later, asked Maddalena, when Mussolini "had died in the way we all know"?[3] The pharmacist was not the only one troubled by the unhappy fate of the Fascist chief. De Monticelli paints a picture of a whole district where, if not nostalgic, people were at least sympathetic, referring not to "Mussolini" but to "Il Duce" and speaking of the mystery of the hidden body "as a sort of local curiosity or privilege."[4]

In Predappio, Mussolini's birthplace, the honor of having produced Il Duce had turned into a heavy burden. According to neo-Fascist journalists of the 1950s, it was "the poorest, most neglected city in Italy, the saddest and most miserable."[5] While that was an exaggeration, it remained true that Predappio, a place of pilgrimage during the Fascist years, had suffered when the regime came to an end. Politically, the town had sought to free itself from its place in Fascist history by rediscovering a left-wing past that predated the March on Rome and had never been entirely wiped out. Thus, when, after the war, it seemed that Mussolini's body might be returned to his family and buried in the Predappio cemetery, the local Socialists and Communists were indignant. "Look," they said, "they want to give him to us as a prize even though he is dead."[6] But even a left-wing local government brought no peace to Predappio. Whether loved or hated, Il Duce lived deep in the hearts of the people there. As late as 1952, photographs of Mussolini still decorated the houses in the town, De Monticelli noted.

De Monticelli knew that the story of Mussolini's dead body had more to do with the living than with mortal remains. Among those living was Mario Proli, a marble cutter at work on a singular sarcophagus. True, the local anti-Fascists had sworn that Il Duce's body would never be buried in the Predappio cemetery, but that hadn't stopped Proli from carving a big slab of tufa stone that would serve as the tomb's cover, and from engraving the fasces that would decorate the corners—pieces the marble cutter proudly showed off to *Epoca*'s photographer. Another local who caught De Monticelli's eye was Don Pietro Zoli, parish priest of the village of San Cassiano, where the Predappio cemetery was located. Eighty years old and not afraid to speak his mind, Father Zoli had been a pupil of Mussolini's mother. "Let Togliatti, Nenni, and Longo say what they will, the point is to bring Il Duce's body back here," he said. "The sarcophagus is ready."[7]

Then there was Giacomo Fabbri, the cemetery custodian. In better times he had been one of the most popular men in Predappio as he took visitors on a guided tour to see the graves of

Mussolini's parents. Now he was a "sad, fat man" who reminded De Monticelli of a reformed alcoholic living in a place thick with cheerful vineyards. Fabbri had his theory about when the body of Mussolini would return to its native soil: it all depended on when the powers in Rome would decide the time had come.

The marble cutter, the parish priest, and the cemetery custodian might have been among the living, but they were people who had outlived their time. In telling the story of Mussolini's afterlife, De Monticelli casts them in the role of minor actors, as if they were pathetic players on a stage:

> They have a certain melancholy in common; there is a certain quality of being undone that makes these figures similar. They are typical secondary characters in a drama played out years ago. History left them behind like a fast train passing an insignificant and forgettable stationmaster. They stayed in place, for what else could they do? What is left for secondary characters when the protagonists have been overwhelmed by catastrophe?[8]

It was not out of ideological sympathy for Fascism that De Monticelli wondered about the fate of Predappio's minor characters or drew eloquent portraits of Fascist bosses who had survived the ruins of the regime, men whose time had run out, who invariably had a bust of Il Duce on their shelves and a drawer full of letters from other men whose time had run out and whose days were too long. Neither was De Monticelli influenced by the conservative press, which urged "pacification" of Fascism's remnants, amounting to something close to amnesia regarding the recent past. Far from wanting readers to forget, De Monticelli felt that his job in reporting on post-Fascist Italy was to conserve memory.

From his origins in the Action Party he had retained, like many fellow Resistance members, the belief that the new Italy could not flourish without having expressed grief for the old. But De Monticelli thought that compassion must be extended to all. The Italian soldiers who died at El Alamein deserved the same attention as the partisans who lost their lives in the Apennines, he thought. The corpses of Fascists buried in the Musocco cemetery seemed just as human to him as the bodies of slain Resistance heroes.

FOR THE MOST part, the Italian left, especially when it came to the Resistance, had difficulty freeing itself from the black-and-white logic expressed by Elio Vittorini in his novel *Men and Not Men,* discussed earlier. Playing and replaying the civil war, the literature of the left, even the most sophisticated, reserved grief mainly for the fallen partisans, depicting any compassion for the dead of the Republic of Salò as absurd or degrading. In the Resistance novel par excellence, *Agnese Goes to Die* by Renata Viganò, a partisan's death represents the fountain of life ("The more they die, the more others come"), while the death of a Salò Fascist opened a sinkhole ("the dead carry away even the living").[9] Just as Manichean was much of novelist Beppe Fenoglio's early writing, in which the dead enemy was condemned to an animal existence in the hereafter, "a beast that disgusts even the God of mercy."[10] Italo Calvino granted the Salò Fascists the status of human beings but denied their dead any pity: it was pointless to bow one's head over the grave of a Blackshirt, for he had been on the wrong side of history. The first important leftist to propose a less brutal dichotomy was Cesare Pavese, an anti-Fascist but one who had not taken to the hills with his gun. His novel *The House on the Hill* concludes with the following memorable words:

I saw the unknown dead, the dead of the Republic of
Salò. They are the ones that woke me. If a man who is not
one of us, an enemy, becomes something like this when
he dies, if he stops us in our tracks and we are afraid to
step over him, it means that even in defeat, the enemy is a
person. Where the dead man lies we too could lie. . . .
There would be no difference, and if we are alive, we owe
that fact to the battered corpse. So every war is a civil war;
every dead body resembles someone alive and demands a
reason why.[11]

In Fenoglio's later works, the novelist learned to look his Fascist
enemies in the face and see their "fleshly and human" attributes.
When, in *Johnny the Partisan*, Fenoglio drops the historical dimension in favor of epic fiction, he finds dignity in the sacrifices of
both sides in the civil war. "Remember that without the dead—
theirs as well as ours—none of this would have meaning," says
Johnny. While Pavese and Fenoglio were widely acknowledged for
their literary talents, anti-Fascists felt uneasy with the way the writers seemed to put Fascists and partisans on the same plane, as if
they were distant antagonists—ancient Greeks and Persians at war.

Could one show compassion for the Fascist dead without becoming a Fascist sympathizer? Would not compassion for the Fascist dead—Mussolini among them—chip away at the foundations
of a democracy attained by the blood of the Resistance? Where
did intellectual considerations about Il Duce's remains end and
"obscene speculation" about a "dishonorable corpse" begin?[12] In
1950s Italy, the sensitive anti-Fascist conscience was troubled by
such questions. "Mother, tell me, is it really evil / To take and
string up a general? / Just one of them, hanging head down / I
won't ask for anything more, this time around," sang the Cantacronache ("the reporters"), forerunners of the left-wing singer-

songwriters of the 1960s. Addressing the fraught issue in song, they treated the moral legitimacy of a republic founded at Piazzale Loreto in a lighter vein.[13] More seriously, the well-known Sicilian poet and Nobel Laureate Salvatore Quasimodo wrote about the same theme in his "Laude, 29 April, 1945." The poem also opens with a son questioning his mother:

> And why, mother, do you spit on a body
> that hangs head down, feet tied
> to the crossbar? Aren't you just as disgusted by the others
> that hang by its side? Oh, that woman,
> her stockings worthy of a crazy can-can,
> her mouth and throat like flowers trod underfoot.
> No, mother, stop: shout at the crowd
> to go away. They are not mourning, they are revelling,
> rejoicing: the horseflies are already buzzing
> at the veins. You fired
> at that face, now: mother, mother, mother.[14]

In the decade after Mussolini and Claretta Petacci were strung up in Piazzale Loreto, no Italian poet—and certainly none on the left, where Quasimodo remained although he distanced himself from the Communists—looked so unflinchingly at the unsavory spectacle of April 29, 1945. No one else wrote about the ferocity of the crowd in Piazzale Loreto with such frankness. As the poem goes on, we learn that the son is questioning his mother from the grave: "You are dead, son / And because you are dead / you can forgive." Quasimodo seems to suggest that the civil war was so terrible as to make pardon possible only for the dead, not for the survivors. And so the son comes to agree with his mother, replying that "the fat green flies / collect in bunches on the meat hooks: rage and blood / rightly flow." Along with this poem, Quasimodo dedicated another, "To the Fifteen of Piazzale Loreto," to the Resistance fighters shot and dumped in the piazza on August 10, 1944. In the memory of the postwar left, that heap of bodies thrown in the square seemed to provide some, if not sufficient, reason for the bodies strung up on the crossbar on the day of the Liberation.

Like Quasimodo, Gaetano Salvemini was one of the few anti-Fascists who dared to lift the taboo from Piazzale Loreto and consider it as one of the keystones of the Italian republic. Even before returning to Italy from exile in America, the aging historian of modern Italy freely crowed over the insult the Resistance had delivered to the ox of the nation: "They hung him up by his feet like a butchered ox in front of the meat shop." Many thought Salvemini's words scandalous, revealing a moral laxity especially unpardonable in a Harvard professor. Scandalous or not, Salvemini's view of Piazzale Loreto was anything but superficial. A longtime anti-Fascist, he had relished the fantasy of Mussolini dead and supported attempts to bring his death about long before April 29, 1945. And after Il Duce's exposure in the piazza, Salvemini did more than simply write a few approving sentences; he searched his conscience, questioning his old attitude toward assassinating Mussolini, a move that during the years of the regime he had considered pointless and risky. "I did not believe that liberty and justice were more sacred than life itself," he wrote after the Liberation, noting that he had trembled with fear in April 1945, to think that the life of Mussolini might continue to be considered sacred.[15]

Salvemini also searched for a justification for the display of Mussolini's body. His quest reminded him of Anteo Zamboni, murdered by a gang of Fascists in Bologna in 1926 after the sixteen-year-old supposedly tried to kill Il Duce. The historian was seeking to respond to the Jesuit publication Civiltà cattolica, which had annoyed him by expressing concern for Mussolini's fate at Piazzale Loreto but none for the victims of Fascist violence. Zamboni's body, he maintained, had been "strung up and exhibited in Bologna for a week."[16] Salvemini was too serious a scholar not to grasp the gravity of this claim. If the young Zamboni's corpse was indeed displayed in Bologna in 1926, then the Fascist practice of exhibiting the bodies of the dead would have in fact begun at least a decade earlier than was generally believed. As it happened, though, the event never took place. The plan to string the body up was nixed by Fascist boss Italo Balbo and the corpse was hastily transported to the Bologna cemetery. Besides, this was not Salvemini's first encounter with Zamboni's body. As early as 1930, in an anti-Fascist tract written with the historian's encouragement, Emilio Lussu referred to the cruel treatment of Zamboni, saying that the body was "dragged through the streets and left for eleven days before it was buried."[17] When Salvemini took up the story after the war, the dragging had become hanging and the delay in burial had become public exhibition of the corpse. The appeal of these charges was obvious: why should the anti-Fascists be ashamed of displaying the body of a war criminal when twenty years earlier the Fascists had done the same to an innocent boy?

When, in a meeting in 1954, Salvemini casually referred to Mussolini "with his feet in the air in Piazzale Loreto," a onetime admirer of the professor, journalist Giovanni Ansaldo, became enraged. In an open letter, Ansaldo published a long list of accusations against him. "What is the point of studying so much, dear professor, what is the point of having seen so many sunrises and so many sunsets," he asked, if historical scholarship and long experience do not produce in the soul "a higher sense of mercy"?[18] True, Mussolini's body had been strung up by the feet. But that was something Italians should never say, or put in print, or even remember; they should "pretend not to know," because what had been done to Mussolini had dishonored Italy in the eyes of the world. Even among the Resistance, no one wanted to take credit for Piazzale Loreto; the perpetrators had vanished into anonymity. And now, ten years later, "for no good reason," Salvemini reminded people of the barbarous act in gleeful tones, as if in his twenty-two years of opposing Fascism, and in the ten years after the Liberation, he had dreamed of nothing else, as if the insult to the corpse were the great event that lit up his life. Salvemini's behavior was enough to make Ansaldo doubt not only the professor's good taste but the worth of his thought:

> If you are still capable of such one-sided cruelty, laughing because Mussolini's corpse was hung up by the feet, one can only wonder about the moral value of your opposition, which endured for so long and appeared so honorable. . . . If you do not understand the damage caused to our country by the memory of that outrage, one can only ask what you could possibly understand about what would really be to Italy's benefit.[19]

More than any other postwar journalist, Ansaldo had thought deeply about the symbolic consequences of Piazzale Loreto. He had begun writing about it in his diary while a military prisoner in Germany and had continued over the years, speaking freely in part because he did not share much of the Resistance ideology. When the company that owned the Piazzale Loreto gas station decided to dismantle the notorious crossbar, Ansaldo wrote a memorable article about the proceedings. Published in *L'Illustrazione italiana*, his story showed how that piece of the piazza had come back to life. After the bodies were taken down, the crossbar remained with its macabre ghosts, since the names of the

Fascist dead had been painted on the metal bar. The gas station reopened after the war and people stopping to refuel would "discuss how much gas and at what price where once dark blood had been spilled." The famous crossbar also stirred fantasies of many would-be executioners, who were always ready to taunt their political adversaries with the threat of hanging them in Piazzale Loreto. Political and union marches filed by the gas station. The terrible crossbar, shameful symbol of the civil war, "risked becoming a monument," according to Ansaldo.[20]

While Salvemini refused to treat Piazzale Loreto as an event to be repressed by the Resistance, Ansaldo feared that the famous square would become sacred. Their disagreement over Mussolini with his feet in the air pointed to two radically different kinds of grief. Salvemini's response—a Jacobin version of grief—involved so unforgiving an approach to Fascism that no room was left for compassion for the people who had brought the country to the brink of ruin. Ansaldo's Thermidor variety of grief was too conscious of the moral ambiguities of the civil war to allow for outbursts of hate. Mourning for the partisan dead had hardened anti-Fascist hearts until they felt indifferently or even pleased about Mussolini's posthumous treatment, while anyone whose grief extended to the Salò dead tended to feel compassion for Il Duce as well. "Historically, everyone has some merit, even the losers, those who were killed and those who were strung up by their feet," Ansaldo wrote.[21] Downplaying the conflict between Fascism and anti-Fascism, Ansaldo's historical relativism fit nicely with the line espoused by Christian Democratic prime minister De Gasperi. But Ansaldo's position annoyed those anti-Fascists who saw the centrist government as a Thermidor takeover of the Italian revolution. Thus Il Duce's story also involved competing versions of grief, one sort of sorrow pitched against another.

Article 1 of the Italian constitution declares the republic to be founded on labor, but it was also founded on grief. This was inevitable, given the deaths Italy suffered in World War II and the subsequent civil war. Even prior to the Liberation, when the partisans were still fighting, notices for the fallen took up a significant amount of space in the clandestine press. Afterward, and particularly after the Christian Democrats won the elections in April 1948, the most thoughtful spokesmen for the moral legacy of the Resistance wanted to go on remembering the partisan dead, even as the conservatives in power urged Italians to put the troublesome past behind them and move on. Anti-Fascist intellectual Piero Calamandrei wrote scores of partisan epitaphs, and his lapidary style established the spirit with which Action Party veterans would look back on their losses. One such veteran, Enzo Enriques Agnoletti, wrote the preface to *Letters from Resistance Fighters Condemned to Death*, a monument to the partisan sacrifice. Much of the writing by partisan survivors took the form of obituaries for their comrades. "The Casket" by Giulio Questi, a story published in Vittorini's *Il Politecnico*, tells of the odyssey of four partisans who have decided to give their comrade a proper burial. They have a cart for a hearse, the glow of the moon, which lights their way—but also risks exposing them—and the conviction of their grief. All the same elements, that is, that stirred the young Domenico Leccisi to steal Mussolini's corpse.

AFTER HIS ARREST in the summer of 1946, Leccisi was sentenced to six years in prison for counterfeiting. He was in fact released on appeal just before the April 1948 elections, having served twenty-one months in all. A few weeks later, his memoir, *I Stole Mussolini's Body*, began appearing in serialized form in *Tempo*, the Milan illustrated weekly. Written in the best swashbuckling style,

Leccisi's account told the exciting tale of digging up Il Duce's corpse, of seeing, and imagining, the body move, of handing the corpse over to the Franciscan friars, and of the body's discovery at the Certosa di Pavia. *Tempo* reproduced a map of the Musocco cemetery and another of the body's route. The magazine also published photos, including one of Mussolini's battered body as it lay in the morgue. "That's how Il Duce looked to me that night," Leccisi informed his readers, "perfectly recognizable even though time had left its mark on his tough face."[22] More than once, Leccisi mentioned how well preserved he found the corpse, as if the lack of decay might suggest, according to time-honored Christian doctrine, a mark of sainthood. The high point of the story is the moment when the band of grave robbers moves the corpse to the waiting automobile. The cemetery, white beneath the moon, the naked body, the undertaker's cart used to transport it—despite their meager tools, the neo-Fascists conceived of their action in the boldest of terms. "Shakespeare," wrote Leccisi, "never imagined a stranger and sadder voyage for the travels of his dead Hamlet."[23]

On July 24, 1948, Leccisi shared the cover of *Tempo* with Antonio Pallante, the man who had just tried to kill Communist leader Palmiro Togliatti. There was no better example of how the popular illustrated weeklies, with their appetite for scandal, reflected the anti-Resistance position of the conservatives than the pairing of these two men. The musicologist Massimo Mila, a well-known anti-Fascist from Turin, reacted with fury. In the days leading up to the attempt on Togliatti's life, said Mila, all the Fascists who should have been "in jail or six feet under" were publishing their stories in pro-government magazines.[24] Certainly, presenting individual Fascists as blameless men of conscience was a useful way for the moderate press to support the government line of "pacification," leaving the past behind. But it would be wrong to infer from this that the centrist press was crypto-Fascist. True, the moderates were more indulgent toward veterans of the Mussolini regime than toward Communists, but this was because they believed that neo-Fascism was merely a residual phenomenon, destined to die out. Thus, in one issue that included Leccisi's recollections, there was an article by Vitaliano Brancati, a famous playwright and novelist, suggesting that the neo-Fascists were "men of the grave," of greater interest to fiction writers than to historians. Neo-Fascism had no political significance, only poetic resonance: there was nothing more melancholy than observing a faith—"already dead in terms of history"— slowly fade away, said Brancati.[25]

The survivors of Salò had a duty to ensure compassion toward the Salò dead: Domenico Leccisi built his political career on this principle. In the five years between his release from prison and his election to Parliament, Leccisi struggled as a sales representative for a chemical company, never forgetting the Fascists buried in the Musocco cemetery, where the graves were periodically vandalized by overzealous anti-Fascists. In the early years of the Italian Social Movement, the question of paying homage to the Fascist dead was an important rallying issue. Thanks to his role as Mussolini's undertaker, Leccisi was able to use it to launch himself politically, especially since he had a healthy appetite for skirmishes in the press. In September 1950, Leccisi's name was back in the papers with the launch of *Lotta d'Italia,* a new neo-Fascist weekly. The first issue was devoted to Leccisi's adventures in the Musocco cemetery, his dealings with Il Duce's body, "cold and stony in the naked composure of death."[26] After this new account appeared, the Communist Party challenged the government in Parliament and Leccisi was charged with promoting Fascism. This was just what the young neo-Fascist had hoped for: in 1951 his newfound notoriety helped elect him to the Milan city council, where he began a campaign to devote a section of the Musocco cemetery to the military and civilian casualties of the Republic of Salò.

Bodies in search of a grave and cemeteries missing their corpses continued to obsess the illustrated weeklies. In the spring of 1952, *Epoca* ran an article suggesting that somewhere in central Italy the remains of numerous Fascists were buried in an unidentified cemetery. A photograph showed a memorial plaque, a bunch of flowers, and a vineyard, but the magazine offered no proof that anyone was actually buried beneath the vines. Had eighteen Fascists and two Germans killed during the Liberation been buried in the Musocco cemetery and then secretly transferred to this vineyard in central Italy? Was it true that the bones of Mussolini's fingers, lost during the theft of his body, had been recovered and given a proper burial in that place? Roberto De Monticelli interviewed Leccisi but received no answers to these questions. Instead, Leccisi did reveal that he had kept a souvenir from his adventures in the cemetery—a "rather small scrap" of the great leader's trousers. Such medieval relics were cherished on all sides. In a last letter by a young martyr of the Resistance, Pedro Ferreira, condemned to death, wrote to his Action Party comrades that he had kept "a piece of the bloodied shirt" of Duccio Galimberti, the legendary military commander of the Piedmont branch of the Justice and Liberty organization. The following day, he planned to ask the commander of the execution squad to soak it in his own blood once he, too, had been shot. Ferreira hoped the scrap would then be preserved by the Action Party as a "historical souvenir of this bloody struggle."[27]

At the end of June 1953, Leccisi went to Rome as a deputy for the Italian Social Movement from the district of Milan-Pavia, having gotten more votes than the local party boss. The neo-Fascist adventurer had become a figure to be reckoned with in his party, having established a national reputation as a leader of the

"I stole the body of Mussolini."—Domenico Leccisi
(*Foto Publifoto/Olympia*)

movement's more radical faction and a reputation in Milan as the chief of the militant gangs. In general, the elections of 1953 marked the passage of the Italian Social Movement from a young party to a mature one. With twenty-nine deputies and nine senators, the party was solidly rooted in the lower middle classes of central and southern Italy. So the republic got its share and more of Fascists. Piero Calamandrei, one of the principal authors of the Italian constitution, greeted the parliamentarians with one of his famous "epitaphs" in his magazine, *Il Ponte*. He addressed his words to the partisan dead, telling them not to suffer because the Fascists were back. The reappearance of these "shameful ghosts" would only serve to remind Italians how evil they really were:

> Too soon we forgot them .
> It is well they are out in view
> On this stage
> So that everyone
> Will recognize their faces
> And remember
> That all that really did happen.[28]

The Fascists on the parliamentary benches were thus a sort of Piazzale Loreto of the living, a display of the enemy to the Italian public.

In the years that followed, the anti-Fascist press depicted Domenico Leccisi as the foolish guardian of an abandoned temple. *Il Ponte*, in particular, made a point of tracking the high points of Leccisi's parliamentary career, among them a lively fight with Communist veteran Giancarlo Pajetta. "Silence, grave digger!" Pajetta shouted. "If it weren't for Audisio, you wouldn't be a deputy. Go back to stealing corpses and shut up."[29] Meanwhile, Leccisi showed that he was on the job by mounting an inquiry into the whereabouts of one of the boots Mussolini wore at the time of death and the rumor that the Milan prosecutor's office had ordered the other boot destroyed. These fetishist initiatives notwithstanding, the young deputy from Milan showed intellectual integrity and even some political courage. As the Italian Social Movement grew more cautious and conservative, seduced by the example of the right-wing Christian Democrats, Leccisi, just two years after his triumphant election, left the party to found the National Corporative Party, which aimed to perpetuate the radical "socializing" spirit of the Salò Fascists. This was the first step in a series of Leccisi's comings and goings—in and out of the Italian Social Movement—over the following decades, as the maverick neo-Fascist obstinately pursued "left-wing" Fascism.

Leccisi, however, was not the mover behind a petition, circulating in December 1954, calling for the return of Mussolini's body to his family and thus also to his devoted followers. The initiative was conceived by Vanni Teodorani, related to Mussolini by marriage, Il Duce's secretary at Salò, and later the founder of an association of Italian Social Republic veterans that had links to the most reactionary elements of the Roman Curia, the Vatican government. Teodorani's contacts made it possible for him to secure the signatures of various notable Christian Democrats. But he failed to obtain the blessing of Rachele Mussolini, who was opposed to exerting pressure on the authorities to return Il Duce's body, nor did he gain Leccisi's support. Teodorani also sought the backing of some anti-Fascist voices, and this step made Leccisi scornful of the whole effort, since it involved people who were directly or indirectly responsible for Il Duce's execution at Giulino di Mezzegra and the shameful spectacle of Piazzale Loreto. "We're of the opinion," said Leccisi, "that the current state of regret by the Resistance bosses does not merit the consideration of the Fascists."[30] As long as Italy remained poisoned by the civil war, the appropriate degree of mercy was a matter of dispute.

"THE WAY A man meets his death will be determined by his character": in the golden days of the Fascist regime, Mussolini subscribed to his own demanding dictum.[31] Fascism, born in the trenches of World War I, saw a "good death" as the great mark that separated one man from another. But as it happened, Mussolini's death was no boon to his posthumous reputation. Whatever one said of what happened at Giulino di Mezzegra, one could not say it fit the Fascist definition of a good death. To be credible, a martyr had to die with style. It was hard to point to the style of a man who had refused to surrender to the Committee of National Liberation—not in order to stage an eleventh-hour defense of Salò but so he could try to sneak across the border and escape.

In the early days after Mussolini's death, the most intellectually honest of the Fascists had confided this unpleasant truth to their diaries. "To lose one's life is serious but morally remediable," observed Giuseppe Bottai, a onetime Fascist minister, of Mussolini. "But there is no remedy for the man who fails to keep a grip on his death."[32] Writing from Africa, where he was serving in the Foreign Legion, Bottai sketched a tender portrait of Il Duce before his arrest, as a man prostrated by fatigue, a man whose gaze was vague and whose jaw was slack. But Bottai did not allow his human, Christian tenderness to affect his moral judgment. What could possibly repair the shame of Mussolini's flight, disguised in a German overcoat and helmet and hidden in a truck? How could he possibly escape the "whorehouse judgment" he had himself invited by dragging Claretta Petacci along to Dongo? There was no way around it, Bottai wrote. Mussolini's last act had been played out without grandeur or nobility.

Imprisoned in Italy, Vincenzo Costa—sentenced after the Liberation for having served as a *federale,* a high-ranking Fascist official, in Milan under the German occupation—also reflected on Mussolini's last days. He wrote of the terrible disappointment Fascists felt in Il Duce's behavior before his death. A few days after Mussolini's excecution, Costa had gone to the shores of Lake Como with other unrepentant militants of Salò to pay homage to

Il Duce. "It shouldn't have ended that way," he wept, "it shouldn't have ended that way."[33]

While a source of embarrassment and shame for the Fascists, the squalid circumstances of Mussolini's death were a consolation to anti-Fascists. This, they felt, was certain to squash any posthumous mythmaking. The end of Il Duce also stood as a cautionary note: his pathetic finale was emblematic of a pathetic life. Gaetano Salvemini spoke for most anti-Fascists when he turned Mussolini's bold declaration about the way a man meets his death against Il Duce himself:

> Il Duce . . . really did die in keeping with his character, that is, he died as he was hightailing it to Switzerland dressed up as a German soldier and hidden under a blanket, with $149,365, 203,705 Swiss francs, 16,593,300 French francs, 10,000 pesetas, 11,000 Portuguese escudos, 27,113 pounds sterling in banknotes, 2,150 pounds in gold, and many, many bundles of Italian lire. Not to mention his girlfriend. . . . She had stuffed precious stones into the seams of her underwear and they had to dig her up later to get the gems back. Nero, in keeping with his character, died a far more dignified death in his day.[34]

From the very first hours and days after the Liberation, that Luftwaffe overcoat worn by Mussolini to escape capture became the symbol and material proof of Il Duce's treason, not to mention one of the spoils of war of the Resistance. One partisan went up and down the shores of Lake Como showing everyone the shameful German greatcoat, and newsreel makers and photographers trained their lenses on it. Mussolini's flight so fueled the collective imagination that fables began to circulate about it. In one, Il Duce ran away dressed in women's clothes; the idea was picked up by a British cartoonist, who depicted Benito and

Adolf trying on ladies' garments in preparation for escape to Argentina. There were even those who, before the event, had predicted that Mussolini would don a disguise and flee. On the morning of April 27—twelve hours before Il Duce was apprehended dressed up as a German—*l'Unità* imagined the dictator trying to run away concealed as a country priest. In the mental hospital where he had been forced to take refuge from the Racial Laws, Renzo Segre, an Italian Jew, reacted to the news that Mussolini had been arrested at Dongo "with all but a fake beard" with disgust.[35] "No one expected Mussolini's get-up would be so pathetic," commented a longtime opponent of the regime.[36] As it turned out, the anti-Fascists could not have hoped for a better outcome, because Il Duce in disguise embodied the Il Duce who had betrayed Italy. *Mussolini, the Traitor* was in fact the title of a 1945 book by the Russian Socialist Angelica Balabanov, who had once been Il Duce's lover before becoming a fierce opponent.

The money Mussolini and his Fascist cronies were carrying was proof of another crime—larceny. While Il Duce was not known as greedy, journalists could not be expected to let this go. One book published in 1946 was titled *The Morality of Mussolini: A Hand in the Till*. As for the gems sewed into Clara Petacci's underwear—"how pitiful the details," wrote Giovanni Ansaldo—what better emblem of the late-empire atmosphere of Il Duce's final days? Even the exhumation of Petacci's body failed to put the legend of the stolen gems to rest. Although the jewelry recovered from her corpse was worth only a paltry sum, a man of Salvemini's stature continued to spin fables about the riches hidden in Claretta Petacci's brassiere as late as 1953.

Then there was the crime of adultery. After tirelessly promoting the sanctity of marriage, the Fascist chief had run away with his mistress, sparing not a thought for his wife. "Mussolini's offense cannot be excused in any way," a former Fascist leader charged.[37] Of course, anti-Fascists were ready to depict the episode in the harshest key. One reporter traced the couple's immorality back to the days when the two would meet at a great pretentious villa on the Via Camilluccia in Rome; according to the reporter, their bedroom was "covered floor to ceiling with mirrors"—a room worthy of a brothel. Long after the war, even civilized left-wing intellectuals persisted in humiliating Claretta Petacci by calling her names. Historian Giorgio Spini deemed her "a slut," while Salvemini confined himself to "lover girl."

THE GERMAN GREATCOAT, the money, and the "lover girl" were images that stuck in anti-Fascist minds as symbols of treason, larceny, and adultery—Mussolini's crimes at Dongo. But in 1950s Italy, anti-Fascist memory existed only among a minority, since opposition to the Fascist regime as well as the armed struggle against the Republic of Salò had been decidedly minority phenomena. In the immortal words of the writer Ennio Flaiano, the Fascists had been "a negligible majority."[38] Under such circumstances, forgiving mercy of the Thermidor variety was bound to win out over the sterner Jacobin approach of the Resistance. This remained true until the passage of time changed the balance between two generations: those who had been adults during the regime, those for whom Fascism was a living memory began to decline, while their children, who had grown up after the war and saw the regime as history, were in the ascendent. The tensions of 1968 can be traced to the dynamic between these two generations. In the 1950s, however, hegemonic Italian culture—epitomized by the popular weeklies, the predecessors of television—rigorously excluded the ideals of the Resistance. At the same time the weeklies vigorously stoked compassion for the fate of Il Duce's body.

The literature of intimate confessions about Mussolini's life and death passed first through the illustrated weeklies and then appeared in book form, expanding the audience. Edda, Mussolini's daughter, was not the only woman in her family to publish her memoirs and keep Mussolini's memory warm; so did her mother, Rachele, and her aunt Edvige. Mussolini's ghost was also revived by the popular history writers of the period. Two small classics of cheap popular literature—Giovanni Artieri's book on the failed attempts on Mussolini's life, and Franco Bandini's book tracing the background of Walter Audisio's mission—got their starts in the illustrated weeklies. A former big name in Fascist journalism, Paolo Monelli, published a short version of his postwar book *Mussolini, Petit Bourgeois,* in the weekly *Europeo.* The sum total of all this recollection, reportage, and storytelling was to sketch an indulgent version of Il Duce's last days, in which the crimes he committed were transmuted into venial sins, to be duly pardoned.

The figure of Mussolini fleeing in a German greatcoat was therefore transformed by a chorus of voices that tended to downplay his cowardice and dismiss his act of treason. Mussolini, it seemed, had always intended to die a good death. In his final days, his Fascist co-conspirators had forced a man who had become "inert . . . still thinking but inert" to run away, the apologists argued.[39] He might have been inert, but when he donned the German coat, Il Duce nonetheless revealed his tortured soul, readers of the weeklies were told; and besides, there was no incontrovertible proof that he ever actually wore the Luftwaffe coat. As for concealing himself in a German transport truck, Il Duce had only acceded to Claretta Petacci's insistence. Should Mussolini have committed suicide as Hitler had done in his bunker? No, it would have been unseemly for the earthy boss from Predappio to end his days in chilly Wagnerian abstraction. In any case, "more than a man's death, what counts is his life," as contemporary writers claimed.[40] This seemed all the more true in the twentieth century, when the Romantic concept of a hero had been mostly expunged by World War II. Had Mussolini betrayed his country? "We are all betrayers," explained one journalist.[41] Italians had to stop punishing themselves for offenses both real and imagined. It was time to stop worrying about pacts with the Germans and civil wars; the histories of many other countries were "rife with Piazzale Loretos and Fosse Ardeatine,"[42] the latter a brutal reprisal in 1944, in which the Germans murdered 335 civilians on the outskirts of Rome.

To counter the shameless picture of Il Duce with his hand in the till, the journalists pulled out an old chestnut of Fascist propaganda, the image of a Mussolini so indifferent to money as to constantly forget his wallet. Mussolini was captured "without a lira in his pocket," the apologists were still—incredibly—writing in 1950.[43] Even the terrible events of Piazzale Loreto were proof of Il Duce's perfect honesty, for not one lira fell from his pocket when the partisans strung him up. Mussolini's hands were also made to look clean after it was learned that some of the money he was carrying, which was seized by the partisans, ended up in the accounts (or in the pockets) of Communist functionaries. Thus, for more than a decade after the fact, the centrist press was writing about the "gold of Dongo" in an anti-Communist, not an anti-Fascist, vein. Among the petty thieves in action on the shores of Lake Como, wrote the weeklies, was a future representative for the Communist Party, Dante Gorreri, charged in the theft of Mussolini's traveling alarm clock and in the murder of a woman, a partisan comrade. Perhaps there was also Walter Audisio, suspected of having taken a wristwatch and a gold cigarette case. In the opinion of a journalist for *Corriere della Sera,* the "double game" of the Resistance had allowed the Communists to pocket in twenty days what the Fascists had taken twenty years to accumulate—meaning the Fascist leadership, not Mussolini. According to one weekly, Il Duce's only material concern before his death was for two of his dressing gowns, "the black one and the velvet one with the fur," which he asked his wife to look after.[44]

The fact that Claretta Petacci shared Mussolini's last hours at Lake Como was corrected in the weeklies after the war with a barrage of stories about Rachele Mussolini. While Il Duce's widow was living in Forio, on the island of Ischia, the weeklies vied with one another to recount the most minute details of her compulsory residence there. The stories were illustrated in high neorealist style with black-and-white pictures of the good housewife living in honest poverty, her neighbors eager to be of help and the whole island admiring her. When she finally got permission to move to Rome, the coverage did not let up during the long wait to reclaim Benito's body. How could they resist publishing a picture of Rachele embroidering the shroud to wrap her husband's body, like a modern Penelope awaiting the day her Ulysses would return as a corpse? Rachele was by no means silent; in addition to making herself available to the photographers, she gave interviews and offered assorted memoirs to the weeklies. Whenever given the chance, she replicated the feat she had accomplished with her 1948 memoir, *My Life with Benito,* which canonized Il Duce in a perfect apologia for the regime. She was helped in this enterprise by her ghostwriter, Giorgio Pini, Mussolini's biographer and the chief repository of Fascist historical memory.

There was no cliché about Mussolini that did not make it into Rachele's version, whether in her two books or in the popular press. There was Mussolini the elementary school teacher who had mesmerized her with his flashing black eyes; Mussolini the young man of integrity, taking on the humblest jobs if it meant keeping his intellectual independence; Mussolini the Socialist bohemian, touring Europe in tattered clothes but always with a stack of books and newspapers; Mussolini the natural-born journalist who could write any article in fifteen minutes. There was Mussolini the true believer, ready to take a 50 percent pay cut as editor of *Avanti!;* Mussolini the lover of culture, so passionate about the theater he would take the maid along when Rachele couldn't attend; Mussolini man of courage, imperturbable when attempts were made on his life; Mussolini man of honor, who wouldn't hesitate to challenge his most vicious political adversaries to a duel. Then there was Mussolini tireless worker, a prime minister so hardworking as to wreak havoc on the placid routines of the Roman bureaucracy; Mussolini the natural athlete, who, kicking the ball around with his children, was capable of breaking the windows at his Villa Torlonia residence; Mussolini the kindhearted Duce, quick to wriggle out of the grasp of his bodyguards and get close to the people. There was Mussolini the leader, whose charisma was such that one or two visitors to Palazzo Venezia would invariably faint; Mussolini the lover of nature, who like a trained gardener pruned the old almond tree near Rocca delle Caminate, his property near Predappio; Mussolini the polyglot, able to converse with world leaders in English, French, Spanish, or German; Mussolini the good father, as much involved in his children's upbringing as in affairs of state.

Above all, Rachele made a point of insisting on the cliché of Mussolini the perfect husband. Il Duce, whose eye never wandered, "fulfilled his conjugal duties right up to the end," she told her readers.[45] It wasn't enough for Rachele to reassure Italians about the frequency of her sexual relations with Benito. She also published a highly edifying letter that she claimed had been written by Il Duce ("with a red pencil") on the eve of his death:

> Dear Rachele,
>
> I have now arrived at the last stage of my life, at the last page of my book. We may not ever see each other again, and so I wanted to write you this letter. I ask your forgiveness for any wrongs that I have involuntarily done you. You know that you were the only woman that I ever really loved. I swear that to you before God and our dear departed son Bruno in this moment of supreme sacrifice. You know that I and the others must go to the Valtellina. You, with the children, should try to reach the Swiss border. Up there you can begin a new life.[46]

As a document attesting to Mussolini's marital, Christian, and patriotic virtues, this letter became a monument to Il Duce's glorious memory. The weeklies printed and reprinted it for a good half century, always ready to accept Rachele Mussolini's explanation for why she no longer had the red-penciled original, which was that she had memorized the words and destroyed it to prevent it from falling into partisan hands. But a few years before she died, Rachele Mussolini finally admitted that the letter was completely invented. She had written it herself, she said, to gain sympathy at a moment when she thought the public favored Claretta Petacci.

Following Rachele's lead, others also sought to minimize Claretta's role in Mussolini's life as a way to lessen the gravity of the crime of adultery. "On the verge of death," wrote Il Duce's sister, Edvige, Benito found himself with Clara at his side, but before his eyes "were the faces of Rachele and his children." The supposed love between Il Duce and Clara was a one-sided passion, asserted another writer. Mussolini had long tried to free himself from his mistress and was constantly unfaithful to her; the only thing he loved about her was her "enormous bosom."[47] Thus Il Duce was supposed to have behaved like a typical middle-class Italian: he had a wife to look after the house and children and a lover so he could feel successful, and he betrayed his lover as frequently as possible. What was the point of dwelling on the liaison between Mussolini and Petacci? For an Italian male there was nothing more routine than accumulating lovers. Committing a few sins was a salutary way to keep evil at bay. The books and weeklies maintained that Il Duce was a libertine, thereby dismissing the scandal about his death beside Claretta.

Unlike the daily papers, subsidized by the state, the weeklies depended on the market. Perhaps, therefore, they can be considered more indicative of postwar Italian taste and orientation. The people who flocked to buy the illustrated weeklies seemed to like their benevolence toward Mussolini. Obviously, readers didn't buy the weeklies solely for their pictures of Il Duce and Rachele Mussolini's memoirs; the magazines also contained photos of film stars and gossipy details about various sordid crime stories. If the black-and-white images from the Fascist period contributed to their popularity, it was for sentimental, not ideological, reasons. Photographs win us over with their aura of time gone by, and even the pictures of Mussolini, images that a whole generation of Italians had been poring over since childhood, partook of that aura. In the 1950s, in a country that was undergoing vast social changes, it was possible to be nostalgic without regretting the demise of Fascism.

The fact that Mussolini's big jaw could appear in the weeklies alongside pictures of "naughty" Brigitte Bardot and the Sicilian bandit Salvatore Giuliano was a sign of the times. That the roles of Il Duce, the pinup girl, and the gunman were interchangeable pointed to the decline of a certain postwar morality, one that the partisans had hoped to impose. If ever it had risen over postwar Italy, the star of the Resistance had set in a hurry.

There was no room for Jacobin grief in the illustrated weeklies—mourning for the victors' dead, as the Resistance veterans would have preferred. When the popular magazines depicted Il Duce as a family man led astray by corrupt Fascist leaders and hunted down by Communist agents, they bolstered an image of Mussolini, dear departed, and popularized the Thermidor version of mercy, offering sorrow for the losers. They also created a climate in which the government could finally decide to return the "restless corpse" to the family. But the mood of forgiveness was at least as useful to the living as it was to the dead. It allowed Italians to measure themselves against Il Duce's memory without feeling uneasy. Absolving Mussolini of the crimes of Dongo—the greatcoat, the money, the lover girl—meant absolving him of the crimes of the regime. And to forgive the crimes of the regime— the political opportunism, the economic corruption, the duplicitous morality—meant forgiving Italians their past as Fascists.

7

THE RETURN OF THE REMAINS

In the days of Piazzale Loreto, Il Duce's remains were the civil war incarnate—a trophy for the partisans, a sacrifice for the Fascists. During the first decade of the Italian republic, the remains generated two competing forms of mercy: the anti-Fascists' harsh brand and the saccharine variety of the anti-anti-Fascists. When, in 1957, Il Duce's body was transferred to the San Casciano cemetery at Predappio, there was yet another occasion for these sentiments to clash. Inside the walls of San Casciano—and elsewhere in Italy— the two souls of the postwar period went to war.

In early 1955, there was a rumor in Predappio that the government was about to return Mussolini's body to his family. Like many other such rumors, this one proved untrue, but it gave the weekly *Il Mondo,* the bible of non-Communist anti-Fascists, a pretext to take up the problem of the wandering corpse. According to the magazine's political editor, the way the government had handled the problem of Mussolini's remains revealed its "inferiority complex" with respect to right- and left-wing oppositions alike.

Christian Democratic leaders had never felt strong enough either to allow the remains to be dispersed or to restore the body to the dictator's family without fuss or negotiations, as if the move were standard bureaucratic procedure. As *Il Mondo* saw it, the word that Prime Minister Mario Scelba was considering returning Mussolini's body to Predappio reflected his desire to secure the backing of the extreme right. The prime minister's deliberations also reflected the Christian Democrats' highly ambivalent approach. Scelba wanted the body to be buried at San Casciano during the night; he feared that a daytime burial would be seen by the left as an intolerable provocation. Scelba wanted to "satisfy the neo-Fascists and at the same time avoid the protests of the anti-Fascists," wrote *Il Mondo;* he wanted to take credit for a gesture of "pacification" and yet ward off scandal—"too many objectives at once, obviously, and we can be sure he won't accomplish any of them."[1]

Il Mondo's characterization of Scelba's motives apply as well to his Christian Democratic successor Adone Zoli, who became prime minister in May 1957. Zoli, too, saw the gesture of restoring Mussolini's corpse to the family as a chance to satisfy neo-Fascists and thus expand the Christian Democrat hegemony over the extreme right. He, too, sought to evade anti-Fascist protests by keeping the decision to return the body quiet. But unlike Scelba, Zoli really did release Il Duce's body. He did so at a highly thorny political moment: the formula the party had devised to rule from the center was failing; the Christian Democrats were unable to maintain a parliamentary majority in their coalition with several small moderate parties. The party was divided between those who favored an opening to the left, that is, the inclusion of the Socialists in the governing coalition, and those who were bargaining, more or less secretly, to embrace the neo-Fascists. Zoli had to seek a combination of support that would give his government a parliamentary majority. The challenge, which was fought out from the end of May to early July 1957, ended with Zoli calling on the body of Il Duce.

In return for supporting the Christian Democrats, the Italian Social Movement demanded the promise that Mussolini's body would be quickly returned to Predappio. It was a charged request for Zoli personally, as his family had its origins in Predappio and the family tomb in the San Casciano cemetery stood only a few meters from the Mussolinis. In his inaugural address to Parliament, Zoli carefully refrained from mentioning Il Duce's body. He presented his government as one of transition, in anticipation of national elections in 1958. Referring discreetly to his anti-Fascist views, Zoli made it clear that he would not deviate from Christian Democratic precedent and allow the Italian Social Movement to be part of the governing majority. "Our record, in the past and in the present," said Zoli, "is too well known and too respected for there to be any doubt that we will depart from it."[2] But the smaller moderate parties and the left failed to endorse his government and Zoli was confirmed with the votes of the monarchist party and the Italian Social Movement. Domenico Leccisi, who had left the neo-Fascists to run as an independent, even spoke up to offer Zoli "the modest vote of a Fascist."[3] For the first time in the history of the republic, neo-Fascist votes become decisive in forming a government.

Right after Zoli's parliamentary majority was confirmed, the Chamber of Deputies was the stage for one of the most animated scenes in the tale of Mussolini's afterlife. The neo-Fascists, arguing that Zoli governed only thanks to their votes, challenged him to step down, as he had said he would not accept the backing of the Italian Social Movement. However, the Christian Democrats calculated that even without the Italian Social Movement they had 281 votes, or one more vote than the bare majority necessary. Leccisi then insisted on being counted as a member of the Italian Social Movement and not as an independent, because, he said, he was a genuine Fascist: "How else can you define a warrior who has even gone so far as to steal the body of Il Duce to protect it from the depredations of the infidels?"[4] Leccisi's political message could not have been more pointed.

The Communist daily, *l'Unità*, echoed that message with a polemical headline: "Leccisi's Vote . . . the Deciding One." The paper offered a scathing description of Christian Democrat ministers trying to deny that Leccisi was a neo-Fascist. Even the *Corriere della Sera*, which usually hewed to a pro-government position, did not try to conceal the embarrassment of the previous day's developments. After some hesitation, Zoli remained as prime minister despite his reliance on the Italian Social Movement—and despite the attacks from the extreme-right press, still angry about the anti-Fascist stance Zoli had taken earlier. Soon the pages of *Il Mondo* were featuring a cartoon by satirist Mino Maccari showing two black boots labeled "the pillars of a right-wing majority."[5]

Riven by disagreement, Zoli's coalition with the neo-Fascists was not so novel as it seemed. From the start of the republic's second legislature in 1953, the Christian Democrats had colluded with the far right. Indeed, it would be only a small stretch to say that the return of Mussolini's corpse to Predappio was the natural outcome of Christian Democratic politics—always more anti-Communist than anti-Fascist. But politics do not explain everything here. Il Duce's body was given back to his family not just because there was a right-wing parliamentary majority but also because the Christian Democrats acted on a popular sentiment they shared with most of the electorate. Theirs was an expiatory kind of patriotism, based on a vague yet widely shared feeling of collective guilt. The Christian Democrats favored an apolitical interpretation of history, involving conciliation and shying away from memories of the Resistance and the attendant social tensions; they exalted the figure of the martyr who pays for others' guilt with his own; and they embraced the Christian notion of forgiveness.

A March 1956 letter from the great Sardinian jurist Salvatore Satta to Prime Minister Antonio Segni suggests the deep roots of this philosophy. The occasion for the letter was Easter, said Satta, when peace was supposed to settle into the hearts of all good Christians. The issue he wanted to take up was Il Duce's body. He was writing to persuade Segni that the "beaten, humiliated" body should be returned to the care of Il Duce's children and his "tender companion." It was not just Mussolini's corpse that was in question, wrote Satta. He was concerned about the fate of all the fallen of the Republic of Salò, all those Italians massacred "out of a sadistic hate that hides behind the decorum of partisanship," all those who lay in mass graves or mountain cemeteries, far from their families. Difficult as it was to make reparations for all the dead, Satta urged Segni to let his Christian charity come to bear at least in the case of Mussolini. Let a stone be laid on the tomb of hatred and bureaucratic inflexibility, let the remains of Il Duce rest in the waiting sarcophagus at Predappio, he pleaded. Whom, after all, were they talking about? About a veteran of World War I, "corporal of the Bersagliere corps Benito Mussolini," Satta wrote, referring to Il Duce's wartime assault unit. Invoking the intense solidarity binding those who have fought in the same trenches or shed blood for the same nation, Satta made his appeal not only as a "onetime Blackshirt" but as a "soldier among soldiers."[6]

Satta's letter is enlightening in its belief that Italy was undergoing "a national death," a decline of any vestige of national unity and prominence.[7] Satta mourned the demise of an Italy that seemed to matter on the world stage, a nation that was baptized at the battle of Vittorio Veneto during World War I and came of age under Mussolini at Piazza Venezia. At the same time, Satta's letter shows that it was possible to urge the return of Mussolini's remains to Predappio without being a Fascist. In his view, the act of forgiveness was meant to serve the cause not of any one group but of suffering humanity. As a good Christian would perforce see it, the skirmish over a cemetery was really Italy's version of Judgment Day. Prime Minister Adone Zoli, despite the tangled circumstances that produced his government, regarded the matter much as Satta did. And Zoli was anything but a Fascist sympathizer. During the Resistance, he had led the Committee of National Liberation in Florence. In 1951 he had helped effect the return to Italy of the Roselli brothers, anti-Fascists murdered in France in 1937. But Zoli was not a man to ask a corpse to show its party membership card.

DURING THE SUMMER of 1957, *Il Secolo d'Italia,* the Italian Social Movement paper, engaged in a vociferous campaign to restore Il Duce's remains to Predappio. By the end of July, working through the mediation of a common friend in Predappio, Rachele Mussolini was negotiating the details of the body's return with Prime Minister Zoli. The government wanted to make the move during the August 15 Ferragosto holiday to take advantage of the fact that Italians would be going on their vacations and the newspapers would not be published the following day. Rachele Mussolini, for her part, said she did not want to bury the body immediately but wished to arrange a funeral ceremony in the little cemetery of San Casciano. On August 30, 1957, fifteen days after the government would have liked and twelve years after his death, the body of Il Duce began the road home. It was escorted by Caio M. Cattabeni, the forensics expert from the University of Milan, who had been called to authenticate the corpse; the former police chief of Milan, Vincenzo Agnesina, whom Zoli had asked to transport the casket to Emilia-Romagna, throwing journalists off the track by using a decoy vehicle; and the Cappuccine monks of the Lombard convent of Cerro Maggiore, where Mussolini's remains had been hidden since 1946.

Despite the government's efforts to keep the proceedings quiet,

Unloaded by several monks from a rented car at the San Casciano cemetery, a wooden crate marked "Church Documents." August 3, 1957.
(Foto Publifoto/Olympia)

the press was on hand, trailing the body virtually minute by minute,
turning the funeral into spectacular entertainment. While the weekly
Oggi bargained for exclusive photo rights, the San Casciano cemetery swarmed with photographers from all over. At the Cerro Maggiore convent, the dailies reported, Mussolini's corpse had been
hidden in the space behind an altar until 1950. When the smell from
the famous trunk in which the remains were sealed became too evident, the trunk itself was sealed in a wooden crate marked "Church
Documents" and moved to a storeroom. This was the crate that several monks unloaded from the rented car at the San Casciano cemetery. Some of the assembled made a point of signing their names on
the crate. And then, at the Mussolini family crypt, a small group of

August 31, 1957. The Mussolini family crypt, where Rachele Mussolini, surrounded by the neo-Fascist faithful, laid the body of Il Duce to rest. (*Foto Publifoto/Olympia*)

men raising their right arms in the Fascist salute succeeded in crowding around the remains of Il Duce and the frail figure of his widow, who had gotten approval to hold a memorial mass before the burial. So on August 31, 1957, the body of Il Duce was finally laid in the simple sarcophagus where it remains today and where the faithful come to sign their names in the guest book.

No sooner had the burial taken place than the protests began. *L'Unità* accused Zoli of having "dared to do the unthinkable."[8] By returning the body to the neo-Fascists, were the Christian Democrats laying the basis for a new clerical-Fascist regime? Less polemically, *Il Borghese* suggested that Zoli had needed to repay the debt of the neo-Fascist votes that had put his government in

The sarcophagus and guest book at the San Casciano cemetery.
(*Michele Bella*)

power. The long postwar rule of the center, it seemed, was finally coming to an end. Meanwhile, the prime minister's desk was piled high with letters about Mussolini's return to Predappio. Most were positive. Praising Zoli's gesture, a farm woman from the province of Mantua wrote that for years she had been tormented by the thought that Il Duce's corpse had no peace. A worker from Emilia-Romagna approved of the wonderfully Christian act of restoring the body to the widow and promised Zoli that "as a local boss, I can get out the vote for you, at least 200 votes at the next election, all for you."[9] In the chorus of applause there were only a few dissenting voices, one of them a woman who decreed it shameful to have moved remains of Mussolini, "the greatest criminal of our times."[10] The woman, who did not sign her letter, wrote that she had lost four sons in 1944 when they were all deported by the Fascists, never to return home.

Enzo Biagi, editor in chief of *Epoca,* took a stern position. Mussolini, he wrote, belonged to the category of dead people who bring votes, and that was why so many had hastened to give a decent burial to the man who had dragged Italy into World War II and why so few had acted to build a memorial to the nameless and blameless, the very victims of that war. But in general the pro-government press tended to be conciliatory toward Zoli. The local correspondent for the *Corriere della Sera* depicted the town of Predappio as united in its desire to see Il Duce's body return. An editorialist for the paper called Zoli's decision a gesture toward making peace with Italy's past. The editor of *Oggi* praised the Italian people for their "noble silence" about Il Duce's new burial place. Even the editorialists of the left—with the exception of the Communists—refrained from painting the events in too dramatic a light. In *Il Ponte,* noted intellectual Riccardo Bauer derided the clumsy way the anti-Fascists had protested the tributes at the tomb. Let the faithful stage their lugubrious ceremonies, but meanwhile young people should know something about Italian history and the "paper hero" who had for so many years deceived and poisoned the country, he wrote. *Il Mondo* offered several modest proposals of Swiftian inspiration. They included a tax on those who wanted to visit the San Casciano cemetery, higher postage for postcards sent from Predappio, and other ways of turning a profit for the public treasury from those who came to worship the remains of Mussolini.

In a more serious vein, *Il Mondo* observed that the political culture of Fascism had always been based on death. The Fascist path followed a straight line that led from 1919 to 1957, from the earliest militants who gathered in Piazza San Sepolcro in Milan to those clustered around the holy sepulchre of Predappio. It wasn't by chance, wrote *Il Mondo*, that in 1946 neo-Fascists made a hero of Domenico Leccisi. Nor was it insignificant that the young neo-Fascist had received twelve thousand votes, thereby defeating illustrious captains of the old Fascist regime: "To the neo-Fascist voters of Milan, the prestige of those who played an august role under Mussolini was nothing compared with the glory attained by an obscure young man who had come to attention for his mortuary high jinks. . . . It reminds one of the Ishmaelite sect, who pay in solid gold the living weight of the Aga Khan. The Fascists would like to pay the dead weight of their Duce in electoral votes." The pilgrims who came from all over Italy to assemble at Mussolini's crypt, observed *Il Mondo*, were the genuine heirs of Domenico Leccisi, "the most sincere Fascist of all time."[11]

The cemetery quickly became a site of pilgrimage. On Sunday, September 8, 1957, thirty-five hundred Fascist faithful turned up to line the pathways of the little country graveyard. They came from all over but especially from Rome and Milan, the younger Fascists predominating over older veterans. Forty-two were charged with offenses under the Scelba Act, which outlawed neo-Fascist demonstrations, for wearing black shirts or making the Fascist salute. Among those arrested were two young men who would play an important role in the neo-Fascist movement: one, a young attorney from Bergamo, Mirko Tremaglia, would one day be a party leader; the other, a Roman militant, Stefano Delle Chiaie, would be implicated in terrorist activities.

The minister of the interior, Christian Democrat Fernando Tambroni, had sent an order barring entry to anyone "dressed in a black shirt."[12] But outlawing black shirts did not resolve the problem. A neo-Fascist from Tuscany was charged with having distributed the text of a poem entitled "Piazzale . . ." The walls of the town were plastered with posters predicting that Il Duce's spirit would rise again. On Sunday, September 22, some seven thousand neo-Fascists converged on Predappio, arriving in fifty buses and hundreds of private cars. Many wore black shirts and most waved neo-Fascist pennants, raised their arms in the Fascist salute, and chanted songs from Mussolini's day. The police, following Tambroni's orders, stopped all those in black shirts at the gates of the cemetery, so that soon the place was crowded with men in their undershirts.

It was hard to ignore the numbers arriving at Mussolini's tomb, especially when their rituals were so explicit. Nevertheless, the anti-Fascist press generally avoided using the occasion to denounce the neo-Fascists. Rather than attack head-on, anti-Fascist opinion makers chose to muse ironically on the celebrations at San Casciano. In the long run, maybe the real beneficiaries of Mussolini's move to Predappio would be the vendors of *piadine*—a kind of local sandwich—and those who sold Fascist memorabilia, *Il Mondo* wrote; in that case, Mussolini could finally take credit for having done something for Italy's humble classes. But comments of this sort—which ultimately proved correct—did not convince everyone. In the fall of 1957, a number of anti-Fascists rallied against the pilgrimages to Predappio, convinced the neo-Fascists were sullying the memory of the Resistance. Their protests were but a tiny ripple in the complicated history of postwar Italy, but these scuffles sowed the seeds for the furious anti-Fascist demonstrations that would erupt all over Italy in 1960 when the government embraced the extreme right. The protests at Predappio were at once spontaneous and organized. On September 29 local Socialist and Communist parties called out their militants to demonstrate at the Predappio cemetery. According to the police, the Communists even went so far as to infiltrate neo-Fascist ranks with provocateurs, hoping to incite trouble. The local Christian Democrats, although they deplored the left-wing militancy, were concerned enough to call for an end to the neo-Fascist reunions.

More daunting than their organized protest was the spontaneous anger of the anti-Fascists at Predappio. Lining the road to the cemetery, local Resistance veterans and left-wing activists had greeted the buses of arriving neo-Fascists with a hail of stones. The effect was such that the local secretary of the Italian Social Movement sent out a letter to neo-Fascists all over Italy advising them how to get to the cemetery without incident—and, above all, how to keep up a vigil rather than running away after fifteen minutes. "Otherwise our visits to places of Mussolini memory will appear hasty and elicit the usual unflattering comments about us," the neo-Fascist party secretary wrote.[13]

The prefect of Forlì, responsible for Predappio, banned anti-Fascist demonstrations planned for September 29 "because of the heated atmosphere created by activists, extremists, and provocateurs of the left."[14] That Sunday, some three thousand Fascists turned up to pay homage at Mussolini's tomb, and the police were mostly able to keep order. In his telegraph to the interior minister, the prefect was able to claim a victory for democratic freedom over the machinations of "Communists and their satellites," who were determined to disturb "the influx of visitors to the famous tomb."[15] For the pilgrims of San Casciano, the prefect of Forlì was the perfect defender, for like other prefects of the 1950s he saw his role as defending Italy from the Communists. When several Communist deputies asked Interior Minister Tambroni why he had not charged Predappio's neo-Fascist visitors with violating the law against forming military associations, the prefect of Forlì offered a helping hand:

> It would be useful to point out that because of the small number (155) who have so far come wearing black shirts,

representing just 6 percent of the visitors (a total of 25,510) in the period from August 31 to September 29, and because of the variety of styles of clothing worn and the absence of pins and buttons, it cannot be said that conditions have been met to apply the aforementioned law."[16]

The battles of San Casciano, with stones hurled and legal codes brandished, was not fought only in the province of Forlì. All of Italy had an opinion on the matter and the telegrams flew. Fascists sent Rachele Mussolini a deluge of condolences, as if Il Duce had just died. Anti-Fascists directed their missives to Tambroni, urging him to apply the spirit and the letter of the constitution and stop the pilgrimages to Predappio.

The clash was also played out on Italy's walls, in the form of political posters. Il Duce, who had controlled the walls for years with Fascist slogans, was back with the controversy over his afterlife. The most violent exchanges took place in Terni, in central Italy. Posters celebrating Mussolini's burial at Predappio were covered with fresh bulletins from the Communists, deploring the "macabre" collusion between Christian Democrats and Fascist followers. The neo-Fascists accused the Communists of wanting to rekindle the civil war "in the name of an anti-Fascism that is by now dead and buried."[17] Each side claimed to smell decay in the other. In Verona, Christian Democrat ex-partisans promised to fight anyone seeking to "draw putrid breath from a corpse to infect the conscience of Italians."[18] Local neo-Fascists replied that Catholics should not forget that the Church commanded mercy, including burial of the dead.

Clearly the Italian Social Movement intended to prolong the Predappio pilgrimages right through the spring, thus putting Il Duce's body to work in the 1958 election campaign. Interior Minister Tambroni decided it was time to intervene. Appealing to the transportation minister, Armando Angelini, he said that he did not want to take extraordinary measures, but urged him to move quickly to stop bus companies from facilitating trips to Predappio. So Tambroni appeared to guarantee freedom of travel around Italy, including freedom to travel to Predappio, while behind the scenes he was maneuvering to stop the visits to Mussolini's grave. On Sunday, October 6, only three buses arrived at San Casciano, but many visitors came in automobiles, so there were still eighteen hundred of them. Still, the number of visitors dropped as the weeks wore, which may well have been due to dropping temperatures rather than to Tambroni's cleverness.

As *Il Mondo* had suggested, the Christian Democrats who laid Mussolini to rest did not get the far right's full approval, nor did they escape the left's furious protests. The neo-Fascists were unhappy about the sneaky, semi-clandestine way the body had been returned to Predappio. The left was convinced that Zoli and especially Tambroni were overriding the constitution and hence were dangerous enemies of the Resistance's achievements. A letter from the National Association of Partisans of Parma to Tambroni seemed to anticipate resentments that would, by 1960, trigger far more significant anti-Fascist uprisings. The veterans of Parma did not protest Mussolini's burial in Predappio. Rather, they challenged the Fascist license to travel across Italy wearing black shirts and singing "Giovinezza," the Fascist hymn. The ex-partisans urged Tambroni to heed the constitution, including the rule forbidding the reconstitution of the Fascist Party. If the police, always ready to block "legal, peaceful, and harmless democratic demonstrations," continued to stand by while the neo-Fascists carried on, the National Association of Partisans would gladly take on the job of "enforcing respect for the constitution and the law."[19]

In the long odyssey of Il Duce's body, the last chapter—the return to Predappio—is of interest for its element of premonition. Tambroni decided to ignore anti-Fascist protests in 1957–58. Three years later, in a historic moment, Tambroni, now prime minister in a government backed by neo-Fascists, defended the Italian Social Movement once more, allowing the party to hold a national congress in Genoa. He did so despite the furious rebellion of that part of Italy which clung to the Resistance. Stones tossed against some buses at San Casciano in September 1957 escalated to war in the streets throughout Italy in July 1960; Tambroni sought to impose his rule—and lost. The anti-Fascist demonstrations were so significant that never again would the Christian Democrats govern with neo-Fascist backing, preferring to seek partners on the left.

It was a moment of dramatic political tensions, and there were fears that Tambroni would attempt a coup d'état. But he was simply a man with an authoritarian vision of the role of the state. His vision was undoubtedly misguided, and he was certainly very stubborn. He had not learned the lesson of the anti-Fascist protests of 1957, which was that Italians were ready to mobilize in the name of a different grief and a different memory from those of the neo-Fascists. In 1958 and 1959, Tambroni had been warned repeatedly not to allow the Resistance to be scorned at the San Casciano cemetery. To those who continued to honor the Resistance, the pilgrimage to Predappio had itself become Fascist mythology. In *La Dolce Vita*, which came out in 1959, director Federico Fellini and fellow screenwriter Ennio Flaiano depict this mythic quality: "From all over Italy, we all came," says the spiffily dressed former Fascist official at the party in the Castelli Romani. "And it was a beautiful ceremony, sad and moving. It was the people—really the people—bringing flowers to their beloved captain."[20] As the years went by, the rites at Predappio showed the small scale of hard-core Il Duce worshippers. There was no longer reason to feel that vague sense of guilt which had prompted many Italians (including ex-Fascists) to worry that Mussolini's body would never find peace. Now the guardians of the flame could be counted, and they were few—unwitting caricatures of distant Fascists. "They're people living with myths that don't hold up anymore," said Fellini of the characters in *La Dolce Vita*.[21]

Only a little more than a decade after the civil war, it was still too soon to take the act of mourning lightly. The corpse of Il Duce still had the power to elicit the veneration of the neo-Fascists, but also the hatred of the guardians of the Resistance. Monuments to partisan dead were still all that was needed to remind many Italians that their republic was founded on sacrifice. And the children of Italy's "economic miracle," the postwar generation, turned out to be profoundly aware of the sacrifices made by their fathers' generation. So the riots of the summer of 1960 were steeped in memories of the dead. When, at the end of June, Genoa rose up against the proposed neo-Fascist party congress, Socialist leader and ex-partisan Sandro Pertini watched the crowds go wild when he said their revolt was inspired by "the fallen of Benedicta" and "the martyrs of the Student Residence Hall"—references to the civil war's Genovese anti-Fascist dead.[22] Even before the neo-Fascist delegates arrived in Genoa, scuffles with police began at the Resistance memorial on Via XX Settembre. Try as they might, the police were unable to prevent the anti-Fascist crowds from laying wreaths at the site. For their part, the congress delegates were no less determined to fight this battle. The neo-Fascists insisted on holding their events at the Teatro Margherita, only a few meters from the partisan memorial.

In Rome, too, on July 6, police and anti-Fascists clashed at the plaque to the partisan dead in Porta San Paolo. Next came the Resistance veterans of Reggio Emilia, who turned out at the Piazza della Libertà to demonstrate at the monument to their fallen comrades. The police fired into the crowd and five demonstrators were killed. "Oh, dead of Reggio Emilia / Come from the grave, / Come out and sing with us, / Bandiera Rossa": the new martyrs of the partisan cause had become the heroes of one of the most powerful political songs of the postwar period.[23]

Epilogue

The fall of the Tambroni government following the anti-Fascist protests of July 1960 marked a sea change for the Christian Democrats. Those in the party who favored a coalition with the left now had the upper hand over those who preferred an alliance with the extreme right. Simultaneously, Tambroni's fall marked the failure of Italian Social Movement secretary Arturo Michelini's attempt to secure a place in the government for the neo-Fascist party and to give it a larger role than that of shadow backer. The events of 1960 created a split within the party, with the radical right bent on subverting democratic institutions and increasingly finding its allies among rogue elements of the secret services ready to engage in terrorist activities. Meanwhile Italian Social Movement leaders sought to "de-Fascistize" the party, eliminating the symbols and the rituals that tied it to the past— black shirts, Fascist flags, and memorial masses for Il Duce. Domenico Leccisi, who had rejoined the party at the end of the 1950s, thought that policy was an attack on the very foundations of neo-Fascist political culture. In 1963, his battle with the leadership came to a head when he was not reelected and was subsequently expelled from the party. In August 1964, Leccisi found himself in Milan's San Vittore prison for tossing fireworks into a crowd that had assembled in the city to mark the death of Communist leader Palmiro Togliatti.

The sixties were hard times for those who worshipped the memory of Mussolini. After the demonstrations of 1960, the Resistance began a process of ideological and moral rehabilitation, and Il Duce ceased to hold an important place in Italian hearts. Not that the illustrated weeklies suddenly ceased publishing their endless stories about the life and death of Mussolini or that writers of popular history books stopped disclosing "revelations" about his last hours, about what happened to the money at Dongo, and about the passions of Claretta. But television was replacing the popular press as the medium that counted. Although state television was cautious when it came to the minefield of contemporary history, the footage that replaced photographs did little for Mussolini's posthumous reputation.

The films of Il Duce delivering his orations in Piazza Venezia, especially, looked different on TV than in still photographs. Mussolini had learned the art of conducting a rally at the beginning of the century, prior to microphones and film crews, at a time when a loud voice and exaggerated stage gestures were necessary. In the years he held power, Il Duce never changed his method of public speaking, and the crowds that turned out to hear him didn't seem to mind his artificial style, or at least they didn't complain on record. In fact, Il Duce's peculiar oratorical style helped cement the powerful hold his physical person had on his followers. Watched thirty years later on television, however, Mussolini's rallies in Piazza Venezia look incongruous, even ridiculous.

The TV version deprived Il Duce of his aura of power, reducing his charisma to a series of grotesque postures, theatrical grimaces, and street hawker's hollering. Unreeling in Italian living rooms like an old comedy, the footage made the dictator look foolish. Who could take seriously that windbag puppet standing on the balcony of Palazzo Venezia? What did his silly theatrics have to say about the malevolent power of a totalitarian regime? In the worried judgment of a young Turinese anti-Fascist writing in 1963, "The laughter distances us from that era, turning it all into pure spectacle . . . and freeing us of it."[1] Both the weeklies of the 1950s and the television documentaries of the 1960s tended to domesticate the memory of Fascism and its chief, the magazines by moving their readers to compassion, television by making people laugh.

If Mussolini no longer frightened anyone, neither did the Resistance. In the 1960s the popular image of the Resistance was simplified, shorn of its elements of hate and violence and softened with stories of heroism rather than references to the civil war. When it came to contemporary history, Italian schoolbooks offered a prudish version of the past. They had little or nothing to say about Mussolini's death and the events of Piazzale Loreto. The schoolbooks of subsequent decades followed suit. Generations of Italian students saw reproductions in their history books of late-eighteenth-century prints depicting the death of Louis XVI—the guillotine, the executioner, the head of the king separated from his body and waved before the crowd. But how many of them learned anything about the terrible lesson of Piazzale Loreto—the crossbar at the gas station, Il Duce strung up by his feet, the bloodthirsty crowd applauding? In the republic born of the Resistance, Italy's most tragic piazza was a place of memory to be forgotten. The legendary merchant who supposedly bought the historic crossbar would never see the day when he could resell it as

Resistance memorabilia rather than as scrap iron. The memory of Piazzale Loreto was kept alive not by ex-partisans but by neo-Fascists fanning the flames of anger.

The far-left militants of 1968 and after did, however, appropriate the image of Il Duce's strung-up body. "We like Almirante better head-down," the demonstrators sang of Giorgio Almirante, leader of the neo-Fascist party.[2] "In the streets and in the squares / All the Fascists with their heads cracked open," they chanted, appropriating the savagery of Piazzale Loreto. But few anti-Fascists embraced such brutal slogans, especially not during the 1970s, marked as they were by terrorism and political violence. In fact, widespread horror at terrorist brutality in Italy cooled enthusiasm for the violence of the Resistance, and it became more difficult to posit Piazzale Loreto as a supreme example of liberation. Even anti-Fascist radicals found the memory of Piazzale Loreto instructive but hard to commemorate. Italo Calvino, in his magnificent essay "Portraits of Il Duce," proposed one possibility: "Having brought about so many deaths where there were no pictures, Mussolini left us his last pictures—of his own death. They are not nice to look at or to remember. However, I wish all dictators who are now in power or who aspire to be, whether 'progressives' or reactionaries, would keep those pictures framed by their bedsides and study them every night."[3]

But between the 1970s and the 1980s, a revisionist trend in Italian historical writing tarnished Resistance rhetoric even further, suggesting that anti-Fascists were poisonously dogmatic and moralistic. The new trend was to see Fascists in an indulgent light, studying their private lives rather than their politics. At the centenary of his birth, in 1983, the former dictator was one of the main beneficiaries of this approach. TV documentaries, newspaper articles, and popular history books revived the cliché of Mussolini as an ardent husband, a devoted father, an affectionate grandfather, not to mention a statesman ready to sacrifice himself for the good of all Italians.

The Resistance point of view was showing signs of wear after years of dominance, in part because the conflicts inherent in Italian democracy after the civil war were now subsiding. Some Resistance veterans began to regret that Mussolini's summary execution had not allowed them to stage an Italian Nuremberg in which the Fascist regime's historical responsibilities would have been exposed and condemned with proper argumentation. Other partisan veterans asked themselves what they would have done in the place of Colonel Valerio, had they found themselves on the shores of Lake Como with Il Duce's life in their hands. One of them was the novelist Luigi Meneghello:

> My first impulse would have been to hide him, so as to give myself time to reflect and then to talk to him. This "talk to him" was something that was always in the planning but never actually took place. In truth I didn't have anything concrete to communicate to Il Duce, and I didn't want to know anything from him. Still, the idea of directing his last hours in captivity—of coming to agreement on the details with him, so as to guarantee the seriousness of what was going to happen—was something that burned bright in me. I wanted his and my acts and words to be thoughtful, to be about what I would call the essence of his life and ours. In short, I wanted to prepare myself well for his death.[4]

Meneghello is torn between competing sentiments. On the one hand, there is the certainty that the body of Il Duce strung from the crossbar of the gas station, his arms spread in a kind of dive as if to plow into the earth, represented poetic justice, bore the seal of a punishment deserved. On the other hand, he feels

Revived, the ardent husband, devoted father, affectionate grandfather (a photomontage from 1942).   (*Istituto Luce*)

regret about the hastiness of the ceremony in Piazzale Loreto, when truth was simplified. "That scarecrow turned upside down," Meneghello writes, "didn't he too quickly become our scapegoat?"[5] In the half century since April 29, 1945, few Italians have pondered the uneasy legacy of Piazzale Loreto as deeply as Meneghello, who dissects the uneasiness of a scene more theatrical than serious, an execution without comment, a sort of Greek tragedy without a chorus.

THE PARTISAN STRUGGLE was in fact made up of radical volunteers, although that was a truth the left had trouble admitting, not wanting to challenge the notion that the Resistance had been a great collective uprising of the Italian people. Hence the Communist Party's caution celebrating Walter Audisio, hence the reticence of partisan literature on the historical problem of Mussolini's execution. Just after Silvio Berlusconi's center-right coalition won the 1994 elections, footage of the scene at Piazzale Loreto filmed by American photographers was broadcast on Italian TV. Furious about the electoral results, editorialists of the center-left attacked those responsible for broadcasting "Combat Film," as the transmission was called. The program's presenter, Vittorio Zucconi, who had commented that "kicking the corpses of Mussolini and Petacci was a stain on Italy's first republic," was attacked by the center-left press as a tool of the new government (which included Alleanza Nazionale, the National Alliance, successor to the Italian Social Movement and heir to the neo-Fascist legacy) and for having "lobotomized the memory" of Italians.[6] Watching "Combat Film," anti-Fascists recognized, unhappily, that times had changed. Three decades after their crowning moment in July 1960, it had once again become possible to claim anything, even that Fascism and the Resistance were moral equivalents, even that Piazzale Loreto and the Nazi murders of 335 civilians at the Fosse Ardeatine were comparable events.

The reaction to "Combat Film" was alarmed and emphatic: historians warned of the danger of translating compassion for the losers into a full-blown revisionist history of Italy. Even a terrible death, wrote one of the most acute historians of neo-Fascism, did not make a wrong cause right.[7] A journalist made fun of the revisionist logic, likening it to Ionesco's syllogism of the absurd ("All cats are mortal; Socrates is mortal; therefore Socrates is a cat"). "Fascists and anti-Fascists are mortal," she continued. "Therefore Mussolini and the Resistance are the same thing. They are both cats."[8]

An intellectual of Jewish origins criticized "Combat Film" not so much for its lionizing of the Blackshirts as for the excuses it made for the great silent middle. Presenting the past as a problem of deaths rather than as a problem of moral choices excused all those who made no choices, those who refused to take sides, he said.[9] A well-known commentator, Guido Ceronetti, suggested that the program showed the crazy power that the death exerted over the living, for the corpse of Mussolini, seen on the TV screen, emanated a disturbing "death energy": "It is strange, the posthumous recognition Mussolini has achieved—there is almost something of an invisible vendetta about it. . . . Mussolini's ghost can only laugh at the secret necro-sadism of several million pairs of eyes fascinated by the gruesome stringing up of two corpses. For his part, he has forgotten the insults and cruelty of Piazzale Loreto, but he enjoys seeing himself as the center of attention, and even of the passions, of his Italians."[10]

It was journalist Giorgio Bocca who put things back in perspective. The passion with which Italians had watched "Combat Film," he suggested, should not be seen only as a symptom of an infectious historical revisionism that humanized Mussolini and granted a historical identity and moral dignity to followers of the Republic of Salò. The dispute needed to be seen in the context of a society dominated by television. "What is and what was do not exist; the only thing that exists is what television allows us to see," wrote Bocca, a former partisan.[11] Half a century after Mussolini's death, the body of Il Duce could come to life only on television.

IS IT REALLY true that in Italy today, Mussolini lives only within the frame of a television screen? The enthusiasm for programs that show footage from Istituto Luce, the historical archive, would suggest that he does. Such footage is often dominated by the figure of Il Duce, by his words and body language. The images split the generations on the question of Mussolini's charisma. Younger viewers are incredulous that the puffed-up haranguer of Piazza Venezia could have so excited their grandparents or parents, while those who were young during the Fascist era seek to explain the strange air one breathed back then. "Anyone who did not experience the atmosphere of Mussolini firsthand," writes journalist Eugenio Scalfari, "probably cannot understand what it was."[12]

At times, though, Il Duce shows signs of life even outside Italian television. A woman claiming to be Mussolini's "secret daughter" went to court in 1998 to ask that Il Duce's body be dug up for DNA testing. Two books dedicated to the last part of Mussolini's life and his death sold many copies in 1996–97. One was the final volume of historian Renzo De Felice's monumental biography, the other, *Mussolini's Last Five Seconds*, an account by neo-Fascist journalist Giorgio Pisanò. There have also been several novels in which Mussolini returns to Italy. In the best of these, *Swamp*, the ghost of Il Duce haunts the city of Latina, which he founded in the 1930s and which remains half faithful to the Fascist chief, half absorbed in its own narrow concerns. Astride his roaring Motoguzzi motorcycle, Mussolini wanders the streets and along the canals, where he stops to fish out the old toilets and bidets that people throw in the water. But Il Duce was not allowed to rise again in the town of Seravezza, near Lucca, where a planned exhibit of art about him drew protests in the summer of 1997. Paintings of Il Duce made during the Fascist era should not be put on display, said the anti-Fascists, especially since Seravezza stands near the town of Sant' Anna di Stazzema, where the Nazis carried out a brutal reprisal in 1944.

Meanwhile, the news from Predappio has been mixed. With the neo-Fascist Italian Social Movement defunct, replaced by the "post-Fascist" National Alliance, it might have been thought that there was no reason for anyone to make the annual pilgrimage to Mussolini's tomb. Why show up in Predappio on the appointed days—Mussolini's birthday, the anniversary of the March on Rome—if the party no longer identified with the founder of Fascism? To avoid mingling with the repudiators from the National Alliance, the hard-core faithful decided to stop visiting the San Casciano cemetery. "I'm not going to Predappio this year," said Domenico Leccisi in 1995. "I don't want to meet the hypocrites who, having betrayed that great man, still dare to present themselves at his grave."[13]

Leccisi's disdain was not enough, however, to keep the faithful from coming to Predappio. Some 100,000 visitors travel to the cemetery every year, in fact. Following the abolition in 1983 of an ordinance forbidding the sale of Fascist memorabilia, there are now several local shops specializing in Duce paraphernalia—not just postcards and reproductions of period photos of Mussolini but metal busts, tapes of his most famous speeches, and belt buckles, pins, T-shirts, watches, necklaces, and key chains deco-

Predappio, 1997. From postcards to metal busts, tapes of speeches, belts, T-shirts, watches, necklaces, and key chains, the body of Il Duce is still selling briskly. (*Michele Bella*)

rated with portraits of Il Duce. If the shop owners' word is anything to go by, the body of Il Duce is still selling briskly.

But a look at the guest book in the Mussolini crypt at San Casciano cemetery suggests that those sales may mean less than they seem. The visitors to Predappio, many of them very young, know nothing about Mussolini, nothing about the Fascist past, which for them points mainly to their own desire for transgression. A typical inscription brings Mussolini magically up to the political present: "Oh, Duce," it reads, "may your enlightened spirit guide us to free our nation from the filthy Communist sewer of the Ulivo that is oppressing us,"[14] referring to the Ulivo, the Olive Tree, the center-left coalition of Italian politics. Messages in adolescent handwriting say things like "I love you," as if the tomb of the Fascist boss belongs to a rock star. Today, the body of Il Duce stirs mostly apolitical dreams.

In the 1990s the same atmosphere suffused www.mussolini.it, a now-defunct Web site. As the home page opened to the sound of a beating heart—suggesting that Mussolini still lived?—viewers saw a starry sky, a virtual heaven of tranquillity from which Il Duce sent out his messages of peace. But anyone who joined this forum of cyber-Fascists found comments no more pointed than those written in the Predappio guest book. The site's creators did little to stir things up, asking such tame questions as, "Who believes that the government will bring back the Eurotax?"—a onetime levy designed to improve Italy's finances before the launch of the euro. The site is no longer accessible; in the twenty-first century, even Mussolini's virtual afterlife is fading.

Notes

These notes have been substantially abridged from the Italian edition.

Prologue

1. Benito Mussolini, "Coccodrilli," *Il Popolo d'Italia*, June 26, 1920.
2. Benito Mussolini, preface to *Dux*, by Margherita Sarfatti (Milan: Mondadori, 1926), p. 7.
3. Benito Mussolini, *Opera omnia* (Florence: La Fenice, 1961), vol. 34, p. 190.
4. Caterina Bianchi, "Il nudo eroico del fascismo," *Gli occhi di Alessandro: Potere sovrano e sacralità del corpo da Alessandro Magno a Ceausescu*, ed. Sergio Bertelli and Cristiano Grottanelli (Florence: Ponte alle Grazie, 1990) p. 160.
5. Dino Biondi, *La fabbrica del duce* (Florence: Vallecchi, 1966), p. 46.
6. See Francesco Longo, "Era veramente di Matteotti il cadavere della Quartarella?" *l'Unità*, January 31, 1947.
7. See Carmelo Briganti, *La fine di un tiranno: Visione d'Oltremondo* (Lecce: La Modernissima, 1945), p. 51.
8. Biondi, *La fabbrica*, p. 131.
9. "Il vindice sacrificio di Giacomo Matteotti celebrato da Filippo Turati," June 27, 1924; "La dichiarazione delle opposizioni alla Camera.

L'ultimo discorso del martire," *Camera dei Deputati,* May 30, 1924 (Rome: Partito Socialista, 1924), p. 3.

10. As recalled by Umberto Clementi, in *Gramsci vivo nelle testimonianze dei suoi contemporanei,* ed. Mimma Paulesu Quercioli (Milan: Feltrinelli, 1977), p. 197.

11. Leonardo Sciascia, *Le parrocchie di Regelpetra* (1956; rpt. Milan: Adelphi, 1991), p. 43.

12. Leonardo Sciascia, "Il ritratto fotografico come entelechia," *Fatti diversi di storia letteraria e civile* (Palermo: Sellerio, 1989), p. 155.

Chapter One: Tough to Eradicate

1. Carlo Villani, "Stile di Mussolini," *Convivium,* November–December 1937, p. 9.

2. Gec [Enrico Gianeri], *Il Cesare di cartapesta: Mussolini nella caricatura* (Turin: Grandi Edizioni Vega, 1945), n.p.

3. Carlo Delcroix, *Un uomo e un popolo* (Florence: Vallecchi, 1928), p. 3.

4. Indro Montanelli, "Mussolini e noi" (1936), *Eia, eia, alalà: La stampa italiana sotto il fascismo,* ed. Oreste del Buono (Milan: Feltrinelli, 1971), pp. 310–11.

5. Giorgio Boatti, ed., *Caro duce: Lettere di donne italiane a Mussolini, 1922–1943* (Milan: Rizzoli, 1989), p. 61.

6. Vitaliano Brancati, "La mia visita a Mussolini," *Critica fascista,* August 1, 1931, p. 295.

7. Quoted in Renzo De Felice, *L'organizzazione dello Stato fascista,* vol. 2 of *Mussolini il fascista* (Turin: Einaudi, 1968), p. 74.

8. Quoted in Renzo De Felice, *Lo Stato totalitario, 1936–1940,* vol. 2 of *Mussolini il duce* (Turin: Einaudi, 1981), p. 278.

9. Gaetano Salvemini, "Il fascismo senza Mussolini" (1926), *Scritti sul fascismo,* vol. 6 of *Opere complete* (Milan: Feltrinelli, 1966), p. 247.

10. Giuseppe Bottai, "Risultanze dell'inchiesta sull'arte fascista," *Critica fascista,* February 15, 1927, p. 63.

11. From undated notes by Sisto Zamboni in the papers of Roberto Vighi in the Museo del Risorgimento in Bologna.

12. Gustavo Trombetti, Gramsci's cellmate in Turi prison, quoted in Mimma Paulesu Quercioli, ed., *Gramsci vivo nelle testimonianze dei suoi contemporanei* (Milan: Feltrinelli, 1977), p. 235.

13. Quoted in De Felice, *L'organizzazione*, p. 362.

14. Quoted in Emilio Gentile, *La via italiana al totalitarismo: Il partito e lo Stato nel regime fascista* (Rome: La Nuova Italia Scientifica, 1995), p. 214.

15. Quoted in Luisa Mangoni, *L'interventismo della cultura: Intellettuali e riviste del fascismo* (Rome-Bari: Laterza, 1974), p. 235.

16. Leonardo Sciascia, preface to *Attenti al Duce: Storie minime dell'Italia fascista, 1927–1938*, ed. Vincenzo Rizzo (Florence: Vallecchi, 1981), p. vi.

17. Adriano Dal Pont and Simonetta Carolini, eds., *L'Italia dissidente e antifascista: Le Ordinanze, le Sentenze istruttorie e le Sentenze in Camera di consiglio emesse dal Tribunale speciale fascista contro gli imputati di antifascismo dall'anno 1927 al 1943* (Milan: La Pietra, 1980), vol. 1, p. 120.

18. Ibid., p. 249.

19. Ibid., pp. 360, 378, 395.

20. Ibid., p. 542.

21. Quoted in Rizzo, *Attenti al Duce*, pp. 51, 62, 65, 127, 131, 82.

22. Emilio Lussu, *La catena, 1930* (Milan: Baldini e Castoldi, 1977), p. 88.

23. Quoted in Rizzo, *Attenti al Duce*, p. 69.

24. Dal Pont and Carolini, *L'Italia dissidente*, vol 2, p. 864.

25. Quoted in Nicola Gallerano, "Gli italiani in guerra, 1940–1943: Appunti per una ricerca," *Italia contemporanea*, no. 160, 1985, p. 90.

26. Angelo Michele Imbriani, *Gli italiani e il Duce: Il mito e l'immagine di Mussolini negli ultimi anni del fascismo (1938–1943)* (Naples: Liguori, 1992), p. 54.

27. Luisa Passerini, *Torino operaia e fascismo* (Rome-Bari: Laterza, 1984), pp. 131–32.

28. Quoted in Pietro Cavallo, *Italiani in guerra: Sentimenti e immagini dal 1940 al 1943* (Bologna: Il Mulino, 1997), p. 266. The letter was written in November 1942.

29. Ibid., p. 362.

30. Giovanni Battista Ranieri, quoted in Nuto Revelli, *La strada del davai* (Turin: Einaudi, 1966), p. 431.

31. Gaetano Salvemini, "L'Italia e la pace separata" (1942), *L'Italia vista dall'America*, vol. 7 of *Opere complete* (Milan: Feltrinelli, 1969), p. 65.

32. Vincenzo Vacirca, *Mussolini: Storia di un cadavere* (New York: La Strada, 1942).

33. Ibid, pp. 208–11.

34. Salvemini, "L'Italia e la pace separata," p. 65.

35. Aldo Palazzeschi, *Tre imperi . . . mancati: Cronaca, 1922–1945* (Florence: Vallecchi, 1946), pp. 129–30, 195.

36. Giovanni Pesce, *Quando cessarono gli spari: 23 aprile–6 maggio 1945: La liberazione di Milano* (Milan: Feltrinelli, 1977), p. 75.

37. Quoted in Ivo Dalla Costa, ed., *L'Italia imbavagliata: Lettere censurate, 1940–43* (Treviso: Pagus, 1990), p. 152.

38. Quoted in Cavallo, *Italiani in guerra,* p. 386.

39. Ibid.

40. Publifoto archive, Milan. I am grateful to Giulia Carrese and Lella Masotti for letting me see these documents.

41. See the recent account by Silvio Bertoldi, *Colpo di stato: 25 luglio '43: Il "ribaltone" del fascismo* (Milan: Rizzoli, 1996), p. 270.

42. Quoted in Enzo Santarelli, *Nenni* (Turin: Utet, 1988), p. 248.

43. Quoted in Renzo De Felice, *La guerra civile, 1943–45,* vol. 2 of *Mussolini l'alleato* (Turin: Einaudi, 1997), p. 19.

44. Quoted in Nicola Gallerano, "Critica e crisi del paradigma antifascista," *Problemi del socialismo,* no. 7, 1986, p. 106.

45. Quoted in Mario Isnenghi, *Intellettuali militanti e intellettuali funzionari: Appunti sulla cultura fascista* (Turin: Einaudi, 1979), p. 272.

46. Commander Ussari, a character in Carlo Mazzantini's *A cercar la bella morte* (Venice: Marsilio, 1995), p. 148.

47. Carlo Mazzantini, *I balilla andarono a Salò: L'armata degli adolescenti che pagò il conto della storia* (Venice: Marsilio, 1995), p. 156.

48. Longanesi's fantasy is reported in Piero Calamandrei, *Diario, 1939–1945* (Florence: La Nuova Italia, 1982), vol. 1, p. 26.

49. Salvatore Satta, *De profundis* (Milan: Adelphi, 1980), pp. 104–05. Completed in 1944–45, the text was not published until 1948.

50. Quoted in Jeffrey T. Schnapp, *Staging Fascism: 18BL and the Theater of Masses for Masses* (Stanford: Stanford University Press, 1996).

51. Benito Mussolini, *Storia di un anno (Il tempo della bastone e della carota)* in *Opera omnia,* vol. 34, p. 396.

52. Ibid., p. 398.

53. Quoted in Pesce, *Quando cessarono gli spari,* p. 129.

54. Quoted in Giovanni Artieri, *Le guerre dimenticate di Mussolini, Etiopia e Spagna* (Milan: Mondadori, 1995), p. 283.

55. Mario Borsa, "Riscossa," *Il Nuovo corriere,* April 26, 1945.

56. Reprinted in Pietro Nenni, *Vento del Nord: Giugno 1944–giugno 1945* (Turin: Einaudi, 1978), pp. 355–56.

57. Unsigned article, "L'uomo e gli vomini," *Rinascita*, April 1945, p. 105.

58. Lampredi's memo was published as "La fine del Duce" in *l'Unità*, January 23, 1996.

59. Giovanni Ansaldo, *Diario di prigionia* (Bologna: Il Mulino, 1993), p. 345.

60. Ibid., pp. 346, 355, 427.

Chapter Two: The Ox of the Nation

1. Corrado Alvaro, *Quasi una vita: Giornale di uno scrittore* (Milan: Bompiani, 1950), p. 354.

2. As witnessed by the Communist partisan Mario Filipponi in Alessandro Portelli, *Biografia di una città: Storia e racconto: Terni, 1830–1985* (Turin: Einaudi, 1985), p. 282.

3. I quote from the diary of a Turinese man of Jewish origin who escaped persecution by taking refuge in an insane asylum in San Maurizio Canavese (Renzo Segre, *Venti mesi* [Palermo: Sellerio, 1995], p. 67).

4. Piero Malvezzi and Giovanni Pirelli, eds., *Lettere di condannati a morte della Resistenza italiana (8 settembre 1943–25 aprile 1945)* (1952; rpt. Turin: Einaudi, 1975), p. 325.

5. Ibid., p. 270.

6. Ibid., p. 170.

7. Ibid., p. 75.

8. As witnessed by Camilla Cederna, a young journalist who would later become well known (*Milano in guerra* [Milan: Feltrinelli, 1979], p. 16).

9. Quoted in Ricciotti Lazzaro, *Le brigate nere* (Milan: Rizzoli, 1983), p. 66.

10. Elio Accrocca and Valerio Volpini, eds., *Antologia poetica della Resistenza italiana* (San Giovanni Valdarno: Landi, 1956), pp. 34, 54, 156, 91.

11. Alfonso Gatto, *La storia delle vittime: Poesie della Resistenza (1943–47, 1963–65)* (Milan: Mondadori, 1966), pp. 72–73.

12. Padre Pacifico Valungani, "Nota cronistorica, 26 aprile 1945," *Nemesi: Dal 25 aprile al 28 aprile 1945: Documenti e testimonianze sulle ultime ore di Mussolini*, ed. Renoto Salvadori (Milan: Gnocchi, 1945), pp. 64–66.

13. Ibid., p. 67.

14. Quoted in Anita Pensotti, *Rachele e Benito: Biografia di Rachele Mussolini* (Milan: Mondadori, 1993), p. 121.

15. I quote a participant in Damiano Damiani's TV documentary *Piazzale Loreto* in the series *Finché dura la memoria* by F. Falcone.

16. The journalist was Gualtiero Jacopetti, as quoted in Angelo Del Boca, *Nostalgia delle colonie*, vol. 4 of *Gli italiani in Africa orientale* (Milan: Mondadori, 1996), p. 91.

17. Oreste Del Buono, *La debolezza di scrivere* (Venice: Marsilio, 1987), p. 53.

18. Ibid., p. 54.

19. Quoted in V. Costa, *L'ultimo federale. Memoirie della guerra civile, 1943–1945* (Bologna: Il Mulino, 1997), pp. 23, 121.

20. Lorenzo Greco, *Censura e scrittura: Vittorini, lo pseudo-Malaparte, Gadda* (Milan: Il Saggiatore, 1983), p. 82.

21. Carlo Mazzantini, *A cercar la bella morte* (Venice: Marsilio, 1995), pp. 298, 299.

22. Caio M. Cattabeni, "Rendiconto di un'autopsia di eccezione" (1945), reprinted in Giorgio Pisanò, *Gli ultimi cinque secondi di Mussolini* (Milan: Il Saggiatore, 1996), p. 196.

23. Curzio Malaparte, "Una partita di ping-pong," *Due anni di battibecco, 1953–1955* (Milan: Garzanti, 1955), p. 28.

24. *Avanti!*, April 30, 1945. See the interpretation of Claudio Pavone, *Una guerra civile: Saggio storico sulla moralità nella Resistenza* (Turin: Bollati Boringhieri, 1991), p. 514.

25. Ibid.

26. An anonymous anti-Fascist eyewitness from Romagna, quoted in Pavone, *Una guerra civile*, p. 513.

27. "Trionfali accoglienze di Milano libera alle truppe alleate che restituiscono vita e dignità all'Italia e all'Europa," *L'Italia libera*, special Milanese ed., April 29, 1945.

28. Gaetano Afeltra, "Quelle quindici foto firmate Fedele Toscani," *Corriere della Sera*, April 13, 1994.

29. Alvaro, *Quasi una vita*, p. 375.

30. State Archives, Milan, Prefecture, Gabinetto, versamento 2, cat. 029, busta 337, *Fotografie di Mussolini e della sua amante dopo la morte: Sequestro*. I quote from a letter dated May 20, 1945, on Comune di Milano letterhead.

31. "Monito" [unsigned], *Rinascita*, April 1945, p. 119.

32. Luigi Meneghello, *Bau-sète!* (1988; rpt. Milan: Bompiani, 1996), p. 38.

33. Mino Caudana, "Edda mi ha detto," *Oggi*, July 1, 1947, p. 9.

34. Quoted in Luisa Passerini, *Torino operaia e fascismo* (Rome-Bari: Laterza, 1984), pp. 119–20.

35. Adolfo Omodeo to Luigi Russo, May 4, 1945, *Lettere, 1910–1946* (Turin: Einaudi, 1963).

36. Meneghello, *Bau-sète!*, p. 20.

37. Il Pontiere [Piero Calamandrei], "Idrometro," *Il Ponte*, June 1945, p. 254.

38. *La Capitale*, April 30, 1945, quoted in Mirco Dondi, "Piazzale Loreto 29 aprile: Aspetti di una pubblica esposizione," *Rivista di storia contemporanea*, 1990, p. 222.

39. Umberto Saba, "Totem e tabù," *Scorciatoie e raccontini* (Milan: Mondadori, 1946), p. 108.

40. Giovanni Ansaldo, *Diario di prigionia* (Bologna: Il Mulino, 1993), p. 348.

41. Aldo Carpi, *Diario di Gusen* (Turin: Einaudi, 1993), p. 159.

42. Giampiero Carocci, *Il campo degli ufficiali* (1954; rpt. Florence: Giunti, 1995), pp. 167–68.

43. E. Benedetto, *Racconti del tempo perduto* (Rome: Arte-Vivà, 1968), pp. 207–08.

44. Central State Archives, Presidenza del Consiglio dei Ministri, 1944–47, folder 1–7 35849, "Fucilazione di Benito Mussolini nel Nord Italia." From the Italian embassy in Paris, May 3, 1945.

45. Ibid. From the Italian embassy in London, May 3, 1945, report signed by Ambassador Niccolò Carandini, a Liberal.

Chapter Three: An Unquiet Grave

1. Marcella Ferrara and Maurizio Ferrara, *Cronache di vita italiana, 1944–1958* (Rome: Editori Riuniti, 1960), p. 77; Giuseppe Fiori, *Vita di Enrico Berlinguer* (Rome-Bari: Laterza, 1989), p. 57.

2. "La Costituente all'ordine del giorno del paese," *Avanti!*, May 11, 1945.

3. Quoted in Agostino Giovagnoli, *La cultura democristiana: Tra Chiesa cattolica e identità italiana, 1918–1948* (Rome-Bari: Laterza, 1991), p. 153.

4. Quoted in Ugo Zatterin, *Al Viminale con il morto. Tra lotte e botte l'Italia di ieri* (Milan: Baldini e Castoldi, 1996), pp. 90–91.

5. Giovanni Artieri, *Umberto II e la crisi della monarchia* (Milan: Mondadori, 1983), p. 57.

6. State Archives, Milan, Prefecture, Gabinetto, second collection, cat. 031, "Affari riservati," 1946, envelope 471. I quote from a letter by Angelo Marco Pagani, mailed in Milan on November 7, 1946.

7. Orio Vergani, *Misure del tempo: Diario 1950–1959* (Milan: Leonardo, 1990), p. 17.

8. "Mussolini-Hitler e viceversa," *Oggi*, August 13, 1946, p. 13.

9. Reprinted in Elio Vittorini, *Gli anni del "Politecnico": Lettere, 1945–1951*, (Turin: Einaudi, 1977), p. 417.

10. Vittorio Gorresio, *Un anno di libertà* (Rome: Edizioni Polilibraria, 1945), p. 106.

11. Angelo Scarpellini, ed., *La Repubblica sociale italiana nelle lettere dei suoi caduti* (1962; rpt. Rimini: l'Ultima Crociata Editrice, 1995), p. 42.

12. From the State Archives, Milan, Prefecture, Gabinetto, second collection, cat. 031, "Affari riservati," 1946, envelope 470.

13. Indro Montanelli, *Qui non riposano* (Milan: Tarantola, 1945), p. 7.

14. Edilio Rusconi, "Per l'uomo della strada," *Oggi*, September 15, 1945.

15. Montanelli, *Qui non riposano*, p. 188; Montanelli, "Antonio Bianchi, sì o no?," *Oggi*, October 6, 1945.

16. State Archives, Milan, Gabinetto 1944–46, envelope 263, folder 23050, "Milano, movimento fascista," April 6, 1946.

17. "Primo atto della riscossa" and "Piazzale Loreto," *Lotta fascista*, March 1946, pp. 1, 4.

18. State Archives, Milan, Gabinetto 1944–46, envelope 263, folder 25464, "Milano, situazione generale," unsigned report, pp. 7–17.

19. Domenico Leccisi Archive, Milan, from clandestine documents of the Democratic Fascist Party, a flyer dated Lake Como, September 15, 1943.

20. Domenico Leccisi, *Con Mussolini prima e dopo Piazzale Loreto* (Rome: Edizioni Settimo Sigillo, 1991), pp. 176–77.

21. Domenico Leccisi, "Continuità nella rivoluzione sociale," *La Repubblica fascista*.

22. "P," "Confisca e vendita dei beni mobili ebraici: Attendiamo risposta," *Brigata Nera Aldo Resega*, April 7, 1945.

23. Leccisi, *Con Mussolini*, pp. 218–19.

24. State Archives, Milan, Gabinetto 1944–46, envelope 218, folder 22620, "Milano, carceri," "Relazione sui fatti di Milano," April 21–24, 1946, p. 16.

25. Tommaso Besozzi, "Qualche cosa di nuovo a Musocco," *Corriere lombardo*, April 25–26, 1946.

26. Domenico Bartoli, "La salma di Mazzini," *Il Tempo*, July 6–13, 1946, p. 6.

27. Ibid.

28. "Nemici della patria," *l'Unità*, May 1, 1946.

29. State Archives, Milan, Gabinetto 1944–46, envelope 218, folder 2262. "Milano, carceri." See also "Relazione di indagini tecniche di polizia giudiziaria, April 28, 1946." Attached to the text is a photograph of the two bones found in the cart.

30. "Relazione sui fatti di Milano," p. 20.

31. Ibid.

32. Vasco Pratolini, *Un eroe del nostro tempo* (1949; rpt. Milan: Mondadori, 1995), p. 188.

33. State Archives, Milan, Gabinetto 1944–46, envelope 226, folder 23050, "Milano, movimento fascista." The undated anonymous letter was sent to the chief of police from the cabinet of the minister of the interior on May 15, 1946.

34. Domenico Leccisi Archive, Judicial documents, 1946–48, Milan Questura, "Procedimento penale contro Leccisi Domenico ed altri," signed by Questore Vincenzo Agnesina, August 12, 1946, p. 5.

35. Ibid., pp. 26–42. See also attached transcripts of the police questioning of Parozzi, Gasparini, and Leccisi.

36. Ibid., p. 43.

37. "Facevano il 'doppio gioco' i due frati Zucca e Parini," *l'Unità*, August 15, 1946.

38. Roberto Di Monticelli, "La tomba di Mussolini: Nebbiose novità arrivano dal Brasile," *Epoca*, October 6, 1951, p. 16.

39. Tommaso Giglio, "Noi fummo gli ultimi a salire il Calvario," *Il Politecnico*, July–August 1946, p. 49.

40. Alberto Parini, "La nostra vicenda," in *Cronistoria di una salma famosa e diario di 42 giorni di carcere*, by Pasquale Scarpa (Milan: Seti, 1947), pp. 61–63.

41. Ibid., p. 165.

42. State Archives, Milan, Gabinetto 1944–46, envelope 263, folder 25464, "Milano, situazione generale," p. 1 of "Quadro generale."

43. Domenico Leccisi Archive, Judicial documents, 1946–48, Milan Questura, "Procedimento penale," pp. 43–45.

44. *Avanti!*, April 5, 1947.

45. Claudio Pavone, "La continuità dello stato: Istituzioni e uomini," *Alle origini della Repubblica: Scritti su fascismo, antifascismo e continuità dello Stato* (Turin: Bollati Boringhieri, 1995), pp. 70–159.

Chapter Four: Mussolini, Dear Departed

1. Indro Montanelli, *Il buonuomo Mussolini* (Milan: Edizioni Riunite, 1947), p. 9.

2. Curzio Malaparte, *Maledetti toscani* (Florence: Vallecchi, 1956), p. 37.

3. Montanelli, *Il buonuomo*, p. 97.

4. Ibid., p. 100.

5. Ibid., pp. 104–05.

6. Indro Montanelli, *Lettere a Longanesi (e ad altri nemici)* (Milan: Longanesi, 1955), p. 254.

7. [Gian Gaetano Cabella], *Testamento politico di Mussolini, dettato corretto siglato da Lui il 22 aprile 1945* (Rome: Tosi, 1948), pp. 2–3.

8. Alberto Giovannini, "Mussolini ordinò al frate di assolverlo," *Oggi*, April 4, 1948, p. 9.

9. G. P., "Dove è finito il diario di Mussolini?," *Epoca*, June 14, 1953, p. 19; Duilio Susmel, "C'è una Maria che sa come finì il camioncino fantasma," *Epoca*, March 28, 1954, pp. 58–59; Susmel, "Il testamento di Mussolini," *Epoca*, May 15, 1955, pp. 22–26.

10. Cabella, *Testamento politico*.

11. Giuseppe Bottai, *Diario, 1944–1948* (Milan: Rizzoli, 1988), p. 546.

12. Giuseppe Bottai, *Diario, 1935–1944* (Milan: Rizzoli, 1982), p. 212.

13. Giuseppe Bottai, *Vent'anni e un giorno (24 luglio 1943)* (1949; rpt. Milan: Garzanti, 1977), p. 32.

14. Ibid., pp. 25–26.

15. Ibid., pp. 27–32.

16. Paolo Monelli, *Roma 1943* (1945; rpt. Turin: Einaudi, 1993), pp. 27–28.

17. Il Pontiere [Piero Calamandrei], "La Maschera," *Il Ponte*, May 1945, pp. 254–55.

18. Aldo Palazzeschi, *Tre imperi . . . mancati: Cronaca (1922–1945)* (Florence: Vallecchi, 1946), p. 264.

19. Ibid., p. 10.

20. Monelli, *Roma 1943*, p. 41.

21. Gadda's own terminology in a review of Palazzeschi's book: Carlo Emilio Gadda, "Tre imperi," *Saggi giornali favole* (Milan: Garzanti, 1991–92), vol. 1, p. 935.

22. Carlo Emilio Gadda, *Il primo libro delle favole, Saggi giornali favole*, vol. 2, pp. 35–36.

23. Ibid., pp. 35–36, 43–44.

24. Ibid., p. 71.

25. Carlo Emilio Gadda, *Fatto personale . . . o quasi, Saggi giornali favole*, vol. 1, p. 496.

26. Carlo Emilio Gadda, *Un testimone, Saggi giornali favole*, vol. 1, pp. 945–46.

27. Carlo Emilio Gadda, *Eros e Priapo (Da furore a cenere)* (1967; rpt. Milan: Garzanti, 1990), pp. 83, 187.

28. Carlo Emilio Gadda, *That Awful Mess on the Via Merulana* (original Italian ed., 1957; Aventura, 1984).

29. Giulio Cattaneo, *Belfagor*, 1957, p. 607.

30. Gadda, *Eros e Priapo*, p. 120.

31. Bottai, *Diario, 1944–1948*, pp. 367–68.

32. Gadda, *That Awful Mess*, p. 81.

33. Carlo Emilio Gadda, from an early version of *Eros e Priapo, Saggi giornali favole*, vol. 2, p. 1008.

34. Corrado Alvaro, *Quasi una vita: Giornale di uno scrittore* (Milan: Bompiani, 1950), p. 387. Alvaro writes: "I didn't think our priapic cult went so far."

35. Goffredo Parise, *Il prete bello* (Milan: Mondadori, 1986), p. 111.

36. Georg Zachariae, *Mussolini si confessa: Rivelazioni del medico tedesco inviato da Hitler al duce* (Milan: Garzanti, 1948), p. 11.

37. Cesare Rossi, *Mussolini com'era. Radioscopia dell'ex dittatore* (Rome: Ruffolo, 1947), p. 280.

38. Antonino Trizzino, *Mussolini ultimo* (Milan: Bietti, 1968), p. 108.

39. Paolo Monelli, *Mussolini piccolo borghese* (1950; rpt. Milan: Garzanti, 1983), p. 229.

40. Gec, Il Cesare di cartapesta, n.p.

41. Curzio Malaparte, *Diario di uno straniero a Parigi* (Florence: Vallecchi, 1966), pp. 195–96.

42. Curzio Malaparte, *The Skin* (original Italian ed. 1949; Chicago: Northwestern University Press, 1997).

43. Ibid., p. 92.

44. Ibid., p. 47.

45. Vitaliano Brancati, "Messe in suffragio," *Il Tempo*, May 24–31, 1947, p. 8.

46. "Messa nera," in the "Taccuino" column of *Il Mondo*, April 14, 1951, p. 2.

47. Rachele Mussolini, "In sogno lo vedo sempre giovane," *Oggi*, November 7, 1957.

48. Carlo Levi, *The Watch* (original Italian ed. 1950; South Royalton: Steerforth Italia, 2000), p. 67.

49. E. Forcella, "L'ora dei cimiteri," *Il Mondo*, April 13, 1954.

50. Piero Caliandro, *Benito Mussolini senza il fascismo: 12 colloqui dall'al di là* (Milan: Agenzia Rateale Editoriale, 1952), pp. 9–22, 163–79.

51. Marco Ramperti, *Benito I imperatore* (Rome: Sciré, 1950), p. 8.

52. Leo Longanesi, *Un morto fra noi* (Milan: Longanesi, 1952), pp. 281–86.

Chapter Five: The Executioner

1. Miriam Mafai, "Un segreto in quei tempi durissimi," *l'Unità*, January 24, 1996.

2. "Caccia al tesoro," *Oggi*, March 25, 1947.

3. Togliatti's comment is from an unsigned article, "L'esecuzione di Mussolini è un grande merito dei partigiani," *l'Unità*, March 14, 1947.

4. Longo made the comment at a rally in Milan's Palazzo dello Sport, and it was reported in "La verità sul 'tesoro di Dongo,'" *l'Unità*, March 18, 1947.

5. "Chi è Walter Audisio? Legalità e moralità dell'esecuzione di Dongo," *l'Unità*, March 23, 1947.

6. Miriam Mafai, *Botteghe Oscure, addio: Com'eravamo comunisti* (Milan: Mondatori, 1996), p. 34.

7. Roberto Faenza and Marco Fini, *Gli americani in Italia* (Milan: Feltrinelli, 1976), p. 250.

8. Franceseca Gori and Silvio Pons, *Dagli archivi di Mosca: L'URSS, il Cominform, il PCi, 1943–1951* (Rome: Carocci, 1998), pp. 326–27.

9. *Candido*, January 11, 1948.

10. Giovanni Artieri, "Scelba e la rivoluzione," *Il Tempo*, November 29–December 6, 1947, p. 3.

11. Ugo Zatterin, "Valerio agguantò il compagno Pajetta per il collo," *Oggi*, June 13, 1948, p. 5.

12. Ilazio Fiore, "Gli ufficialetti della morte," *Settimana Incom*, March 5, 1949, p. 8.

13. Giulio Salierno, *Autobiografia di un picchiatore fascista* (Turin: Einaudi, 1976), p. 109.

14. Ibid., p. 134.

15. "De Gasperi di fronte alla sua più dura prova," *Il Tempo*, July 2–9, 1953, p. 9.

Chapter Six: The Quality of Mercy

1. "La salma di Mussolini è tumulata al Verano" and [Benso Fini], "Paura di che?," *Corriere lombardo*, October 29–30, 1949.

2. Roberto De Monticelli, *L'educazione teatrale* (Milan: Garzanti, 1986), p. 75.

3. Roberto De Monticelli, "La tomba di Mussolini: A Pavia c'è una firma sul registro dei visitatori," *Epoca*, October 27, 1951, p. 61.

4. Ibid.

5. Vittore Querel, *Il paese di Benito: Cronache di Predappio e dintorni* (Roma: Corso, 1954), p. 22. Querel was the editor in chief of the *Gazzetta dell'Emilia* during the Republic of Salò.

6. Ferrante Azzali, "Il neo Sherlock Holmes scopre i tesori di Mussolini," *Il Tempo*, December 20–27, 1947, p. 21.

7. Alfredo Panicucci, "Celebrano la Messa sulla tomba di Mussolini," *Epoca*, November 7, 1954, p. 30.

8. Roberto De Monticelli, "Tutto è pronto a Predappio," *Epoca*, April 26, 1952, p. 16.

9. Renata Viganò, *L'Agnese va a morire* (Turin: Einaudi, 1954), p. 328.

10. Beppe Fenoglio, *Appunti partigiani, 1944–1945* (Turin: Einaudi, 1994), p. 39.

11. Cesare Pavese, *The House on the Hill*, in *The Selected Works of Cesare Pavese* (New York: New York Review Books, 2001), p. 26.

12. Riccardo Bauer, "Lasciamo dimenticare," *Il Ponte*, April–May 1955, pp. 762–63.

13. The song is "Raffaele," words by Dario Baraldi, music by Fausto Amodei.

14. Salvatore Quasimodo, *Complete Poems* (New York: Schocken, 1983), p. 32.

15. Gaetano Salvemini, "Terrorismo e attentati individuali," *Controcorrente*, March 1947, p. 11.

16. Gaetano Salvemini, "Le voci del cuore," *Belfagor*, 1946, p. 744.

17. Emilio Lussu, *La catena* (1930; rpt. Milan: Baldini e Castoldi, 1997), p. 17.

18. Giovanni Ansaldo, "'Coi piedi per aria': Lettera al professor Salvemini," *Il Borghese*, December 31, 1954, p. 875.

19. Ibid.

20. R. C. [Giovanni Ansaldo], *L'Illustrazione italiana*, September 19, 1948, p. 377.

21. Giovanni Ansaldo, "'Coi piedi per aria,'" p. 875.

22. Domenico Leccisi, "Apparve la sua testa," *Il Tempo*, July 24–31, 1948, p. 9.

23. Domenico Leccisi, "Ci sorprese l'alba," *Il Tempo*, July 31–August 7, 1948, p. 10.

24. Massimo Mila, "Antifascisti, si ricomincia!" (1948), *Scritti civili* (Turin: Einaudi, 1995), p. 274.

25. Vitaliano Brancati, "Uomini-tombe: Soggetti poetici," *Il Tempo*, March 1–8, 1947, p. 5.

26. Domenico Leccisi, "Dalle tenebre alla luce: Difendiamoci," *Lotta d'Italia*, September 16, 1950, p. 1.

27. Piero Malvezzi and Giovanni Pirelli, eds., *Lettere di condannati a morte della Resistenza italiana (8 settembre 1943–25 aprile 1945)* (1952; rpt. Turin: Einaudi, 1975), p. 110.

28. *Il Ponte*, June 1953, p. 729.

29. Unsigned, in the column "Bollettino della libertà della cultura, delle informazioni e delle opinioni," *Il Ponte*, November 1953, p. 1607.

30. Undated press release of the Autonomous Italian Social Movement, the name first assumed by the splinter group to which Leccisi belonged after leaving the Italian Social Movement (Domenico Leccisi Archive, Milan).

31. Emil Ludwig, *Colloqui con Mussolini* (1932; rpt. Milan: Mondadori, 1950), p. 225.

32. Giuseppe Bottai, *Diario, 1944–1948* (Milan: Rizzoli, 1988), pp. 396, 177.

33. Vincenzo Costa, *L'ultimo federale: Memorie della guerra civile, 1943–1945* (Bologna: Il Mulino, 1997), p. 282.

34. Gaetano Salvemini, "Ludwig e Mussolini" (1953), *Scritti vari (1900–1957)* (Milan: Feltrinelli, 1978), p. 281.

35. Renzo Segre, *Venti mesi* (Palermo: Sellerio, 1995), p. 116.

36. Gian Dauli [Ugo G. Nalato], *Mussolini, l'uomo, l'avventuriero, il criminale* (Milan: Lucchi, 1946).

37. Cesare Rossi, *Mussolini com'era: Radioscopia dell'ex-dittatore* (Rome: Ruffolo, 1947), p. 209.

38. Ennio Flaiano, *Diario notturno* (1956), *Opere, 1947–1972* (Milan: Bompiani, 1990), p. 445.

39. "Guardò per l'ultima volta l'obiettivo," *Il Tempo*, September 6–13, 1947, p. 3.

40. Yvon De Begnac, *Palazzo Venezia: Storia di un regime* (Rome: La Rocca, 1950), p. 26.

41. Manlio Lupinacci, "Siamo tutti traditori," *Epoca*, November 29, 1953, p. 49.

42. Manlio Lupinacci, "Hanno tutti un 8 settembre," *Epoca*, September 13, 1953, p. 47.

43. Paolo Monelli, *Mussolini piccolo borghese* (1950; rpt. Milan: Garzanti, 1983), p. 142.

44. From a letter (certainly apocryphal) quoted in "Camicia nera 'a fiori': Estrema divisa," *Settimana Incom*, November 19, 1949, p. 20.

45. Anita Pensotti, *Rachele e Benito: Biografia di Rachele Mussolini* (Milan: Mondadori, 1993), p. 116.

46. Rachele Mussolini, *La mia vita con Benito* (Milan: Mondadori, 1948), p. 267.

47. Rosetta Ricci Crisolini, "'Vidi piangere le innamorate di Benito': Le memorie di Edvige Mussolini," *Epoca*, March 14, 1953, p. 46.

Chapter Seven: The Return of the Remains

1. "Errante per l'Italia," *Il Mondo*, January 18, 1955, p. 2.

2. *I programmi dei governi repubblicani dal 1946 al 1978* (Rome: Centro Romano Editoriale, 1978), p. 160.

3. Parliamentary Acts, Second Legislature, Chamber of Deputies, *Discussione*, June 7, 1957.

4. "I fascisti dopo il voto beffeggiano i ministri che cercano scusanti per non dimettersi," *l'Unità*, June 8, 1957.

5. *Il Mondo*, July 2, 1957, p. 16.

6. The letter, dated Naples, March 30, 1956, is in the archives of Palazzo Chigi, Prime Minister's Office, 1955, folder 1–7 14274, subfolder 5–2, "Benito Mussolini e famiglia. Resti del corpo: Richieste varie."

7. Salvatore Satta, *De profundis* (Milan: Adelfi, 1980), p. 16. Written in 1944–45, the book was published in 1948.

8. Ulisse [Davide Lajolo], "La promessa di Zoli," *l'Unità*, August 31, 1957.

9. Letter, signed Benito Crisafulli, August 30, 1957, in the archives of Palazzo Chigi, Prime Minister's Office, 1955, folder 1–7 14274, subfolder 5–2, "Benito Mussolini e famiglia. Resti del corpo: Richieste varie."

10. Ibid., letter sent September 10, 1957.

11. [Enzo Forcella], "Passione cadaverica," *Il Mondo*, September 10, 1957, p. 2.

12. State Archives, Milan, Cabinet of the Interior Ministry 1957–60, envelope 42, folder 11220, "Mussolini, famiglia-carteggio-salma," subfolder 11220/3, "Mussolini salma." Note from the minister written on a telegram dated September 8, 1957, from the Forlì prefect.

13. Ibid., from a letter signed by Primo Giunchi, dated Forlì, October 2, 1957.

14. Ibid., from a telegram to Interior Minister Tambroni, dated Forlì, September 27, 1957.

15. Ibid., telegram dated Forlì, September 29, 1957.

16. State Archives, Milan, Cabinet of the Interior Ministry 1957–60, envelope 42, folder 11220, "Mussolini, famiglia-carteggio-salma," subfolder 11220/3, "Mussolini salma," from a communication marked "Riservatissima," dated Forlì, September 30, 1957.

17. Ibid., prefect's announcement, dated Terni, September 13, 1957.

18. Ibid., prefect's announcement, dated Verona, September 24, 1957.

19. Ibid., letter from the provincial executive committee of the National Association of Partisans, dated Parma, September 27, 1957.

20. Screenplay of *La Dolce Vita*, written by Federico Fellini, Ennio Flaiano, and Tullio Pinelli.

21. Quoted in Guido Crainz, *Storia del miracolo italiano: Culture, identità, trasformazioni fra anni cinquanta e sessanta* (Rome: Donzelli, 1996), p. 151.

22. Ibid., p. 168.

23. "Per i morti di Reggio Emilia," sung by the Cantacronache. See Paolo Jachia, *La canzone d'autore italiana, 1958–1997: Avventure della parola cantata* (Milan: Feltrinelli, 1998), pp. 33–35.

Epilogue

1. "Open letter" from Enrico Sturani to his grandfather Augusto Monti, *Belfagor*, 1963, cited in Guido Crainz, "La 'legittimazione' della Resistenza: Dalla crisi del centrismo alla vigilia del '68," *Problemi del Socialismo* 7 (1986): 86.

2. Mirko Dondi, "Piazzale Loreto," *I luoghi della memoria: Miti e simboli dell'Italia unita*, ed. Mario Isnenghi (Rome-Bari: Laterza, 1996), p. 491.

3. Italo Calvino, "I ritratti del Duce" (1983), *Saggi 1945–1985*, vol. 1 (Milan: Mondadori, 1995), p. 2891.

4. Luigi Meneghello, *Bau-sète!* (1988; rpt. Milan: Bompiani, 1996), p. 39.

5. Ibid., p. 40.

6. Norma Rangieri, "Combat film, rapsodia in nero," *Il Manifesto*, April 7, 1994.

7. Franco Ferraresi, "La storia 'sfregiata' per sensazionalismo" *Corriere della Sera*, April 9, 1994.

8. Barbara Spinelli, "La TV e l'Italia malata," *La Stampa*, April 8, 1994.

9. Interview with Stefano Levi della Torre, "Quando avanza la zona grigia," *Il Manifesto*, April 13, 1994.

10. Guido Ceronetti, "Lo spettro funest," *La Stampa*, April 7, 1994.

11. Giorgio Bocca, "I due falsi storici del 25 aprile," *La Repubblica*, April 14, 1994.

12. Eugenio Scalfari, "Aria di Mussolini," *Il Venerdì* (weekly magazine of *La Repubblica*), February 27, 1998, pp. 33–34.

13. Domenico Leccisi, "Ai lettori," *Alternative: Agenzia di informazione per la stampa*, March 1995, p. 4.

14. From the guest book, crypt at San Casciano, January 1997.

Acknowledgments

Many people helped me during the years of research. My first thanks go to Ugo Berti Arnoaldi, whose generous advice was matched by his profound knowledge of the routes that link Italian history and memory during the twentieth century. I am equally indebted to Domenico Leccisi, one of the principal actors in Mussolini's afterlife, who shared with me his archives and his store of memories. I am all the more grateful for his willingness to help given the great gulf in our political beliefs.

The children of two other prominent figures in this story offered help and information about their fathers; my thanks, therefore, to Giovan Battista Ansaldo and Roberta De Monticelli. Journalist Mario Proli supplied background on modern-day Predappio; it gives me pleasure to thank him and his mother, Rosanna Proli, who showed me around the relevant Mussolini sites. On the day I visited I was accompainied by Michele Bella, a photographer, who produced the images from Predappio and helped me choose material from the Publifoto archives. My thanks also go to those who made the American edition of this book possible. In the first place to Frederika Randall, who brought to the translation not only her literary talent but also a thorough knowledge of Italian society and culture, past and present. And to the staff of Metropolitan Books, in particular to Sara Bershtel, who believed in this project with contagious enthusiasm, and to Riva Hocherman, who edited the book with the greatest of skill and patience.

When I first set out to track the odyssey of Il Duce's body, I was encouraged by the best historian in the field, Mario Isnenghi, whom I thank for our initial conversations and for his comments on the Italian edition. Antonio Gibelli not only offered a critical reading of the text but an ongoing dialogue about the book's concerns. To Paolo Viola, finally, I owe more than thanks. I owe to him my methods and my motives for the study of history.

Index

Entries in *italics* refer to illustrations.

About the Author

SERGIO LUZZATTO is a professor of modern history at the University of Turin, Italy. He is the author of four works of history and is a regular contributor to the leading Italian dailies *La Stampa* and *Corriere della Sera*.